Fascinating Facts from American History

Bill Lawrence

J. WESTON WALCH PUBLISHER

PORTLAND, MAINE

A Note on Maps

The maps in Chapters 5 and 21 were taken from the *Atlas of American History*. The western map in Chapter 10 is a composite taken from the frontispiece of *Gold Dust* (Knopf, 1980) by Donald Dale Jackson and from pages 247, 259 and 269 in *The Plains Across* (University of Illinois Press, 1979) by John D. Unruh, Jr.

1   2   3   4   5   6   7   8   9   10

ISBN 0-8251-2707-6

Copyright © 1982, 1995
J. Weston Walch, Publisher
P. O. Box 658 • Portland, Maine 04104-0658

Printed in the United States of America

Contents

Introduction

In *1066 And All That* two Oxford University professors set out to describe what English history seems like to the average Briton who retains in mind only a confused jumble of names, dates, and places. The result is an incomparably funny book that went through six printings the first month of publication alone. "History," the authors explained in the preface, "is not what you thought. It is what you remember."

In other words, history that isn't remembered isn't history at all. It is like the old conundrum of the tree that fell in the forest: Did the falling of the tree make a sound if there was no one there to hear it? I don't know the answer to that question, but don't worry—I have not attempted any Big Explanations in this book. I am, like Barbara Tuchman, "a seeker of the small facts . . . a narrator, not a philosopher."

I like to learn history not by the pound, but by the ounce. For me, it is detail that makes history interesting, even fascinating, and corroborative detail that makes it memorable. I look especially for the significant little things, such as finding that the friendship between the Pilgrims and Massasoit began to bloom after the newcomers cured the chief of severe constipation. Or that Richard Nixon had a small presidential seal on each tee of his private golf course at San Clemente. Without Massasoit's friendship the Plymouth Colony might not have survived, while the presidential seal on the golf tees tells more about the character of Richard Nixon—and why his presidency went down the drain—than all the memoirs penned by those trapped in the Watergate mess.

I fill *Fascinating Facts From American History* with details in hopes that teachers can use them to help students remember more about their country's past than 1776, the Civil War, and Watergate. It is also for older or more advanced students, as well as for any adult, to read themselves.

It took me seventeen months and a heart attack to finish this book, so please use it with care.

—*Bill Lawrence*

Chapter 1

The First Americans

Hollywood vs. Reality

NATIVE AMERICANS used to be called "red," though many are not that color. Their complexions range from almost black to almost white, with most of them having a bronze cast. Thanks to Hollywood movies and the novels of James Fenimore Cooper, Native Americans are thought of as tall, muscular, and brave. Though many did have exceptionally well-developed bodies, some were short and pudgy and some were cowards.

Natives of the East had muscular legs because of so much walking. Those living near streams and lakes had tremendous arms and shoulders caused by rowing. In the Northwest they grew bowlegged from sitting in dugout canoes.

Thanks to countless movies, it seems as if all American natives rode horses and lived in tepees. Those east of the Mississippi River never had horses[1] and only Plains Indians used tepees. Those in the Northeast lived in "long houses," large structures covered with bark and tree branches and held in place by long tree branches. Several families lived together in one long house.

Forest tribes in many areas lived in wigwams, frameworks of bent poles covered with bark or rush mats. Southeastern natives had thatched huts with grass roofs. In the Northern Plains there were earth lodges, round dwellings made of strong poles and covered with large chunks of sod. In the Southwest there were the famous pueblos of sunbaked clay, some built one on top of another so that when the ladders were pulled up they became forts. One pueblo has been found with 800 rooms.

Native Americans were not impressed by the houses European settlers built, but they were fascinated by the doors. Some might spend hours just opening and closing one.

Some Aspects of Life . . . and Death

THE "NAKED" NATIVES

The first Europeans who came to America often described Native Americans as "naked." In some cases this probably was true, but most of them wore around their loins a breechcloth made of cloth, grass, or hide. To proper Europeans, who wore all the clothes the law would allow, this was the same as being naked.

What Native Americans wore depended on where they lived and what time of year it was. Cotton clothing was common in the Southeast where the art of spinning and weaving was known. Most clothes were made of hide, especially deer hide. In the West the buffalo provided robes both to wear and to sleep on.

Buffalo robes were not limited to the West, however. Even beyond the colonial period buffalo roamed in parts of the East. There were a good many of them in Pennsylvania, with the last one being sighted there in 1799. The woolly beasts roamed New York State, where a city was named for them. The last one was chased out of the city of Buffalo in 1803.

Whatever Native Americans wore to protect themselves from cold weather, they were smarter than Europeans or today's Americans: they wore the fur inside for warmth, rather than outside for looks.

In the summer, men and women went naked above the waist. Women wore a skirt of hide or feathers. In addition to a breechcloth, men might wear leggings reaching far up the thigh to protect their legs from underbrush. Everyone wore moccasins of tanned hide.

WEAPONS AND WAR

The bow and arrow was the basic weapon, but Native Americans also used tomahawks, stone knives, clubs, and blowguns. Bows of the forest tribes were so large and strong few Europeans could pull them. In wet weather the strings would draw up and render the weapon useless, causing the war to be postponed for a while. Sometimes when one tribe had won but neither side had gotten its fill of fighting, weapons were redistributed and the battle recommenced.

Clubs were used often, and could be employed effectively in more ways than simply bashing an enemy's head. Many clubs were enormous and shaped like a paddle, except bigger in the middle and very heavy. Their sharp edges could split open a head, and it was probably one of these that was to have ended the life of the redoubtable Captain John Smith before Pocahontas intervened (assuming the famous tale is true).

Some warriors purposely left their fingernails long in order to claw an enemy's face. Some mutilated the bodies of fallen opponents by scalping them, cutting off all their limbs and breaking every bone in their bodies, and finally shooting arrows into what was left of the bodies. Why the arrows? To keep the enemy's soul from escaping and haunting the victor for the rest of his life.

A prisoner of war could expect to be tortured, sometimes horribly. The prisoner not only expected it, but might be disappointed if he was not. Torture was a chance to show bravery, something very important to every warrior.

FARMING AND FOOD

Corn was the staple crop of most North American natives, in many instances so important it was considered sacred. Corn was replaced by another crop only in the Midwest, where wheat grew in incredible abundance. The French explorers Marquette and Joliet were astonished to see the inhabitants harvesting wheat by paddling through the inundated fields and shaking it into their boats.

In general, Native Americans were not good farmers. Tending crops was not considered proper work for warriors and hunters. So women and children did most of the work, with the old people posted in wooden towers to keep birds and scavenging animals away.

Farming implements were crude, most of them made of stone or wood. When Henry Hudson found a New York tribe tilling the soil with sharp sticks, he sought to win their friendship by giving the chief a small iron plowshare; when he returned he found the chief wearing the plowshare around his neck. Despite crude methods and indifferent care, crops were usually bountiful. The incredible fertility of the soil saw to that.

Fish was the most common food of tribes along the coasts or inland waterways. In New England, cod was as essential for the natives as it later was for Europeans. Besides a hook and line, fish were caught by shooting them with arrows, striking them with a club, spearing them, trapping them with a basket, and sometimes by diving in with a bright object to attract the fish and catching them by hand. And there was the lazy man's method of poisoning the water with roots and scooping dead fish off the surface.

Alligator meat was a favorite dish in the South, but catching an alligator was not a simple matter. If the creature was on land, the natives ran a pole down its gullet, flipped it on its back to expose the soft underbelly, and then shot it with arrows or beat it to death with clubs. An occasional brave soul caught one by swimming past with a thick branch and when the alligator opened its great jaws, the warrior jammed the branch into its gaping mouth and propped it open. The alligator, thinking the branch was the brave's arm, crunched down so hard its long lower teeth pierced the upper jaw and locked its jaws together. The reptile could then be pulled from the water safely as long as the warrior stayed away from its large and mobile tail. The meat of its underbelly was considered a delicacy.

Native Americans have left a long line of popular foods: pumpkins, squash (not popular in all quarters), white and sweet potatoes, peanuts, pecans ("little walnuts," the early settlers called them), peppers, avocados, and tomatoes. It was well into the nineteenth century, however, before other Americans began eating tomatoes—until then they were thought to be poisonous.

DISEASE AND DEATH

Native Americans were susceptible to common European diseases they had never before been exposed to, especially measles, whooping cough, mumps, and smallpox. They had built up no immunity to these diseases—as Europeans had—and they died by the thousands. Some tribes were virtually wiped out. On the other hand, some historians suspect Native Americans brought back by Columbus took the first syphilis to Europe; apparently the disease had existed for so long in the New World that Native Americans were immune.

Treating the sick sometimes consisted of cutting the skin of the forehead and sucking out blood, the idea being that this would get rid of the evil spirit that had taken possession of the patient. Afterwards the body was purified by holding one's head over a fire of burning seeds or tobacco and breathing smoke into the lungs.

Some natives believed rattlesnake oil was a cure for many ailments. A pregnant woman wearing a rattlesnake belt should find delivery easier. Cherokees and Hopis considered the rattlesnake sacred.

Some tribes purged their bodies by partaking of the "black drink," a strong, caffeine-filled stimulant made from the yaupon leaf. In large quantities the drink worked as an emetic, causing users to throw up and thereby rid themselves of anything in the digestive system that might make them sick.

The black drink was accompanied by a ritual including an hour or two in a "hot house"—a primitive steam room—and then drinking until the patient vomited. The one who threw up the farthest won a prize. The drink was also used on such ceremonial occasions as weddings or funerals, and before going off on hunting or fighting expeditions.

Funerals for important tribesmen were attended with great pomp and circumstance. The mourning period could last for days or even weeks. Priests were in charge of burial preparations, including removal of the deceased's flesh—usually by placing the body on a raised platform beneath a smoldering fire. Some tribes buried the body in a grave lined with clay, which when set afire both destroyed the body and baked a container for it. In a few tribes it was customary to dig up the body a few days after burial so that relatives could eat any remaining flesh.

Chapter 2

Discovery and Exploration

The Vikings

THE FIRST EUROPEAN to see America, as far as anyone can prove, was Bjarni Herjulfsson, who sailed along parts of the Canadian coast after being blown off course on a trip from Iceland to Greenland, both sites of Viking colonies. Although Bjarni did not set foot on the continent, the eminent historian Samuel Eliot Morison calls him "the earliest, Number One, indubitable European discoverer of America."

Shortly afterwards, probably in A.D. 992, Leif Ericsson and a thirty-five man crew set out in Bjarni's boat to look for the land Bjarni had found. Following Bjarni's route in reverse, the expedition came first to an island they named Helluland (Land of Stones), where there were glaciers and no grass. Next they reached a flat wooded country with white sandy beaches, which they named Markland (Land of Forests). Finally the explorers came to the land they called Vinland, where they decided to spend the winter. The land was grassy and there was plenty of timber for building huts. The salmon were bigger than any the Vikings had ever seen.

When Leif returned to Greenland in the spring, his brother, Thorvald, decided to seek out this new land and explore it further. He and thirty men spent two winters in Vinland. While exploring farther south along the coastline, they found what appeared to be several small mounds on shore. On closer inspection the mounds turned out to be boats made of skin, turned upside down. From under each of the mounds sprang three dark-skinned natives, the first known to have been seen by Europeans. The Norsemen promptly massacred all but one of the "skraelings," as they called the natives. The one survivor escaped to warn his people. Thorvald's men were then attacked by a large force of skraelings in skin boats, and Thorvald himself was mortally wounded by an arrow. The survivors—how many isn't known—buried their leader on the shore and returned to Greenland.

Next, a rich trader named Thorfinn Karlsefni decided to try his luck in Vinland— perhaps there was wealth to be gained in commerce with these skraelings. Thorfinn arrived with a party of about 160 settlers, including some women, and all kinds of livestock. They spent the winter without event, and in the spring a large force of natives appeared out of the forest bearing sableskins and furs, apparently intent on doing just what Thorfinn had hoped they would do. Suddenly the cows began to moo and a bull to bellow loudly, causing the skraelings, who had never seen such strange creatures before, to drop their wares and run straight to Thorfinn's house, hoping to get inside to safety. As best he could in sign language, the trader explained that the cattle were indeed docile beasts and there was nothing to fear from them.

The natives then proffered their wares, obviously hoping to trade them for the white men's weapons, but Thorfinn forbade that. Then an idea occurred to him, the result of which is described in the sagas this way:

> *He told the women to carry out milk to them and the moment they saw the milk, that was the one thing they wanted to buy, nothing else. So that was what came of the skraelings' trading; they carried away what they bought in their bellies, while Karlsefni and his comrades kept their bales and their furs.*

Eventually there was trouble. An Indian tried to steal weapons and a fight broke out. Several Indians were killed before the remainder fled into the woods. Unsettled by this turn of events, Thorfinn abandoned the project and went home.

A final attempt at settlement of Vinland came to nought because of dissension among the would-be colonists themselves. This expedition had been organized by Leif's sister, Freydis, and when fighting broke out among its members she personally murdered two of the men and hacked to death with an axe all five of the women.

Columbus

It is not true, though the rumor persists, that most people in Columbus's day thought the world to be flat. Educated people of the day believed it to be round and all universities taught that it was. Some scholars, in fact, had computed the earth's size close to its actual dimensions. The influence of these learned men on the crowned heads of Europe was one reason Columbus had so much trouble finding people to back his expedition. They knew the world must be twice as large as this Genoese navigator thought it was, and that the Indies would therefore be twice as far away.

To allay the fears of his crew Columbus kept two logs, one showing the actual distance travelled, the other showing a shorter distance. The odd thing was that the "false" journal was much closer to the truth.

After a month at sea Columbus promised that if land was not sighted in three more days he would turn back. Two hours into the third day, the *Pinta's* lookout shouted that he had seen a dark outline on the horizion. Columbus had offered a reward to the first sailor to sight land, but the *Pinta's* lookout didn't get it: Columbus claimed he found land first because he had seen a light the night before. Gypped of his reward, the sailor later emigrated to Africa and became a Mohammedan.

When the expedition landed on San Salvador, Columbus thrust a sword in the ground and claimed the land for Spain, ignoring the fact that if his calculations were correct the land already belonged to somebody—the Grand Khan of China. (Europeans, still reading Marco Polo's thirteenth-century account of the Far East, did not know the Khan dynasty had been overthrown more than a century earlier.) To a Spaniard in those days—and Columbus was a naturalized Spaniard—it did not matter to whom the land belonged. Besides, the Grand Khan, not having the good fortune to be a Christian, did not count . . . or such was the thinking of the day.

On this first voyage Columbus discovered the Bahamas, Cuba, and Haiti. Most of the natives he found friendly and curious, and many of them smoked that strange "tabac" leaf. But they did not smoke it in the long peace pipe made famous by other Indians in later times; these natives rolled the leaf into a cigar shape and smoked it in their noses.

The Caribs, who gave their name to the sea thereabouts, were cannibals. Somewhat later these Indians cooked a priest and ate him, which made them sick. Not enjoying their first taste of the white man's religion, the Caribs never again looked with a hungry eye on a man of the cloth.

Columbus returned home claiming he had found the Indies, bringing Indians, gorgeously plumed parrots, and an alligator to prove it. Queen Isabella promptly dubbed him "The Very Magnificent Admiral of the Ocean Seas."

ADMIRAL OF THE MOSQUITOES

When Spain and Portugal, the only countries westward-hoing at the moment, began arguing about who owned what among the new discoveries, the Pope drew the Line of Demarcation through the Atlantic Ocean, giving Spain everything west of the line and Portugal everything east of it. Spain ended up with the entire Western Hemisphere except Brazil, while Portugal got that country (when it was later discovered), the Canaries, the Azores, and other islands.

Though Queen Isabella had treated Columbus as a hero after his first voyage, when three more trips failed to turn up the riches of the Orient, Spain treated him like an Italian. He was brought home from one trip in chains, which he kept in his chambers for the rest of his life as a reminder.

After the fourth voyage he returned to Spain to live out his days struggling with crippling arthritis. Isabella, his champion, had died and Ferdinand was not interested in Columbus's extravagant claims to the wealth that was due him as the discoverer of what by this time was realized to be a new continent. The once "Magnificent Admiral" was now the "Admiral of the Mosquitoes." Hardly anyone came to his funeral. His chains, at his request, were buried with him.

Columbus was odd in some ways. He could endure hardships with incredible patience, but might fly off the handle at slight misfortunes. He was deeply religious, once claiming God had told him he had done as much for Him as Moses or Abraham. He would not allow his crewmen to cuss, which probably was an awful hardship for the poor sailors. He thought Haiti was the Land of Sheba and that Venezuela—the most beautiful land he had ever seen—was the Garden of Eden. He imagined that the earth had a bump on it around Venezuela to bring this terrestrial paradise closer to heaven.

When we in this country hear the words, "Columbus discovered America," we naturally think of the United States. But in four trips to this hemisphere Columbus never saw any part of what is now the U.S. The closest he got was the Bahamas.

Hernando de Soto and Francisco Coronado

Except for Juan Ponce de Leon's brief excursion into Florida and the wanderings of the shipwrecked Cabeza de Vaca, the first explorers to see America's natural wonders—which they saw only as obstacles to be overcome in pursuit of gold and jewels—were Hernando de Soto and Francisco Coronado.

De Soto's travels took him from Florida to just beyond the Mississippi River. With him were a pack of fighting bloodhounds and—to begin with—thirteen pigs. Before he had been long in the wilderness the pigs numbered in the hundreds, mainly because de Soto was saving them for emergency rations and would not allow his men to slaughter them for food.

Tribespeople of the Southeast were fascinated by the odd creatures, watching with glee as the pigs rooted and squealed their way through the forests. Natives would pop one in a pot if they got the chance. It was an adage among the Spaniards that when a warrior sneaked up on one of their encampments he carried three ropes—one for a soldier, one for a pig, and one for a horse.

Some of the pigs escaped into the forests to become, according to popular belief, ancestors of the wild pigs later known as razorbacks or piney woods rooters. However, this might be only a legend, for Francisco Coronado's men reported seeing small wild swine as they trudged through the deserts of the Southwest at the same time de Soto was in the Southeast.

These wild pigs were vicious beasts and hard to catch; but few wanted to eat one anyway, for they gave off an odor like a polecat's. Some natives, though, enjoyed wild swine meat best of all. They knew the offensive smell came from a gland on the animal's back, and they had a special way of cooking them in a pit while drawing off the odor with a cane tube.

In northern Mississippi the Chickasaw tribe fire-attacked the Spanish camp one night and about 400 pigs became roast pork. The forest smelled of bacon grease for weeks. When de Soto died, his share of the pigs alone amounted to 700, all of which were quickly auctioned off and feasted upon by his men.

'WAY DOWN UPON THE SUWANNEE RIVER

De Soto had his first serious encounter with Native Americans on the Suwannee River in northern Florida. A band of braves laid down their arms in a forest clearing and asked, by signs, for a peace parley. De Soto knew, however, that other braves lay in hiding and he sent his cavalry to circle around behind them. When the hidden braves rushed out, the horsemen followed them, ambushing the would-be ambushers. Most of the survivors fled into the woods, but a few made the mistake of jumping into a lake. Swimming out beyond crossbow range, they taunted the Spaniards until sundown. As there was no way they could get out of the lake without being killed, morning found them still treading water, weary but undaunted. De Soto's soldiers hauled them out and put them in chains, to serve ever after as beasts of burden.

When they crossed into Georgia, the land of the Creek tribes, the conquistadors were amazed to find great fields of corn and wild flax that stretched as far as the eye could see. Thatched cabins, bright with a whitewash made of ground oyster shells, dotted the landscape. Here indeed was no land of primitive people. It was, by Native American standards, an affluent society.

Some of the Creek chiefs were women. One of them, called by de Soto's chroniclers the "Princess of Cofitachequi," came calling on the Spanish commander borne on a litter carried by several braves. The Spaniards had heard tales of gold in the land of the princess, but they found only copper that had filtered down from the Lake Superior region, the ancient smelting pot of the continent. If there had been gold around, the natives still probably would have preferred copper—they loved its smell.

De Soto took the princess prisoner, forcing her to come with the expedition and order her subjects along the route to carry the Spaniards' equipment and supplies. The princess apparently was a clever and resourceful monarch and calmly bided her time until she found a way to escape. One day she simply walked away, vanishing into the forest. Soldiers quickly pursued her, but could find no trace of the mysterious lady.

PEARLS OF NO GREAT PRICE

Moving north and slightly east, the expedition passed through southern South Carolina, bits of North Carolina and Tennessee, and started south again into Alabama. The gold they sought always seemed to be around the next bend, as the Native Americans had early learned the trick of telling the Spaniards there were riches beyond imagining in this land—but always a bit farther on. Eventually the expedition would spend four years pushing "farther on," finding no riches of any kind except fresh-water pearls. Most of the pearls were flawed because the natives had a frustrating habit of cooking mussels before removing the pearls. For whatever they were worth, the soldiers gathered up several hundred pounds of them, sometimes by robbing graves. Some tribes buried their dead with pearls in the eyes, ears, and nose, and in slits in the arms and legs.

After de Soto had been in the field for a year, he still had nothing to show for it except the bags of mostly worthless pearls. So determined was he to find great wealth like that in Mexico and Peru, he refused to give up. Even when news reached him that his ships were waiting in the Gulf, he hid the report from his men and ordered them to about-face and march north again.

De Soto learned too late that he was now in the land of the Choctaws, a tribe as fierce as angry cougars. Upon entering their territory, the general was greeted by the Choctaw chief, Tuscaloosa, who apparently wanted to be friends. De Soto, in his usual high-handed fashion, had the chief taken captive and ordered him to take the army to his capital, Mauvilla, near modern Mobile, where de Soto had heard there was a great deal of food.

Secretly the old chief had sent runners ahead, and when the Spaniards reached the town, hundreds of warriors lay in wait for them. As the Spanish column passed through the gates, a bevy of dancing girls began putting on a show to divert the white men. Then the warriors leaped out from hiding and the battle was on. With their captors preoccupied, the Indian porters fled into the town, taking with them the bulk of Spanish equipment. When de Soto discovered this turn of events, he ordered the town put to the torch, even though it meant most of his equipment would be destroyed.

Still the Choctaws fought on in what turned out to be the fiercest battle these Spaniards would engage in. When the smoke cleared, there were 22 dead and 148 wounded, some of the wounded having so many arrows in them they looked like porcupines. De Soto took an arrow in the only part of his body not armored: the seat of his pants. He had to finish fighting standing up in the stirrups. His men dressed their wounds with the fat of dead Choctaws and moved into Mississippi and Arkansas. From the battle of Mauvilla on, it was downhill for the Spaniards, their fortunes growing worse until de Soto's death and the return to Mexico of a handful of survivors.

THE TURK TALKS

The world is full of big liars, but some have changed the course of history. "The Turk" was one of those: an unmitigated liar whose monumental fibs helped decide the conquest of North America. His fantastic tales of great wealth, magnificent cities, and glorious rulers—none of which existed except in his imagination—kept Coronado's expedition pushing farther and farther into the American wilderness.

Who was the Turk? History doesn't know, but Coronado's records suggest he was a Pawnee tribesman snatched away from his home in the Midwest not long before Coronado came up from Mexico. He was a slave of his captors when the conquistador met him near what is now Pecos, New Mexico. The soldiers dubbed him "El Turco" because, they said, "he looked like one."

The Turk could speak no Spanish, but he was a master of the parley of the plains—sign language. A few sweeps of his expressive hands fired the imaginations of greedy Spaniards to fever glow. He wove marvelous tales of great golden cities on the plains (the fabled Seven Cities of Cibola, gasped the Spaniards!) and majestic rivers two leagues wide, crammed with fish as big as horses. On the rivers, he said, were huge canoes with golden oarlocks, and the nobles who rode in them lolled under canopies bedecked with precious jewels. The natives of this fabulous land dined with silver table service from dishes of silver and gold. The great king Tatarrax took his siesta under a tree from which hung many silver bells.

The Turk built a small fire in the hearts of the Spaniards and fanned it until it was a conflagration. As their interest grew, so did his stories. At first the Spaniards, though more than willing to believe these tales, were suspicious. To test him they showed him tin and copper. It was not gold, said the Turk. He had never seen gold, but he knew what it looked like: he could see it on the fingers of the soldiers. The Turk claimed he had given a gold ornament and jewels to his friend, an aged Indian the Spaniards called Bigotes ("Whiskers").

Whiskers denied it—and what's more, he said, that rascal was lying about everything else. Even after the Spaniards loosed bloodhounds on him, Whiskers still denied it.

Coronado ordered his guide put in irons, and the expedition headed north for a region the Turk called Quivira. Along the way he picked up two more guides, both of whom agreed the Turk was pulling Coronado's leg. But the Spaniards still wanted to believe their prisoner—he told them the things they wanted to hear. Besides, many of the soldiers had come to believe the Turk was a sort of a witch doctor; one of his jailers claimed to have seen him talking to the devil in a water jug.

THE TURK REACHES THE END OF HIS ROPE

The expedition swung through Texas, the Oklahoma panhandle, and into Kansas. So far no Cibola—only thatched or mud huts and poor, starving Indians. As they marched across the monotonous plains it became obvious to all that the Turk had been lying through his teeth. At the Turk's hometown they met Tatarrax, the glorious monarch they expected to be another Montezuma. He was an ordinary chieftain, dressed in his birthday suit, his only wealth a copper ornament around his neck. Tatarrax, it turned out, was not even his name, but the Wichita word for chief.

The Turk confessed. He had led them astray, he said, because the Pecos chiefs had promised him freedom if he lured the hated invaders from their land. He was placed under close guard while Coronado figured out what to do with him. But the wily captive had one more trick up his sleeve. Secretly he talked to the leaders of his people and convinced them they should not give the white men maize for their horses. The fearsome beasts would die, and without their mounts the Spaniards would be easy prey for Quivira's warriors. Coronado heard of the plot and sent soldiers to kill the prisoner, but the Turk convinced them of the truth of a new whopper. The reason he had brought them to Quivira, he lied, was to fetch his wife; the land they sought was still farther on.

But El Turco's luck had run out. The story didn't work this time, for the soldiers had had enough of him and his wild tales and wanted only to return to Mexico. While the others held him, one soldier stepped behind the Turk and dropped a rope over his head. Thrusting a rod through a loop in the rope, he began twisting . . .

Thus ended the career of one of history's great liars. But without those lies Coronado might never have gone so far north, might never have seen the majesty of the Grand Canyon, the awesome herds of buffalo, or the rolling plains of the great American West.

Chapter 3

The Earliest Settlers

Roanoke

SIR WALTER RALEIGH, who is said to have spread his cloak over a mud hole to protect Queen Elizabeth's dainty foot, is also the man who tried to give his queen a first foothold in America. He tried and failed twice, but his efforts are worthy of note.

Both of the short-lived attempts were on Roanoke Island off the coast of North Carolina, and the second one ended in tragedy—or did it? Until it was officially changed to Virginia, the whole area was called by the Native American name "Windgandcon" (or some variation of it). The name resulted from a mistake on the part of the first Englishmen when they noticed the natives on Roanoke kept saying the word over and over. The English assumed the natives were referring to their land, when actually they were saying, "What pretty clothes you are wearing." Mistakes like these were made often by early settlers.

While the tiny colony was still trying to exist, the natives under Chief Wingina decided to wipe the whites out. But the whites got word of his plan and struck first, killing Wingina and cutting off his head. The act did nothing to help relations, so when Sir Francis Drake—fresh from a highly successful raid on the Spanish Main—happened along, the 103 English survivors got aboard and went home.

Two years later, in 1587, Raleigh tried again, and for a time the little colonial seed seemed about to sprout. Raleigh's governor, John White, came home to round up supplies and new colonists. While he was there, Spain was inconsiderate enough to send her celebrated Armada against his homeland and White was unable to return to Virginia for almost two years. When he did, he found his settlers gone and the settlement taken over by weeds.

There was one clue to the mystery, a clue that has been the source of considerable speculation ever since. On a tree, "in faire Romane letters," was carved CRO, and on a post at the entrance to the fort was the word CROATOAN "in faire capitall letters." White had expected his colony to move to the nearby island of Croatoan, and he had enjoined them to leave a carved message if they did, and if they left "in distresse" to include a Maltese cross.

It appeared that the settlers had of their own volition gone to Croatoan, where lived the friendly chief Manteo. (The natives of Roanoke, remembering the fate of Wingina, certainly could not have been too hospitable.) White and his party set out for Croatoan but were turned back by a severe storm and—somewhat unaccountably, it would seem today—went back to England instead.

What really became of the "Lost Colony"? It isn't likely we will ever know, but Samuel Eliot Morison believes the legend that has followed the colony is probably true: The settlers did repair to the island and were amalgamated into the Croatoan tribe, which later moved to the interior of North Carolina. It is known that among the tribe there were blue-eyed and fair-haired types, and that Elizabethan words and English surnames were used.

Jamestown

As soon as the Jamestown settlers stepped off the boats they made their first mistake: choosing a malarial swamp as the site of their colony. From then on their fortunes went from bad to worse.

The leaders bickered endlessly among themselves, and the "gentlemen" refused to work. They had all heard the Native Americans used golden chamberpots encrusted with jewels, and they wanted to find some of those treasures for themselves. There was not a single farmer, the type of settler needed most among them. For nine years there was not even a plow in the colony.

Most history books imply the little colony might have perished had it not been for the redoubtable John Smith. It may be true, however, that the colony survived more *in spite of* Captain Smith than *because* of him. Smith seems to have been a heavy-handed leader with a special knack for creating dissension. Take, for example, that celebrated occasion when Smith told the laggards they must work if they expected to eat. The "gentlemen" set to work all right, but they cursed their fate every step they took. Annoyed by this blasphemy, Smith ordered each man's oaths numbered, and at night while the reluctant workers lay sleeping he had water dumped upon them, a bucket for each oath. What the books neglect to mention is that this punishment only increased the cussing.

To strike up better relations with the natives, Smith and Captain Christopher Newport, skipper of the ships that brought the settlers, took gifts to Powhatan, chief of the tribes in that region. The gifts were a coat and hat, a greyhound, and an English boy. The lad was probably an indentured servant; and his name, oddly enough, was Thomas Savage. Not to be outdone by foreigners, Powhatan gave the English one of his twenty sons. (He also had twelve daughters, one of whom was Pocahontas.)

Later Smith and Newport came calling again, this time with a crown just arrived from England. An elaborate coronation ceremony, the two captains thought, would put them high in the esteem of the old gentleman. But the chief, who had never bent a leg to anyone, refused to kneel, so Newport had to sneak around behind him and push his shoulders down while Smith clapped the crown on his head. As a token of his regard, Powhatan gave them a pair of his old shoes.

The Pocahontas Tale: Fact or Fancy?

No one tells the tale of Pocahontas's rescue of John Smith except the captain himself, so there is no way of knowing whether it is true. In the first book about his adventures in Virginia, Smith told this story of his capture.

While exploring the Chickahominy River he and his small party were attacked by natives. Two of his men were killed, and Smith escaped death by falling into a bog, allowing the natives to capture him instead. His captors took him before Opechancanough, a subchief and Powhatan's brother, whom he promptly captivated with a compass set in an ivory ball. While the chief sat entranced by the movement of the little needle, Smith delivered unto him a lesson in cosmography, discoursing on "The sunne, moone, starres, and planets . . . the greatnesse of the Land and Sea, the diversities of Nations . . . the roundness of the Earth, and how we are to them Antipodes." How he got such a lesson across in sign language he does not explain.

Confused but impressed, Opechancanough took the captain up to Werowocomoco, the capital, where Smith repeated his magic act. He was wined and dined for several days before being sent back to Jamestown with a four-man escort.

To his second account, written after Pocahontas had come to England and made a hit with royalty, Smith added the rescue story. The captain, who referred to himself in the third person, described it thus: "Pocahontas, the King's dearest daughter, when no entreaty would prevail, got his head in her arms, and laid her own upon his to save him from death." That's all. On that single brief sentence rests the entire legend of John Smith and Pocahontas.

As the daughter of a king, Pocahontas was treated as royalty herself during her stay in England. While preparing to return to America she died suddenly of either pneumonia or tuberculosis. She was only twenty-two.

The Pilgrims

Most of what we know about the Pilgrims comes from the *Journal* of William Bradford, the governor of Plymouth Colony for thirty years. But Bradford gives only 700 words to the Atlantic crossing, so we can only surmise what it must have been like.

We do know that although the wayfarers did not want for food, as did the Jamestown settlers, what they had was not very appetizing and often spoiled. The flour went moldy and the passengers would wait until after dark to eat their biscuits in order not to see the weevils and maggots. The crew made sport of the situation by tapping bits of biscuit loose on the table and betting on which bit walked away first

There were two births and one death among the passengers, and one member of the company was washed overboard and miraculously washed on board again. One young crew member met death after making fun of the Pilgrims, saying they were all sure to die and he would get their belongings. He died "desperately," but Bradford does not say of what cause.

Claims are that the timbers from the *Mayflower* are now in a barn in Buckinghamshire and a chapel in Oxfordshire.

Oh, for a McDonald's

The Pilgrims did not just sail into Cape Cod Bay and step off onto that famous rock; they cruised around the bay for some time and made several landfalls before settling for good. The women got off to wash, the men to scout around and look for food. Finding clams numerous along the shore, the settlers-to-be—who had had no fresh food in over two months—gorged themselves on them, so much that they "made themselves to cast and scour" (sick as dogs, in other words).

They also made off with the corn Native Americans had stored in mounds, which Captain Myles Standish's scouting party had discovered. The Pilgrims, being honorable souls, made themselves a promise to pay the natives later when they were more provident. And they did, when later they met Massasoit and the chief set a price on what they had taken (by which time they had raided a second cache).

The new settlers were to have food problems throughout the early months at Plimouth (sic) Plantation (the English of the time called any colony a "plantation"). Despite the abundance of food for the taking—deer, partridge, turkey, clams, lobster, duck, cod, fat eels—the colonists were often near starvation. Problem was, they were Englishmen through and through and they did not want food they were not accustomed to eating. Most distrusted shellfish because a few of their number had been almost fatally poisoned by Cape Cod mussels. Making matters worse, the fishing hooks they had brought with them were too large and virtually useless.

Enter Squanto

It was the Native American called Squanto (real name: Tisquantum), as every schoolchild knows, who helped the Pilgrims out of their food predicament and many other predicaments as well. He knew English ways and spoke both English and Spanish, and he had been baptized a Christian.

Explorer George Weymouth had taken Squanto to England in 1605, although there is no record of what he did while there. A few years later he returned to America as an interpreter for John Smith, who was mapping the New England coast. When Smith sailed for home he left Squanto in his native land, but the unfortunate man was lured aboard a slave ship with several other natives and was sold in the slave market in Spain. Friendly friars took him under their wing and instructed him in the Christian faith.

Somehow Squanto made his way back to London, where he lived with a merchant for a time. The merchant dispatched him as a guide on a Newfoundland expedition; then the governor of Newfoundland lent him to a captain who was exploring the New England coast. The captain dropped Squanto off—again—in his native land, where he found that his entire tribe had been wiped out by the plague.

Squanto taught the ignorant Pilgrims how to dig for eels with their toes and, as we all learn in grammar school, how to fertilize a row of corn with fish: three herrings to a hole, placed spokewise.

Squanto was without peer as an interpreter and general Man Friday. He once saved the little colony from possible extinction when he warned a band of hostiles that the Pilgrims had the plague hidden under the storehouse and would let it loose on them if they did not behave.

Little known is the fact that at one time Squanto worked a primitive version of the protection racket: He took payoffs from various Indian groups in return for a promise to make sure the white men, with their terrifying "boom sticks," did not attack them. When Pilgrim leaders found out about his little game, Squanto promised to behave himself.

Not generally known either is that another brave, one Hobamock, hung around the palisades much of the time and for all we know may have been as helpful to the Pilgrims as Squanto. (Squanto has merely had better press.) Bradford's *Journal* implies that Hobamock and Squanto vied with each other for the favor of their white benefactors.

Other Friends and Enemies

Squanto was not the first friendly Native American the Pilgrims met. That honor belongs to Samoset, who had learned English—and a bad habit or two—from traders along the coast. He casually strolled into camp one day, said "Me Samoset," and asked for a beer. Having no beer on hand, the settlers gave him a noggin of gin or brandy, cheese, a biscuit with butter, and a little pudding.

Embarrassed by the stranger's "nakedness"—he apparently was wearing the natives' uniform of the day, a small breechcloth—they also gave him a red horseman's coat, which pleased him mightily. He stayed all night and talked their ears off.

After introducing Squanto to the Pilgrims, Samoset disappears from history and Massasoit enters. The chief appeared with ninety braves and was given bread and butter, two knives, a jewel of some sort, and a "pot of strong water." Massasoit tried to down the entire pot of "strong water" in one gulp, which Bradford said "made him sweat all the time thereafter."

In due time Massasoit made with the Pilgrims a treaty of peace and mutual assistance which, when renewed by his sons, lasted fifty-five years.

No such agreement existed with other Native Americans of the area, however, and one time the Narragansett chief, Canonicus, decided to attack the little settlement. Following native custom, he sent the Pilgrims a snakeskin full of arrows as a symbol of his intentions. When the white men sent the snakeskin back filled with powder and shot, Canonicus decided discretion was the better part of valor and called off the attack.

Thanksgiving . . . Giving . . . Giving

The first Thanksgiving feast in Plymouth lasted three days and was held sometime between the first of October and the first week in November. (The Thanksgiving date we know today would be somewhat late for a harvest celebration.) Massasoit's ninety braves, his standard retinue apparently, went into the forest and shot five deer. Then Native American and settler alike feasted on venison, roast duck, roast goose, turkey, cod, eel, clams, leeks, watercress, and stewed fruit—all washed down with plenty of red and white wine. The records don't mention cranberries, although there were acres of them nearby.

Thanksgiving was merely a local celebration for many years, gradually becoming regional by the 1800s. In 1863, in trying to help heal the wounds of civil war, Abraham Lincoln made the celebration a national observance and set aside the last Thursday in November for it. He did so at the insistent urging of Mrs. Sarah Josepha Hale, a magazine editor and author of "Mary Had a Little Lamb."

Because Thanksgiving was made a national holiday and observed once each year, and because schoolchildren grow up pasting pictures of Pilgrim fathers, Pilgrim mothers, Pilgrim children, and Pilgrim dogs in their classroom windows each year, Americans tend to forget that the Jamestown settlers were here first. No American history student should be left to assume that the Pilgrims were either the first or the most important English settlers of this land.

The Pilgrims Arrive— 200 Years Later

Furthermore, the Pilgrims were not the Pilgrims for more than 200 years. They called themselves "Saints." The others on the *Mayflower* who were not members of the church or had been to Holland with them were known as "Strangers." They borrowed both names from a sentence in Paul's Epistle to the Romans: "They confessed that they were saints and strangers on earth."

One of their descendants, in a speech on Forefathers' Day sometime in the 1790s, first referred to the Saints as "Pilgrims" and "Pilgrim Fathers." This name too came from a line in the same Epistle, one quoted by William Bradford: "They knew they were pilgrims." The appellation did not come into general use, however, until the 1840s, after Bradford's *Journal* was found in England. It had disappeared during the Revolution, but in 1840 it turned up in the summer home of the Bishop of London. No one knows how it got there. The discovery brought about a renewed interest in the all-but-forgotten Saints, a recognition spurred on ardently by Northern historians as civil war seemed imminent.

As for that famous rock, no one paid much attention to it for more than a hundred years, and there is no evidence that it was used by anyone as a stepping stone to a new world and a new life. The first mention of it was in 1741 when Ruling Elder Thomas Faunce, age ninety-five, told a group that when he was a boy his father had pointed out the rock and told him that one of the Saints had told *him* that the first landing had been made there. It seems to have been a second-second-second-hand story.

In 1774 someone decided to put chains around the boulder and, using thirty pairs of oxen, hauled it to the higher beach. The rock broke in two, the larger part sinking into the sand. The smaller part was hauled to the town square and left there until 1834, when it was brought to a pit in front of Pilgrim Hall and fenced in. About 1859 a search began for the other half, which was found under a warehouse. The warehouse was pulled down, and an ornate Renaissance arch was erected over that half of the rock. Finally, in 1880, the two pieces were joined together (you can see the split). In 1920, on the three-hundredth anniversary of the landing, the arch was destroyed and a Greek temple was built over the whole piece.[1]

The Slave Trade

Some of the first settlers did not come to this land by choice. Black men were with Balboa, Cortez, Pizarro, and other early explorers, and the first shipload of African slaves arrived in Jamestown in 1619, only twelve years after the founding of English America.

Commerce in slaves was known as the "Middle Passage": Europe to the Guinea coast of Africa, then to America, and back to Europe. Africans seem to have thought nothing of the trade—a tribal chieftain might sell hundreds of his own people for a few of the white man's baubles. The victims were marched to the coast in long rows, linked together at the neck and with their feet so fettered they could barely stumble along. Some died before seeing the hold of a slave ship, especially women who, not being as heavily shackled, killed themselves by eating large amounts of clay. Before boarding ship the "merchandise" was branded.

Life aboard a slaver strains credulity. Male adults were shackled two by two, the right wrist and ankle of one to the left wrist and ankle of the other. They were packed like sardines into the hold, with each man's space five or six feet long and about sixteen inches wide. Women and children were generally allowed free run of the ship.

Slaves brought such fantastic prices in America it wasn't long before slave traders found a way of doubling the usual number on their ships. It was a platform, called the "'tween deck," between the deck and the floor of the hold. The 'tween deck was usually hastily built of unplaned lumber, which in a few days wore the skin off nearly to the bone.

Slaves had to go to the "latrines"—nothing more than a few large buckets— in pairs and walk over their brothers on the way. The trip sometimes was more trouble than it was worth, especially when one was bitten on the leg by those trodden upon, so slaves often answered the call of nature where they lay. In a short time the stench below decks was unbearable and some were fatally overcome by the noxious gases, especially in foul weather when the few small portholes were closed. Some suffocated, while others went mad and hacked a neighbor to death with their fingernails.

CARE AND FEEDING

In a typical day aboard a slaver, the "cargo" was brought up on deck in the morning for the first of two daily meals, most of which consisted of nothing but horse beans, the cheapest food in Europe. The beans were boiled to a pulp and covered with a mixture of water, flour, palm oil, and red pepper, a concoction the sailors called "slabber sauce." If a slave refused to eat, crewmen forced his mouth open with hot coals or pried his teeth apart with a chisel-like "mouth-opener," then poured the sauce down his throat with a funnel.

Afterwards came the "dance," when slaves were forced to "jump in their irons" to the sound of a musical instrument, usually a drum or bagpipe. The "dance" was for exercise and as a specific against what a slave trader feared most—"fixed melancholy." That was a condition in which the slave lost all will to live and in a remarkably short time simply "pined away."

Others were carried off by smallpox, measles, malaria, yellow fever, syphilis, and especially scurvy and the "bloody flux" (dysentery). The dead were immediately thrown overboard. Some of those who lived threw themselves overboard, if they got the chance.

Late in the afternoon the slaves were brought up for their second meal, then returned to the hold, which had been scoured down in their absence with water and vinegar. On some ships this cleaning was done cursorily or not at all.

By the time a load of slaves arrived in port, nearly all of them were emaciated and probably half were injured or diseased. One onlooker described them as "walking skeletons covered over with a piece of tanned leather." If possible, they were fattened up before being put on the auction block, and the traders used various ploys to try to hide the fact that many were diseased. For example, they found that skin lesions caused by certain ailments, such as yaws, could be temporarily disguised with a mixture of iron rust and gunpowder. Those obviously in poor condition were sold by the "candle inch": they were lined up beside a lighted candle and auctioned off quickly to the highest bidder until an inch of candle had burned. These "refuse" slaves might sell for as little as $2.

By the end of the colonial period, slavery showed definite signs of dying out. Then a simple invention by a man named Eli Whitney gave it new vigor. From the invention of the cotton gin in 1793, it was almost a century before the evil institution disappeared, and then only after four bloody years of civil war.

 Chapter 4

Colonial Life

Creature Comforts

HOMES

COLONISTS FOUND IT HARD to get two home-building items we could not do without today: glass and nails. In place of glass many of the simpler homes used oiled paper, which kept out wind and rain, but let in some light. Wooden pegs, which the home-builders made themselves, took the place of nails. Many homes were built not only with no nails, but with nothing else made of iron. Iron nails were so precious that homes built with them were sometimes burned by their owners when they moved out—just so the nails could be retrieved and reused. This became such a common practice some colonies passed laws against it.

The kitchen was the main room in the house of the common folk: it had the only fireplace and was therefore the warmest room as well as the brightest and most cheerful. New England homes commonly had a "keeping-room," a combination kitchen-sitting-dining room. A common piece of furniture found there was the "settle," a rude wooden sofa with a narrow seat and a high back that would keep the cold air off one's own back.

Bedrooms were cold, and families did what they could to warm up their beds. A heated flat-iron could be run around under the sheets, or if the family could afford one, a flat copper pan filled with hot coals, known as a "bed-warmer," was used. Feather mattresses were popular as much for the warmth as for the comfort they provided. Oddly, it would seem today, it was common practice to sleep in a half-reclining posture, with head and back propped up on goose-feather pillows. That's why many colonial beds that can be seen today are shorter than ours.

Such a bed saved space, which was at a premium in the average home. A "jack-bed" saved space by being built into a corner, while many children slept in "trundle-beds" that slipped under the big bed during the day.

COOKING AND DINING

Most cooking was done in the fireplace, which was often enormous. Benches, where people could sit and warm up, were sometimes placed at either end.

Food was most often roasted because that was the easiest way. All food for the day might be dumped into the big "bake-kettle" and cooked together. By heating it up once a day, it could be kept from spoiling for a time. One method of roasting was with the "clock-jack," a device with a hook on the end for the meat. This was suspended from the roof of the fireplace and spun around once in a while so the meat roasted evenly. Another way of roasting was to put the meat on a spit and have the children turn it.

The colonial housewife baked bread in a large brick oven built into the front wall of the fireplace. After heating the oven red-hot, she used a large wooden paddle to place the bread inside, often on large green leaves. She did this in the evening, and next morning the bread was ready to eat. It was delicious, bearing no resemblance to the soft white stuff many of us eat today.

Much eating was done with the fingers. There weren't many forks in the colonies for some time, and some who had them didn't use them often. Meat might be cut with a hunting knife right out of the sheath. The main instrument was a spoon, and for that reason hashes, stews, and soups were the dishes most often found on the colonial table. Meat pies were popular, too, but the most common dish was a corn meal mush called "hasty pudding." (To the colonists "pudding" was not a dessert.) You remember the reference to this dish in the first stanza of *Yankee Doodle*:

> *Father and I went down to camp,*
> *Along with Captain Goodin'.*
> *There we saw the men and boys*
> *As thick as hasty puddin'.*

Many folk, especially the poor, had only wooden table utensils. The "trencher," a wooden block with a hollowed-out place in the middle, served as a plate. Some trenchers were double, with two diners eating out of two hollowed-out places. In some cases the whole family ate out of one large trencher or even straight out of the pot the food was cooked in!

In these homes the table was a wide board set on top of wooden structures we would call sawhorses. The head of the table sat at one end of the "table-board," as they called it, with his wife beside him. A large covered dish known as the "salt-saler" (today incorrectly called a "salt-cellar") might be in the middle of the table as a sort of dividing line. The more important people sat "above the salt," those less so "below the salt." Some people ate out of holes in the tableboard itself.

In some communities, especially those where Puritan influence was strong, children took their meals at a separate table or stood behind the adults and had their plates passed back to them. They were expected to eat in silence and leave the room as soon as they were finished.

Many colonials, including those who could afford it, did not like to use china. John Hancock refused to have any in the house because of the clatter it made.

Since glass was hard to get and expensive, many drinking vessels were made of wood, leather, or animal horn. Tankards and noggins were the most common; some of these would hold a quart or more and might be passed around for all at the table to drink from. (The colonists had never heard of germs.) A much larger vessel was the bombard, and from its name you can imagine how large it was.

Some vessels were made of pewter, as was other table service. When shined up—which had to be done often because of the lead content—pewterware served as decoration and helped reflect light.

DRINKS AND DRINKING

What did the colonists drink from these containers? It certainly wasn't water, for they were fond of what they all called "ardent spirits." Beer, ale, wine, rum, gin, whiskey—these were the "good creatures of God" to both men and women of the age. In some communities it was traditional to seal a bottle of whiskey in the cornerstone of a new church or public building. Taverns were not just licensed to sell liquor, but were required by the same law to keep enough on hand to meet the demand.

The age was famous for its marathon drinking bouts, and rare indeed was the funeral, wedding, birth, or christening that was not celebrated with copious amounts of booze. Doctors prescribed hard liquor for everything from painful teething to the aches of old age. Rum and milk was supposed to be good for pregnant women and nursing mothers, and rum-soaked cherries were said to prevent colds. Most cure-alls contained mainly alcohol and colored water.

For most early Americans, the day began with a tumbler of "ardent spirits" of some sort—"taking our bitters," they called it. In the North it was probably rum or hard cider, in the South a fruit cordial or perhaps mint-flavored whiskey. Other spirits were known by various names: "applejack," "blue ruin," "Jersey Lightnin'," and a potent Dutch gin called "strip-and-go-naked."

Even the abstemious John Adams took his bitters in the form of a tankard of hard cider. George Washington and also William Penn had their own distilleries. The austere Puritans, while frowning upon drinking to excess, quaffed with the rest. They defined excess as "more than half a pint at one time."

Facts of Life

CRIME AND PUNISHMENT

Drinking then, as today, was a main cause of trouble with the law. Unlike today, justice was swift and public.

The whipping post was the most common form of punishment, but the best-known forms were the stocks and pillory. A person in the pillory stood up and put both hands, or head and hands, through holes in a locked board. In the stocks the offender sat with feet, or hands and feet in the board. Some people today mistakenly call both of these devices the stocks.

Often the punishment symbolized the offense, such as cutting off the hand of a thief or thrusting a hot poker through the tongue of a blasphemer. For less serious offenses one could be branded with a letter representing the crime. If the offender was a woman, she might be allowed to wear the letter around her neck or, as did Hester Prynne in Hawthorne's *The Scarlet Letter*, stitched to her dress.

Women judged to be scolds and gossips could find themselves in the ducking stool, a chair at the end of a pole in which they were repeatedly ducked in a stream or pond.

Some towns had a special time, called Lecture Day, when all the week's public punishments were carried out. Everyone was expected to turn out and jeer the unfortunate offenders—it was part of the punishment. It also provided entertainment for fun-starved colonists. And a hanging became a circus-like affair, with people coming from many miles away to see the sight.

MEDICINE—AND ITS RESULTS

Medicine was a rudimentary science at best and surgery was scarcely practiced at all. The chief surgical technique was bloodletting; it was commonly believed that if enough blood was let out of the body, whatever disorder affected the patient (evil spirits, perhaps) would leave with it. Since there were few doctors, the local barber, who had the tools for it, was the obvious choice to perform surgery or "chirurgery," as it was spelled then. The "barber and chirurgeon" advertised his trade with a red and white pole—red for blood, white for bandages. The blue added in later times was either for patriotic reasons or, perhaps, to indicate the condition of the patient after the "chirurgery."

The great killer of colonial times was smallpox, and those lucky enough to survive the disease bore its scars for life, as the pockmarked face of George Washington testifies. Second only to smallpox was tuberculosis, or "consumption," as it was called then.

Malaria, or the "ague," was so common that those suffering from it scarcely considered themselves sick.

Yellow fever—"American distemper"—was thought to be caused by "bad air" and the breath of those afflicted. One tried to ward it off by covering the face with a vinegar-soaked rag, wearing a bag of camphor around the neck, or chewing garlic. To keep yellow fever out of the home, interior walls were whitewashed and the floors sprinkled with vinegar. Children at play added a second verse to "Jack and Jill":

> *Up Jack got and home did trot*
> *As fast as he could caper.*
> *They put him to bed and plastered his head*
> *With vinegar and brown paper.*

With public sanitation almost nonexistent, typhoid fever often raged throughout whole cities. Dysentery caused by foul drink and uncooked food was common, and children died like flies from measles, whooping cough, mumps, and diphtheria. Infant mortality was so high a family with ten children could consider itself lucky if five survived to be adults.

In their almost total ignorance of the cause and treatment of disease, many colonists apparently thought these remedies might work:

- For cancer: Anoint the affected area several times a day with the juice of a woolly-headed thistle.

- For arthritis: Carry a new potato as close to the painful spot as possible.

- For diptheria: Gargle with fluid from the stool of a cow.

- For asthma: Put the pelt of a muskrat on the chest, furry side down.

- For chicken pox: Lie down in the chicken house and wait for a black hen to pass over.

- For headache: Take snuff made of dried and powdered moss. If that doesn't work, put a buckwheat cake on the head.

- For warts: Rub a potato on them and bury the potato; or spit on them every morning; or put cobwebs on them and set fire to the cobwebs.

- For toothache: Prick the tooth with a sliver from a pine tree that has been struck by lightning, or press cow manure—fresh manure only—to the affected side of the face.

DEATH AND FUNERALS

Medical science being what it was, it should come as no surprise to learn that people died of quite mundane causes. And the medical ignorance of the people at large led to hundreds of superstitions concerning death and dying. Some harbingers of death were said to be

- A rose blooming twice the same year.

- A white dove circling the house three times.

- Dreaming of a white horse, or dreaming of a sick person plowing downhill. (If dreamed of plowing uphill, the afflicted one would live.)

- Seeing a lighted candle moving about in the night. (It was called a "corpse candle.")

- Hearing a rooster crow followed by all the other roosters.

- Dropping an umbrella on the floor. (The death in this case would be by murder.)

- Taking ashes out of a stove after sundown.

One also had to be careful when attending a funeral or the next one would be his or her own. Things to beware of included

- Going to a funeral if pregnant.

- Not covering all mirrors, for the person who saw his or her own image would be the next victim.

- Wearing anything new, especially shoes.

- Taking the corpse out head first; if the face looked backward the deceased was beckoning someone to join him or her.

- Meeting white chickens on the way.

- Funerals on Friday—that was bad luck.

- Burying a woman all in black—she would return to haunt the family.

Funerals were a medium for social intercourse, being one of the few times a large number of people got together. Funerals could be lavish affairs and some families almost went broke putting a loved one under the sod in the proper fashion. Even paupers had a funeral, paid for out of the public treasury.

The colonial funeral was likely to be held at night. One did not go, however, without an invitation, which arrived with a gift of some sort: gloves, a scarf, or perhaps a ring with a skull and crossbones on it.

Homes were decorated for the occasion, with appropriate new wallpaper if the family could afford it. Refreshments were served, the beverages all alcoholic of course. If the vanity of the family required it, they could hire professional mourners to sit down in front and wail plaintively.

In Puritan circles, where death was a glorious event, children were often pallbearers, because it was felt they should be properly impressed with the significance of death. Dying, to a Puritan, was the greatest thing in life.

Given these circumstances, it is odd to note how some colonials treated the recently departed with callous disrespect, as these epitaphs from the age indicate:

Here is where poor Henry lies,
Nobody weeps and nobody cries.
Where he went and how he fares,
Nobody knows and nobody cares.

(For an infant girl)
Since she was so quickly done for,
I wonder what she was begun for.

Under this sod and under these trees,
Here lies the body of Solomon Pease.
The peas are not here,
 There's only the pod,
The peas shelled out and went up to God.

Here lies John Racket
In his wooden jacket,
He kept neither horses nor mules.
He lived like a hog,
He died like a dog,
And left all his money to fools.

MARRIAGE AND FAMILY

Courting a girl was not an easy task in those days, as most of it had to be done under the watchful eyes of her parents. One device used by young couples for greater intimacy was the "whispering stick," a hollow pole through which they could whisper "sweet nothings" to each other. Another was a curious custom known as "bundling," which was condoned by a surprisingly large number of adult supervisors. The courting couple got into bed, fully clothed, and said their sweet nothings there in cuddly comfort. There probably was, however, a "bundling board" between them. Bundling, a custom shared by adults as well, was popular because homes were so cold.

Marriage came early for most colonial youngsters, especially girls. Girls usually were preparing for it by the time they were thirteen; boys were somewhat older, and many men did not take the plunge until they were in their thirties. A girl dreaded not getting married worse than anything, and if she wasn't wed by the age of twenty-one she was not an old maid, but an "antique maid." Weddings generally were performed not by a minister in a church, but by some civil official in the bride's home.

Families were large, for several reasons:

1. Effective birth-control methods did not exist.

2. There was so much work to be done, and so little machinery, that the more hands to do it the better.

3. Disease and a hard life took such a toll that any couple intending to bring up a sizeable family had to plan on an oversized one to begin with.

Paul Revere had seventeen children (now you know why he rode off at midnight). The record as far as anyone knows was held by a South Carolina mother who gave birth to thirty-four children.

It has already been mentioned that infant mortality was high, but mothers often died young as well. Many of these large families were the products of one father and two or three successive wives. With so much work to be done in the house and fields and so many children to care for, a man did not tarry long after the death of one wife before taking another.

Bear in mind also that there were never too many children at home at one time. Some died; others married early and moved away. Epidemics might wipe out entire families or even generations of families.

Spirit and Mind

RELIGION

Contrary to popular belief, the majority of colonists never officially affiliated themselves with any church. Neither were most of them fired with religious zeal, an idea we may get from too much study of Pilgrims and Puritans. George Washington could more often be found riding to hounds on a Sunday than in church. Despite his moralizing as "Poor Richard," Benjamin Franklin was not a religious man, and many intellectuals, such as Thomas Jefferson, were deists who believed God and Nature were the same.

Other than those who came to America specifically for religious reasons and those from non-English-speaking countries, most colonials considered themselves of the Anglican (Church of England) faith. By far the majority in the southern and middle colonies, except William Penn's Quakers and Lord Baltimore's Catholics, were Anglicans.

In Puritan New England, religion, not bread, was the staff of life and the rule of the church was absolute. Music, considered too frivolous, was anathema; hymns were simply read or chanted. Sermons were as long as three hours, prayers sometimes an hour or more. Services could last all day, with a "nooning" taken in the "Sabba-house," a building next door kept warm for the horses.

Puritan churches were not comfortable places—one was not expected to be comfortable while worshipping the Lord. There was no heat, and to keep warm one had to wear several layers of clothes and muffle up the head and neck. A foot warmer, a metal box filled with hot coals, might keep the tootsies comfortable. Some churches allowed dogs in to lie on their owners feet.

The "pues" were narrow and hard. Everyone was assigned to a pew and was expected to be in it on Sunday morning. In a Puritan community absence from divine services was not just a breach of faith, but a breach of the law. The "tithing man" (so called because he looked after ten families) checked homes and especially taverns for any scoundrels trying to escape their weekly soul-lashing. He also made sure everyone stayed awake; those who didn't received a sharp rap with his long stick. It was said that if a cat caught a mouse on Sunday it would be hanged on Monday.

The Puritans were strict Calvinists, believing only the chosen few would escape hellfire and damnation—and that there was little anyone could do to change his or her fate. Trouble was, no one could be sure who was among the chosen, or as a wit put it in this famous verse:

> *You can and you can't,*
> *You will and you won't,*
> *You'll be damned if you do,*
> *You'll be damned if you don't.*

The Pilgrims were more rational in religious matters than the Puritans, but they too had their peculiarities. They did not celebrate Christmas, considering it a Papist invention, or Easter, for the simple reason that Christ never did!

EDUCATION

There were few colleges in the colonies for more than a hundred years, and those were founded primarily to train ministers. An early president of Harvard, the first college, was expelled for whipping teachers.

Boys and girls weren't likely to get much schooling. In the South a few plantation owners might get together and hire a teacher who would work in some building on the estate. This was called an "old fields" school. "Dame schools" were those held by a woman in her home.

Most schools were run by a man, the master, who would teach not three Rs, but four: readin', writin', 'rithmetic, and religion. Rules were strictly enforced, and if a young scholar fell behind in his work the master worked on his behind.

All the students might be taught the same thing from the same book, regardless of their age and level of learning. In some schools the seats were rude wooden benches or blocks of wood. The desks might be rough-hewn wooden tables or merely slabs of wood driven into the wall and held up by pegs.

If there was no paper or pen, students worked with whatever was available: charcoal on birchbark or a stick on the dirt floor. Most studies were rote learning, but many a youngster developed beautiful handwriting from so much copying from books. The "hornbook," a paddle-shaped board covered with a thin sheet of animal horn, is a symbol of colonial education. On the hornbook were the ABCs and perhaps a Bible verse, such as:

> *In Adam's fall*
> *We sinned all.*

This was a good way to learn the alphabet and religion at the same time. Rhymes were also a good way to remember things, as in this one still in use today:

> *Thirty days hath September,*
> *April, June and November . . .*

Much of colonial children's schoolwork would be a mystery to us today. For example, try to figure out this arithmetic problem:

> *Deduct the tare and trett. Divide the suttle by amount given. The quotient will be the cloff, which subtract from the suttle. The remainder will be the neat.*

Is your remainder neat?

 Chapter 5

The Revolution

Personality Profiles

GEORGE WASHINGTON

WASHINGTON WAS AN IMPOSING MAN with a tall (six-foot-four-inch) but thin frame. He commanded attention, but he was a man more to be revered than loved. He was warm with family and friends, but with others he could be cold and aloof. He shook no hands at his inauguration—he did not like to be touched—and as President he required all who came to see him to remain standing in his presence, causing some to say he was "indomitable in war, insufferable in peace." When he asked to be called "His Mightiness," some feared the country had exchanged George III for George I.

Although Washington was indeed fond of the ladies, biographers have been able to find little evidence of charm in the man—and almost no sense of humor.

Neither was he a thinker. At meetings of the Second Continental Congress—before leaving to take command of the Army—he said nothing, but merely sat there in his Virginia militia uniform (he was the only member of Congress to wear a uniform). Although he presided over the Constitutional Convention with a firm hand, he contributed little to its deliberations. His mere presence, however, lent an air of purpose to the gathering.

His country was the only thing Washington was father of; he and Martha were without issue. He did, however, adopt Martha's two grandchildren (Martha's first husband had died). The granddaughter, Eleanor, was a particular treasure to George, and he was frequently in hot water with Martha over what she considered his indulgence of the girl. Nelly was a high-spirited lass who would rather ride half-broken colts than learn to sew or play the harpsichord—and that is why her step-grandfather loved her so. He ended every wartime letter with "Give my love to Nelly."

Martha Custis was a rich widow, and she and George were married in one of her homes called the White House. Was that an omen of things to come? No, for the first president served his two terms first in New York then in Philadelphia, while Washington City (as it was first called) was being built from the ground up.

The old story that Washington never told a lie is a lie. A hack writer of the day, Mason Locke Weems, invented the story out of whole cloth. Just after Washington's death, Weems dashed off a slender volume entitled *The Life of George Washington: With Curious Anecdotes, Equally Honourable* [sic] *to Himself and Exemplary to His Young Country- men.* As the title implies, the book was intended for children, and it had more "curious anecdotes" than anything else, chief among which was the famous cherry tree tale. Weems told it like this:

> *"I can't tell a lie, Pa. You know I can't tell a lie. I did it with my little hatchet."*
>
> *"Run to my arms, you dearest boy,"* cried his father in transports. *"Run to my arms. Glad am I, George, that you killed my tree, for you have paid for it a thousand fold. Such an act of heroism in my son is worth more than a thou- sand trees, though blossomed with silver and their fruits of purest gold."*[1]

Had George really chopped down the tree and lied about it, perhaps it wouldn't have mattered; he was going into politics anyway.

THOMAS JEFFERSON

Jefferson was perhaps the most brilliant American in a whole generation of bril- liant Americans. He was interested in everything: politics, government, literature, philosophy, painting, architecture, astronomy, botany, zoology, chemistry, law, and many, many others. His favorite study was probably architecture. He designed and built his magnificent home, Monticello (pronounced "Montichello" and meaning "Little Mountain"), and did the planning for the University of Virginia.

Jefferson was intrigued by gadgets. In addition to making improvements on clocks, calendars, desks, stoves, wagons, and plows, he invented the dumbwaiter and the swivel chair and seems to have been the first to think of the idea of closets. He wrote the Decla- ration of Independence on a portable desk of his own contrivance.

Jefferson was the most intellectually inclined of all the Founding Fathers. He spoke and wrote Greek, Latin, French, Italian, Spanish, and Old English. He was far ahead of his time in advocating public libraries and free public schools. His own library at Monti- cello was the finest in the country, but after retiring from the presidency almost broke, he had to sell all 10,000 volumes in order to live—and only a public conscription saved his beloved home.

After Jefferson died, Monticello finally had to be sold to pay his debts. He and John Adams died the same day: July 4, 1826, the fiftieth anniversary of the adoption of the Declaration of Independence, which both had so much to do with.

Jefferson is considered the founder of the Democratic Party, and he was in succes- sion the first Secretary of State, then Vice-President and President. Before that he had been twice governor of Virginia and had succeeded Benjamin Franklin as minister to France.

He was a democrat to the core of his being. He believed emphatically in the intelligence and dignity of the common people. He considered the farmer the backbone of any society, and was proud to list himself a farmer before all else. His vision failed, however, when he saw the future United States as a nation of farmers.

Jefferson's epitaph, which he wrote himself, makes no mention of his having held three of the nation's highest offices. It reads: "Here lies Thomas Jefferson, author of the Declaration of Independence, of the Statute of Virginia for Religious Freedom and Father of the University of Virginia."

BENJAMIN FRANKLIN

Ben Franklin is the closest America has come to producing a Universal Man: like Jefferson, he was interested in everything. He founded the American postal system, started the first circulating library, began an academy that grew into the University of Pennsylvania, and founded a newspaper that became America's longest-running magazine, the *Saturday Evening Post*.

He was one of the world's foremost authorities on electricity, but he did not "discover" it, as some say. By his famous kite experiment he merely proved that lightning was electricity. He was so well known for this experiment that while he was minister to France chic Parisian women affected a hat style with a long rod—called a "Franklin wire"—hanging from the hat far down the back.

The French, even more than the British when he was colonial representative to the Court of St. James, loved Ben for his intelligence and wit. When Jefferson arrived to take his place, the French asked if he had come to replace Dr. Franklin. "I have come to *succeed* Dr. Franklin," Jefferson replied. "No one can replace him."

His publication of *Poor Richard's Almanack* was alone enough to make Franklin famous. Everyone has heard Poor Richard's epigrams, many of which are quoted today: "A penny saved is a penny earned," "Time is money," "Keep your nose to the grindstone," and so on. Some that aren't so often quoted perhaps should be, such as "Fish and visitors smell in three days."

Franklin was the only man who could easily make George Washington laugh. The story the general liked best was Ben's reply to the stuffy Englishman who protested that it wasn't cricket for the Minutemen to fire at British soldiers from behind stone walls. "Why?" said Ben. "Didn't those walls have two sides?"

Ben married his landlady's daughter, who was almost illiterate, and this in particular kept him out of Philadelphia's upper crust. Ben Franklin didn't care; he accepted everyone, and he anticipated another amiable and funny American, Will Rogers, who said, "I never met a man I didn't like."

JOHN HANCOCK

Because of his bold signature on the Declaration of Independence, John Hancock's name has become synonymous with the word "signature." He wrote it large, he said, so King George could see the name without his spectacles. There was at least one other reason: Hancock was vain, considering himself of special importance. Handwriting experts claim Hancock's large letters—and especially the flourish underneath—show a person who thinks highly of himself and has a great desire for recognition.

The facts bear out this appraisal. Hancock was greatly pleased when chosen president of the Second Continental Congress, but mortified when he was not picked as commander-in-chief of the Continental Army, a position he fully expected to receive. (It is likely he would have, had it not been for certain political considerations. So far all the ruckus had been up North, and Congress was afraid that if it appointed a northerner to command the army the southern colonies might not join the movement.) Hancock was also furious when he learned the price the British had put on his head was only £500.

Hancock was born into a poor family, but he inherited a large fortune, a dowry he improved upon by a little honest smuggling in tea and wine. As incensed as they were with British trade regulations, most colonists did not consider smuggling a crime.

Many books use one of the John S. Copley portraits of John Hancock, the full-length one showing him seated in a chair. If you look closely at it, you will be startled by his resemblance to Bob Hope in a wig.

SAMUEL ADAMS

Books today call Sam Adams the "Father of the American Revolution," but at the time he was known as the "Grand Incendiary." The latter is a more apt description, for he was a fire-eating revolutionary, an uncompromising rebel. When he spoke he trembled; when he was excited he stuttered.

He organized the Boston Committee of Correspondence, taken as a model throughout the colonies. He was the leader of the Boston Sons of Liberty, and most authorities agree he must have been the man behind the Boston Tea Party, and probably the chief instigator of the Boston Massacre.

But revolution seemed to be the only thing poor Sam was good at. All his business ventures failed. He couldn't handle money and was once relieved of his post as tax collector at Boston because of a shortage of funds. No one accused Sam of taking the money: he was the soul of honesty and everyone knew it. With a lot of help from his friends, he paid back the money. His friends also bought him a new suit—all his own were threadbare—when he was elected to Congress.

Samuel Adams was always a man in search of a cause, and when the Revolution ended there were no more causes to fight for. His later life was without distinction.

PAUL REVERE'S RIDE

Ask most Americans why Paul Revere made his celebrated ride and they will say, "To warn the people the British were coming." Ask them where he rode and they can't tell you. Ask them where the British came from, where they were going, and why, and they can't tell you. Ask them what Revere's signal was and they will say, "Oh, it was one if by land and two if by sea." Ask what "by land" and "by sea" mean and they don't know. Ask who the signal was for and they will say, "For Paul Revere, of course"—and they will be wrong, of course. In other words, most people don't know anything about Paul Revere's ride, although they thought they did before you questioned them.

Revere rode to warn Samuel Adams and John Hancock, who were hiding in Lexington, then on to warn the Minutemen in Concord that a British expedition was coming to seize their supplies. The British soldiers could leave Boston either of two ways: by the narrow neck of land that connects Boston to the mainland—that is "one if by land"—or by taking small boats across the Charles River to the mainland—that is "two if by sea." The lights in the belfry of Old North Church (Christ's Church at the time) were not for Paul Revere; he was the one who had them put there.

Too bad Americans so often learn their history from movies, television shows, romanticized novels, and—alas—poetry. For it was Henry Wadsworth Longfellow who immortalized the ride—almost a hundred years after the fact—and at the same time immortalized some bad mistakes.

Revere, still in Boston, found out which direction the British were taking and had a helper hang two lanterns in the church belfry so the men in Charlestown across the river would know as well. So Longfellow is inaccurate when he says in lines 57-59 of the poem:

> . . . impatient to mount and ride,
> Booted and spurred, with a heavy stride
> On the opposite shore walked Paul Revere.

Revere's problem was not which route the soldiers were taking—he already knew—but how to row across the Charles right under the nose of a sixty-four-gun British man-of-war without being seen or heard. He and two friends made it, thanks to a woman friend of one of the others whose contribution to the Revolution was a petticoat to muffle the sound of their oars in the oarlocks. If Paul did not make it, his accomplices in Charlestown would have had to send someone else—hence the importance of the lights. Longfellow's most grievous error is in lines 101-102:

> It was two by the village clock
> When he came to the bridge in Concord town.

Unfortunately for history, poesy, and Paul Revere, he never made it to Concord town. He was caught by a British patrol beyond Lexington and later released to return to that town.

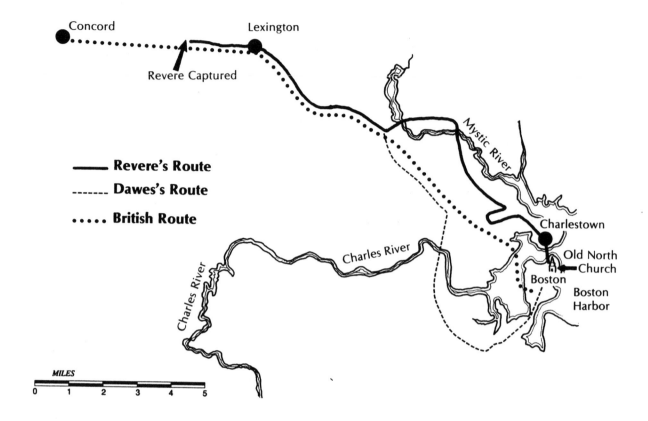

Longfellow doesn't mention the other two riders at all, perhaps because their names are not lyrical enough. William Dawes also galloped out of Boston on the same errand, going by the all-land route and arriving in Lexington half an hour after Revere. He also started out for Concord, but Revere warned him of the patrol and he returned to Lexington. The other rider—the only one to complete the ride Revere is famous for—was Samuel Prescott, a young doctor who asked to accompany the two from Lexington to Concord and who escaped the patrol.

Longfellow published the poem in 1860, and the Civil War, which made everyone more patriotic than usual, helped boost its popularity. Until then Revere had been famous only for his silverware. His name first appeared in a biographical reference book in 1872, a few years after Longfellow's poem was published, but almost a hundred years after the ride. Paul Revere made numerous other rides, but no one knows of them because no poet wrote about them.

THE DECLARATION OF INDEPENDENCE

Ask those same people you questioned about Paul Revere's ride what happened on July 4, 1776, that caused this nation to celebrate that date as Independence Day ever since, and you will get mostly wrong answers again. They will probably say, "The Declaration of Independence was signed," but that is incorrect.

There are three important dates concerning American independence and the document that proclaimed it:

July 2—The Second Continental Congress *voted for independence.*
July 4—Congress *voted on and approved the Declaration of Independence.*
August 2—Most members of Congress *signed the Declaration.*

The entire independence business began on June 7 when Richard Henry Lee, delegate from Virginia, offered Congress a resolution that

> *These United Colonies are, and of right ought to be, free and independent states; that they are absolved from all allegiance to the British crown; and that all political connection between them and the State of Great Britain is, and ought to be, totally dissolved.*

Debate raged for several days until all the colonies were lined up in favor of the resolution except New York, whose delegates awaited instructions from home. Meanwhile, a committee headed by Thomas Jefferson went ahead with drafting a declaration of independence. On July 2 the resolution passed.

WHEN *IS* INDEPENDENCE DAY?

Was this day, July 2, really Independence Day? The delegates thought it would be. John Adams wrote his wife: "The second day of July, 1776, will be the most memorable . . . in the history of America. I am apt to believe that it will be celebrated by succeeding generations as the great anniversary festival."

But it was not to be: Americans would celebrate not the act of independence, but the day that act was proclaimed to the world. On the famous Fourth, the Congress approved—but *did not sign*—a final version of Jefferson's masterpiece and ordered it printed. Only John Hancock, as president of the Congress, put his John Hancock on it that day except for Charles Thomson (sic), the secretary, who signed merely to attest Hancock's signature. On July 19, after hearing the New York legislature had approved their action, the Congress ordered the Declaration embossed on parchment. Now it could be entitled *The Unanimous Declaration of Independence of the United States of America*—and now it could be signed.

The formal signing ceremony was held on August 2, but some members who were not there that day signed it later. (It is believed about fifty of the fifty-five signers were present.) Some who signed were not members on July 2 and had not voted for it, while some who had voted on that date were no longer members and did not sign it.

WHY THE FOURTH?

The question still remains: Why do we celebrate July 4 instead of July 2? All that happened on the Fourth was official sanction of a document explaining why thirteen

American colonies had declared their independence from Great Britain. One reason is that the people didn't know yet what had happened on July 2; meetings of the Congress were secret—after all, what they were doing was treason. Hancock stepped down from the chair and the voting was done informally so that no records needed to be kept. Because of this, Richard Henry Lee's resolution went unnoticed for years.

The Declaration, on the other hand, was a full and ringing statement for all the world to hear. For most citizens of the new republic, it was, indeed, the first knowledge they had of what had gone on in Philadelphia's old State House. As far as the general body politic was concerned, July 4 *was* Independence Day.

In later years, after the July 4 tradition was firmly established, the Congress even doctored its own records to indicate the signing took place that day. Not until the secret *Journals* of the Congress were ordered printed by the United States Congress in 1821 did the facts become known.

The first known reading of the Declaration of Independence was on July 8 in Philadelphia—from a scaffold. The Liberty Bell did not ring out the news, as legend insists; nor did it crack at that time. It cracked while tolling for the death of John Marshall, the long-time Chief Justice of the Supreme Court, on July 6, 1835.

The Liberty Bell legend began in 1847 with the publication of the book *Washington and His Generals or Legends of the Revolution* by George Lippard, said to be the most popular writer of his day. Lippard, like Weems before him, made up the story out of whole cloth. The anti-slavery movement, trying to marshal all its forces at the time, adopted the bell as a symbol and distributed the first pictures of it. They first called it the "Liberty Bell," using its inscription, "Proclaim Liberty to all the Land and all the Inhabitants thereof," as a reference to slavery rather than to American independence.[2]

CHRISTMAS AT TRENTON

Americans were angered when they heard Britain had enlisted Indians, Negroes, and Hessians to fight against them. We don't mind a struggle that pits Englishmen against Englishmen, they said, but we don't like fighting savages, slaves, and foreigners.

The Hessians were subjects of the ruler of the German state called Hesse-Cassel, who rented out armies at $550,000 a year, plus $55 for every man killed and $12 for every one wounded. The soldiers had no choice in the matter, and often had little stomach for fighting; 8,000 deserted to become American farmers.

American soldiers had heard of these mercenaries before they arrived and believed the tales that they were all seven feet tall and had four rows of teeth, the better to eat them with. It turned out the only odd things about them were their pigtails and fierce black mustaches. The pigtails were plastered with flour and tallow and reached to the waist. The mustaches, waxed with the same substance used on their boots, stuck out horizontally like sword points.

On the night of December 25-26, 1776, Washington crossed the Delaware River to give these despised foes a Yuletide present. Emanuel Leutze's painting of the crossing, the most famous painting of the war, is inaccurate in several respects:

1. It was not broad daylight. The army crossed in the dark, while snow and freezing rain fell.

2. A soldier is holding "Old Glory," which would not be designed until the next year.

3. There are twelve men crammed into a boat about fourteen feet long, which would have made it next to impossible to row or do much of anything else.[3]

4. Washington is shown standing. If he had done so on such a perilous trip, we would now honor someone else as the Father of His Country. An artist, of course, must have his prominent figure stand out from the rest, so perhaps we may forgive Leutze for this oversight.

After making sketches of Washington, Leutze went home to finish the painting, using his German countrymen as models for the other men. Here we have, then, a boatload of Germans crossing a river to fight another bunch of Germans in the *American Revolution*.

One man in the real boat was Henry Knox, Washington's enormously fat friend and chief of artillery. In a rare burst of humor, the general told Knox, "Shift your weight, Harry, or you'll swamp the boat." Soldiers passed the story down the line, the joke helping to relieve the agony of this bitter night.

Sometime after midnight all the men had crossed and the march on the sleeping Hessians began. Someone had betrayed the American plan, and the Hessian commander, Colonel Johann Rahl, knew an attack was in the offing and had alerted his men, but an odd coincidence prompted him to relax his vigil. A small band of Americans, without orders, attacked a Hessian outpost, killing three men and wounding several others. Thinking this was the attack he had heard about—and finding the Americans had fled into the woods—Rahl told his men to forget it and enjoy Christmas.

Since a German soldier's Christmas celebration involved heavy drinking, the Hessians were snoring soundly when the real attack came about dawn on December 26. These modern verses explain how the battle went:

A Visit From St. George

'Twas the night of Christmas
When all through the camp
Not a Hessian was sober,
But all lit like a lamp.
Their clothes were all hung
By the fire without care

Never dreaming that Washington
Would ever come there.
And while they lay sleeping
All snug in their beds,
Visions of beer sausages
Danced in their heads.

When outside the barracks
  There arose such a clatter
They sprang from their bunks
  To see what was the matter.
And what did their bloodshot
  Eyes there behold,
But a diminutive army,
  Two thousand all told.
It swarmed in all screaming
  So swift and so bold,
The Hessians in their longies
  Rushed out in the cold.
More rapid than eagles,
  The Americans they came,
And a man whistled and shouted
  And called them by name:
"Now Stirling, now Sullivan,
  Now Knox and Nat Greene,
Move quickly, brave lads,
  And a victory'll be seen.
Up over the ramparts
  And up over the wall,
Dash out! Dash out!
  Dash out their brains all!"
With this the Hessians,
  Now lively and quick,

Knew that their visitor
  Wasn't jolly St. Nick.
'Twas the Old Fox himself,
  With his bag full of tricks,
Who'd crossed the broad Delaware
  Their wagons to fix.
His uniform was wet,
  And all dirty and wrinkled,
But on spying the Hessians
  His eyes how they twinkled.
So the Old Fox the Hessian stocking
  Did fill,
While scarcely a drop of patriot blood
  Did he spill,
For a mere two men
  Were lost in the fight,
And, sad to relate,
  Both of these from frostbite.
Then he sprang to his horse,
  To his troops gave an order,
And away they all marched
  To the New Jersey border.
He was heard to exclaim,
  'Ere he rode out of sight,
"Merry Christmas to all,
  And to all a good fight!"

—Bill Lawrence

Chapter 6

Growing Pains

Lewis and Clark

WHEN THE YOUNG NATION expanded its borders to include the Louisiana Territory, no one in the United States was quite sure what we had bought. President Jefferson sent Meriwether Lewis and William Clark to find out.

The Lewis and Clark expedition was a remarkable exploring venture, and one of the most remarkable aspects of it was that despite trouble with the Native Americans, bears, rapids, and other pitfalls, the men came through almost unscathed. The only fatality was Sergeant Floyd, who died of what was probably a ruptured appendix.

Lewis, nominally in charge but sharing the leadership with his friend Clark, almost met his maker on two occasions. The first was when a bear chased him until he managed to elude the beast by diving into a river. He later learned, to his chagrin, that the rugged monster was only an adolescent.

The second occasion was when Private Cruzat, blind in one eye and nearsighted in the other, shot Lewis in the place where he sits. Lewis was clad from head to foot in buckskin, and Cruzat said he thought his commander was a deer. Although Cruzat had never shown signs of resentment or disobedience—indeed, he had proved a valuable member of the expedition and his fiddle playing had broken the melancholy of many a lonely night—Lewis seemed never to be sure he had not been shot on purpose. In his final report of the expedition for President Jefferson, he made no mention of the fiddler's sterling qualities—although he praised all the others under his command.

Another who had trouble with bears was Sergeant Ordway, who remained treed all of one day until the bear got tired of waiting for him to come down and wandered off in search of more pedestrian prey.

There was surprisingly little that needed to be done in the way of discipline, for the men had not been long on the trail before they found themselves a very close-knit group, each member feeling a deep sense of brotherhood with the others. Punishment for those who got out of line was usually the lash, an act the Native Americans they met along the route thought atrocious. Although they themselves used punishments we would consider much crueler, the natives considered whipping the worst sort of ignominy.

The explorers, in turn, were equally appalled by the Indians' treatment of one another, especially these three ways Sioux chiefs dealt with unfaithful wives:

1. Removing the hair from the nape of the neck to the brow, then taking the skin near the middle of the top of the head and pulling it down to the ears.

2. Cutting the body up into small pieces and taking the tongue home as a remembrance.

3. Slipping a charge of gunpowder into the folds of her blanket and waiting for her to sit down at a campfire.

BLUE BEADS AND A BLACK MAN

Before an expedition was far into Indian country the explorers found they had made a mistake: they had not brought along enough blue beads. Beads of all description were among the gifts for the natives, and although they loved all of them, their favorites were blue—they would even fight over blue ones. Other favorite gifts were knives, hatchets, cocked hats, coats or coat buttons, jews' harps, bows and ribbons, flags, and, of course, whiskey. The expedition started out with forty gallons of whiskey, which natives so relished they would suck the bottle or lick the glass when it was empty. They called it "milk of the Great Father."

Lewis and Clark distributed the gifts in return for certain favors: food, horses, or information. They could also win such favors by showing the natives York, Clark's black bond servant, whom the Indians called the "black white man." Most Native Americans had seen or heard of white men (mostly Canadian *voyageurs*), but they did not believe a man could be black. They were sure he was a white man painted black, and they would rub their moistened fingers over his skin trying to find out. Most tribes would do anything for a chance to see York—and to watch him dance. Fortunately, York seemed to enjoy this attention and would always put on a good show.

GOING TO THE DOGS

Lewis and Clark sometimes bought dogs to eat from the Indians. Long before the expedition was over they had eaten so much dog flesh they had become fond of it, a fact that made the Nez Percé contemptuous of them, they being the only tribe encountered that did not eat dog. Lewis said he learned to like dog better than venison or elk, and Clark liked it better than anything except horse. (Once, the men tired of struggling with a particularly wild horse they had bought from the Indians and decided to eat him instead.)

Although there was sometimes nothing to eat, the party never followed the example of some Native Americans, who ate the inner bark of the pine tree; and they certainly didn't follow the example of the Mandans, who favored the most putrid parts of the buffalo. In one case, though, three hunters lost in the woods survived for two days on the carcass of a wolf. On another occasion the entire party managed to stay alive by eating only bear oil and twenty pounds of candles. After reaching the Pacific Coast they bought 300 pounds of blubber and a few gallons of oil from natives who had found a whale stranded on shore. In his journal Lewis remarked that Providence had been "more kind to us than he was to Jonah, having sent this monster to be eaten by us, rather than swallowing of us."

Scannon, Lewis's 150-pound Newfoundland dog, was valuable in securing food. He caught waterfowl, small game, and on one occasion a deer. Indians stole him once, and the party turned out in force to get him back before the tribe had him in their pot. Although near starvation several times, the men never cast a hungry eye on Scannon. Indeed, they even shared their rations with him.

On the return trip the tobacco supply ran out, for most of the men a disaster worse than lack of food. In desperation the nicotine addicts smoked or chewed the inner bark of trees, especially favoring crabtree and red willow brands. Some cut up the tobacco-soaked handles of their pipes and chewed that.

MURDER OR SUICIDE?

After the grand trip Lewis was appointed governor of Louisiana Territory, but he did not prove a competent administrator and was soon embroiled in financial and political difficulties. On the way to Washington to explain his position he either committed suicide or was killed. He had stopped for the night at a lonely inn on the Natchez Trace in Tennessee. With him were a Chickasaw Indian agent named John (some reports say James) Neely, a servant called Captain Tom, and John Pernia, a Creole ne'er-do-well the governor had befriended.

When two shots rang out in the middle of the night, Captain Tom and Pernia, who were sleeping in a stable behind the inn, seemed not to have heard them. The whereabouts of Neely is unknown. Lewis, mortally wounded with a bullet in his side and with part of his forehead blown away, staggered to the kitchen door and asked the innkeeper's wife (the innkeeper appears to have been away) for water. The woman, peering fearfully through cracks in the door, refused to give him water and would not come out of the kitchen. Lewis staggered across the road and fell. In a few minutes he was back asking for water again, and again he was refused. He staggered off to die.

Incredibly, there was never an investigation, official or unofficial. There was a coroner's inquest, which ruled the death a suicide; apparently there was not enough evidence to rule otherwise. Neely seems to have carried off Lewis's two pistols, dagger, and pipe-tomahawk; there was no way to find out whether the pistols had been fired. A sizeable sum of money the governor carried was never found.

Today most students of the matter are convinced it was murder.

Life on the Early Frontier

It would be a long time before settlers followed in the footsteps of Lewis and Clark. But by the time of that epic adventure many pioneers had already moved into the trans-Allegheny West. What was life like for them in that untamed wilderness? What sort of pioneer did it take to tame it?

Too often Hollywood and historical novelists have idealized the American frontiersman, showing him as honest, God-fearing, courageous, self-reliant, and well versed in what he needed to know to survive. Granted, there were pioneers who fit that description, but the average frontiersman was illiterate, shiftless, foul-mouthed, belligerent, and unwashed. There were no clear-cut dividing lines, but frontiersmen generally fell into three categories:

1. *The true pioneer.* A hunter and trailblazer, this first venturer into the wilderness would put up a rude shelter of some kind and clear a little patch for corn. He might own one cow and perhaps a scrawny nag or two. In manner and lifestyle he was often more like a Native American than a European.

2. *The first farmer.* He was probably unlettered, and a bit of a loafer and drunkard, but he would build a better abode and clear a little more land, at least enough for more than one crop. Eventually most of these early farmers went broke and lost their farms to creditors.

3. *The true farmer.* Probably the buyer of the first farmer's property, this man had more money, more know-how, and more equipment. He built a house instead of a cabin and put up a good barn to shelter several animals. His crops were well tended, his fences mended. His descendants may still be living on this land.

CAMPS AND CABINS

The rough shelter of the first pioneer was probably a "half-faced camp." Sinking forked poles in the ground, he leaned logs against them, and formed the roof with more logs and bark. The front of the shelter was open; the rear was a small hill or rise in the ground.

The second settler lived in the famous log cabin, which most people think is a distinctively American innovation, not realizing it was an idea brought over by the Swedes who settled Delaware. All the neighbors, if any, pitched in to put up a cabin in as short a time as possible; of course this activity was called a "house-raising." It took about four days to throw up a log cabin, each person having a particular job to do. Some cut the trees and trimmed them; some notched the ends of the logs so they could be fitted together; some put up the walls and the roof. The men made frequent trips to the jug for the pause that refreshes: a swig of hard cider or corn liquor. The women cooked and served all day. At night there was fiddling and dancing—and even more trips to the jug.

Some cabins had no windows; if there were any they were covered with wooden shutters. Many settlers used the Native American method of defense—cutting holes in the walls big enough to fire a rifle through, then covering the hole on the outside with plaster. The hole was circled on the inside so that in case of attack the plaster could be punched out and the hole fired through.

FRONTIER FOOD

Corn, thanks to the Native American, was the frontier's staple food. Settlers watched anxiously for the corn to come up and began eating it while it was still green. When it reached the half-hard state they grated it, usually for mush, and when it became too hard for the grater they broke it up in a hominy block. This was a section of hollowed-out log into which the corn was put and pounded with the flattened end of a pole or stave. Afterwards the kernels were softened with water and lye. Yes—lye! It was a trick the settlers learned from the natives; the lye apparently never harmed anyone. The cook then washed the soft kernels, removed the hulls, and washed them again. This hominy, thanks to the lye, puffed up and turned white when boiled and was served as a mush. Coarsely ground hominy became known as "grits," which are still popular in some parts of the country today.

Bread was one of two kinds: corn pone or "johnnycake." Both were made with soda, salt, and buttermilk or sour milk. An egg might be put in the pone, but not in the johnnycake, for it was to be used, originally, for traveling and the egg would make it dry out. (Its real name was "journeycake.")

More than likely, meat would turn up on the table as "potpie," which today would be known as stew with dumplings. Potpie was quick and easy to make and could be eaten with a spoon, which might be the only eating instrument available.

A family usually had at least one cow, but the frontiersman liked his milk sour, as well he might, since without any way to keep it cold it would turn sour anyway. He poured down copious amounts of cider and whiskey and looked down on tea and coffee as "slops that don't stick to your ribs."

The frontiersman shot his own deer, elk, wild turkey, buffalo, and occasionally a panther. Some said panthers were good eating, tasting like veal or rattlesnake. Frontiersmen knew how to preserve meat by soaking it in brine, but getting the salt to do this was a constant problem. The easiest way to preserve it was to cut the meat into strips and dry it before a fire—this was the famous "jerky."

HANGINGS AND OTHER SOCIAL EVENTS

Frontier people were starved for entertainment and they used any excuse to get together: church doings, weddings, funerals, husking and quilting bees, trials—especially trials—and, they could hope, a satisfying hanging.

Perhaps the number one social occasion was a wedding. Nuptials were a time for feasting, drinking, and various forms of play and horseplay. The custom was for the bride's father to set a quart of whiskey on his doorstep and to have all male guests race from a mile away to see who got to it first, the winner taking it to the groom for the first drink. The men also might try to kidnap the groom on his way to the ceremony, and sometimes the women attempted the same stunt with the bride.

The evening following the wedding the newly united couple retired to their bed while the guests partied all night, with occasional visits to the bedside. Another party followed on the second night, and on the third night friends of the bride and groom organized a "shivaree." The celebrants arrived in couples, bringing along anything that would make noise. They surrounded the house and on a signal suddenly began to make such a din the woods shook with the noise. This was the start of a third, and final, all-night party.

The shivaree marked the end of the wedding festival—everyone was too tuckered out for any more celebration.

Chapter 7

The War of 1812

Why Another War?

ONE CANNOT GROW, say the psychologists, without some pain. In the case of our young nation's growth, the pain involved another war with Great Britain. Trouble at sea with Britain—especially the galling practice of impressment used by the British Navy—was perhaps the main cause of the war. But the War Hawks of the West had little interest in the impressment imbroglio; they wanted Canada, which at the time seemed to them easy pickings. Thus it was that a war fought for "freedom of the seas" began with an American invasion of its northern neighbor.

The War of 1812 is a war few Americans know much about, yet as obscure as it may seem today, it enriched this nation with four priceless additions to its heritage:

1. A name for the president's home—"White House."

2. A national anthem—"The Star-Spangled Banner."

3. Our most famous fighting ship—"Old Ironsides."

4. Our cartoon symbol—"Uncle Sam."

Two Major Campaigns

THE CHESAPEAKE CAMPAIGN

Initially the attack on Canada was an abject failure. American armies attacked on three fronts and all were thrown back—sometimes by the same British troops.

Later, American arms were more successful—at Chippewa, Lundy's Lane, and the Thames River—and an army under General Henry Dearborn marched into York (now Toronto), the capital of Upper Canada, and accepted the city's surrender. Alas, Dearborn did not like the surrender agreement and held up his approval of it while his troops ransacked the Parliament building and other places. Dearborn himself made off with the parliamentary mace.

In retaliation for the sacking of York, a British fleet and army began harassing the shores of Chesapeake Bay and eventually marched on Washington. There was not much to Washington at the time. The Capitol and the President's Mansion were unfinished, and the entire setting was so rustic that quail and partridge could be flushed out of the grounds of both.

In command of the fleet was Admiral Sir George Cockburn (pronounced "Coburn"), whom Americans despised for his tactics and his mouth. ("Americans should be treated like spaniels," he had said.) The troops were commanded by General Robert Ross, a more gallant officer. Opposing them was a larger force of 6,000 militia under General William Winder, a lawyer. The militia were, as always, poorly trained and poorly disciplined. Winder sought to stop the British advance on the capital by drawing up his lines at the nearby village of Bladensburg.

The British had a new weapon never seen in America—the rocket. It was little more than a giant firecracker and did little damage, but its noise terrified the panicky militia. As the British lines advanced, the militiamen turned tail and ran. They fled *en masse* and did not stop until they were sixteen miles on the other side of the city. The only casualty was was officer who died of exhaustion—he had run himself to death.

TURN ABOUT IS FIRE PLAY

The British then prepared to enter Washington and—in revenge for the burning of York—put it to the torch. President James "Little Jemmy" Madison—standing five feet four inches tall—was among the troops that fled and afterward wandered around the hills, spending one night in a henhouse. In the meantime, at the President's home, his wife Dolley (the correct spelling) knew what she had to do. Into a wagon she quickly loaded the President's papers, books, silver, four ornamental eagles, and the red velvet curtains from the drawing room. Next came the Gilbert Stuart portrait of George Washington, which was screwed to the wall. Having no time to unscrew it, she had a servant smash the heavy wooden frame with an axe but cautioned him not to roll it up. After another servant fetched her pet parrot, she lit out in a carriage.

British troops set fire to the Capitol, which at the time had no wings or dome, but the building proved so well built it seemed to defy destruction. They finally succeeded in partly burning it by chopping up the furniture into kindling and setting fire to it using rocket powder.

It is probably not true that the troops found the table at the President's Mansion perfectly set for forty guests and that the officers sat down and helped themselves to the meal. But the officers did help themselves to anything that could be taken as a souvenir. Cockburn took one of the President's hats and a cushion from Mrs. Madison's chair, joking that the cushion would remind him of her seat. Soon the building went up in flames. It too was only partly burned, but all the presidential papers and old records going back to the Revolution were destroyed. Some soldiers discovered a fireproof vault on the ground floor but were disappointed when all it contained were more old files. When the building was later repainted it became known as the White House.

The troops then proceeded to the offices of the *National Intelligencer*, a newspaper that had called Cockburn, among other things, a "choleric beast." The admiral ordered all the paper's offices destroyed and, according to legend, specifically ordered every letter "C" in the type cases destroyed so there would be no more abuse of the name Cockburn. General Ross intended to keep a copy of the paper that assured its readers the city was safe from British attack, but couldn't find a place for it because his pockets were already full of Madison's love letters to Dolley.

As 200 troops marched to Greenleaf's Point to destroy an arsenal, someone carelessly tossed a lighted torch into what he thought was a dry well. The well was not only dry, it was packed with powder kegs the Americans had hidden there. The resulting explosion rocked the countryside for miles around, killing at least twelve British soldiers and leaving upwards of fifty seriously wounded.

As the invaders finished up their work of destruction, a summer shower began to fall. The rain did little to quench the larger fires, but it did prevent them from spreading. As the troops prepared for their long march back to the ships in Chesapeake Bay, the sky suddenly grew dark and a storm of close to hurricane force swept across the flaming city. The soldiers then began to beat an even hastier retreat, some seeming to believe the storm was God's retribution for their dastardly deeds. For one unfortunate cavalryman it was: a small tornado spawned by the storm blew him and his horse away, neither ever to be seen again.

What So Proudly He Hailed

The invading force intended to give Baltimore, the new nation's third largest city and an important port, the same sort of going over, but this time they failed. Baltimoreans turned out in droves to help the army put up earthworks (fortifications of logs and dirt), and when an attack came at North Point below the city it was, although successful at first, eventually driven off. General Ross was wounded in the fighting and later died, his body preserved for the trip home in 129 gallons of good Jamaica rum. In the last hours, their grapeshot (clusters of small balls) used up, Americans fired from their cannon anything available: old locks, bits of broken muskets, horseshoes, nails.

After a naval bombardment failed to reduce Fort McHenry, which defended Baltimore's southern approaches, the British gave up the attempt and retired from the Chesapeake. It was while anxiously watching the firing on McHenry that Francis Scott Key, a lawyer by trade, began scribbling down the inspired lines that would become "The Star-Spangled Banner."

Key was on board one of the British ships trying to effect the release of his friend, a sixty-five-year-old doctor named William Beanes, whom the British were holding prisoner. The British had Beanes bagged because he had jailed in his own house some stragglers from the army on its way back from attacking Washington. They detained Key on board until the firing ended.

The ship was eight miles from the fort, and some have questioned whether Key could have seen the flag from so far away, even with the spyglass he used. The flag was certainly big enough: it was forty-two by thirty feet and was flying from high above the ramparts. The War Department had ordered it made so there would be one "so large the British would have no trouble seeing it from a distance." It cost $405.90, a considerable sum in those days. You can see it today in the Smithsonian Institution.

After an unsuccessful attack, the British released Key, Dr. Beanes, and John S. Skinner, an American prisoner-exchange agent who had accompanied Key. In his room at Baltimore's Indian Queen Hotel, Key finished his poem and set it to the music of "To Anachreon in Heaven," a well-known English drinking song. Robert Treat Paine, a signer of the Declaration of Independence, had recently used the same melody for a popular air called "Adams and Liberty." Key himself had used the tune in 1805 for a song about the heroes of the war with the pirates of Tripoli. The new song was an immediate hit, and it was sung as an informal anthem until 1931, when it was made the official national anthem.

A National Ship and a National Nickname

"OLD IRONSIDES"

The great ship *Constitution* got her nickname while engaged with the British *Guerrière* off Halifax, Nova Scotia. Much of the fighting was at close range, and the *Constitution*'s crew was astounded to see cannon balls bounce off her thick oaken sides. From then on she was "Old Ironsides."

Old Ironsides was a national ship. Her timbers were of white oak from Massachusetts and Maine, live oak from Georgia, and yellow pine from South Carolina and Georgia. Paul Revere made the castings, spikes, and copper bolts that fastened the timbers together. Her complement was 400 men—22 officers and 378 petty officers, seamen, and marines. It took 180 of those—90 on the spar deck, 90 on the gun deck—just to hoist her anchor.

Several times the *Constitution* has been saved from the scrap heap. The first was when the Navy planned to scuttle her in 1830, but a poem by Oliver Wendell Holmes whipped up public sentiment. The poem began:

> *Ay, tear her tattered ensign down!*
> *Long has it waved on high,*
> *And many an eye has danced to see*
> *That banner in the sky.*

The last time was in the 1920s, when schoolchildren across the land contributed their nickels, dimes, and pennies to save her.

The *Constitution* still is a commissioned ship of the United States Navy, listed on the rolls as the flagship of the Commandant, First Naval District. She is a floating museum tied up to a dock in the old Boston Naval Yard. Once a year she makes a "turn-around cruise" in the harbor to keep her in sailing trim and to weather her evenly on both sides.

"UNCLE SAM"

There really *was* an Uncle Sam. His name was Samuel Wilson and he was an inspector of meat for a contractor supplying the Army with beef and salt pork during the War of 1812. His workers called him "Uncle Sam" Wilson.

The meat, then as now, had to be stamped "U.S." to show that it had been approved. The nation was scarcely twenty years old and although everyone was acquainted with the name "United States," not all were familiar with the initials. A worker stamping meat asked another, "What does this 'U.S.' stand for, anyway?" The other replied, "Uncle Sam, I guess." The story has been disputed by many historians, but it has stuck.

The first recorded use of the initials was in a Troy, New York, newspaper in September 1813. Uncle Sam first appeared as a cartoon in 1830, but he had no beard and did not wear the clothes we associate with him today. By the time of the Civil War, however, the character was sporting a goatee, striped pants, and a star-studded hatband. The costume was based on the one worn by a comic cartoon character of the day, Major Jack Downing. Major Jack was soon forgotten, but Uncle Sam persisted.

Not much else is known about Samuel Wilson. As a boy he ran away from home and became a drummer in the Continental Army. At one time during his youth he played with another lad named John Chapman, who also would find his way into the history books as Johnny Appleseed.

Congress passed a resolution in 1961 making the Uncle Sam character an official symbol of the United States of America.

Chapter 8

Roads, Rivers, and Rails

Stagecoach Days

WHEN GEORGE WASHINGTON traveled from Mount Vernon to New York for his inaugural in 1789, there were no hard-surfaced roads, only narrow, winding, rutted tracks. Here and there a farmer had thrown rocks into the path, but these only made the road bumpier and more dangerous.

The first decent road in the country was the Lancaster Turnpike, a thirty-six-mile stretch from Lancaster, Pennsylvania, to Philadelphia. The first federally built highway, the National Road, ran eventually from Baltimore to Vandalia, Illinois. Both roads used the new English method developed by John McAdam, laying down a foot of crushed stone topped with gravel that would be pounded hard by the wheels of coaches and wagons.

The stagecoach was the only means of public transportation. When the National Road opened its first segment—Baltimore to Wheeling on the Ohio River—the fare for the full trip was $17.25, meals and lodging not included. VIPs usually traveled free, the driver making a white chalk mark on their hats. Coaches traveled day and night on a schedule so tight one could set a watch by their passing. Fresh horses replaced tired ones every twelve miles, with the change taking no more than a minute or two. At the longer, steeper hills, a groom waited with two extra horses to be hitched up to the usual four.

For passengers spending the night along the line, there were two types of hostelries: wagon stands and stage houses. At a wagon stand the passenger slept on the floor and paid three cents a glass for whiskey; at a stage house he could sleep in a bed, but whiskey was five cents a glass.

At the hostelries meals were served boardinghouse style—all there was to eat went on the table. The customer paid a flat fee and took what he wanted. In the evening passengers sat around and drank, swapped stories, drank, sang songs, drank. Evenings were short because the coachman's signal—a blast on a conch shell—brought passengers tumbling out of bed before dawn. Everyone piled outside to share a common washbasin and more likely than not a common towel. Some stopped off at the bar for an eye-opener before breakfast, perhaps without bothering to wash first. As a bit of verse had it:

> *Our fathers of old, they lived like goats,*
> *Washing their eyes and then their throats.*
> *But we, their sons, have grown more wise*
> *We wash our throats before our eyes.*

Coachmen were considered important people, and many a boy yearned to be one when he grew up. A passenger could consider himself honored if allowed to sit out front beside the driver, as did such notables as William Henry Harrison, Andrew Jackson, Zachary Taylor, and Henry Clay.

Drivers were "characters" even in a day when individualism was the rule. Many were impressive physical specimens, such as the six-foot-six-inch Redding Bunting. Although the Express Line got its nickname, "Shake Gut Line," because of a coach that set a record of eleven miles an hour for a 130-mile run, there were those who liked to think the nickname came from a coachman named Montgomery Hemming, who weighed in on the hay scale at 460 pounds.

Steamboats A-Comin'

"POOR JOHN FITCH"

Although anyone who has ever studied American history knows of Robert Fulton, the real inventor of the steamboat was a man named John Fitch— or as he was called by those who ridiculed him and his inventions, "poor John Fitch." His story is a tragic one.

Fitch began experimenting with steam power in 1786, and if the roads hadn't been so bad in those days he might have been our first automobile maker. Fitch knew no steam engine could pull a wagon through two feet of mud. Boats, though, should be no trouble to propel across smooth water. Fitch's first boat, however, had no engine. It was a skiff just big enough for himself. On each side there were three vertical paddles attached to a chain that turned on sprockets designed for him by a watchmaker friend named Henry Voight. Fitch would move the sprockets by turning a crank. He merely wanted to find out if his idea was sound before mounting a steam engine to do the work of the crank. In the meantime he applied for the exclusive right to operate steam-driven vessels on the waterways of New Jersey. It cost them nothing, so the state legislature agreed to humor this crackpot. Fitch launched his strange-looking craft on the Delaware River near Philadelphia, and the experiment became the first of a long line of heart-breaking failures. The boat proved completely unmanageable, spinning around like a drunken waterbug. A group of waterfront idlers laughed Fitch all the way home.

But Fitch and his friend did not give up. Before long they had built another boat, a longer one with six oars on each side propelled by a small steam engine they had built in Voight's shop. Again the onlookers sneered, but the two builders did not mind—this boat worked. Off went Fitch to Delaware, Pennsylvania, New York, and Virginia, and came home with grants like New Jersey's from all those states. Armed with these, Fitch was able to scare up some money, enough to build a new boat—same plan but larger.

It was now the summer of 1787 and the Constitutional Convention was assembling in Philadelphia. Fitch persuaded some of the members to go along on the first ride in his new craft. This boat failed, too. It wouldn't steer properly because of a rudder that was too long, and it ended up stuck in a mudbank. Poor John Fitch had failed again.

FITCH SUCCEEDS—AND FAILS

Undaunted, the two inventors built a lighter and slimmer boat with paddles at the stern. The new craft made its maiden voyage twenty miles up the Delaware River from Philadelphia to Burlington, New Jersey. Leaving grinning spectators behind, the boat got up speed and was soon making four miles an hour. As the houses on the shoreline fell behind them, Fitch and Voight felt that at last they had triumphed. At Dunk's Ferry upriver some of their friends fired off a brass cannon from the Revolutionary War.

As Burlington hove into sight, the two became overenthusiastic and began feeding more and more wood into the furnace. The boat turned in toward the shore and a great cheer went up from the welcoming committee. Suddenly an ear-shattering explosion rent the air. It wasn't another cannon firing in salute—the boiler had blown up. Knowing little about the operation of steam engines, the two inventors had not made their boiler strong enough. When Voight fed in more wood, the pressure built up until the boiler couldn't take any more and blew apart at the seams. The boat slowed down . . . then stopped . . . then began drifting back downstream.

But again Fitch corrected the boat's faults, and in the summer of 1790, after four years of public ridicule, he launched the ship on the first regular service in the United States—a forty-mile run between Philadelphia and Trenton. It made the trip three times a week at a price of five shillings (about $1.25). To encourage more passengers, Fitch offered free sausages and beer. The boat made at least thirty-one trips totaling over 1,000 miles, and once made eighty miles in one day. It went at least two miles an hour faster than Robert Fulton's *Clermont* did on its maiden voyage up the Hudson in 1807.

The ship did not pay for itself and had to be given up. No longer would anyone agree to back Fitch's efforts with money for fear of subjecting themselves to the same ridicule as he received.

Fitch wandered out to Kentucky where he had bought land, only to find his property overrun with squatters. By this time he was a sick man, constantly racked with pain. He took his land claims to court, but before the issue was settled poor John Fitch died. He had saved up the pain pills the doctor gave him, and one night in 1798 he took them all.

Found in his room was a model steam engine mounted on a small truck with flanged wheels. If he had lived, this "visionary madman" might have been the father of the American railroad.

FULTON'S SUCCESSES AND FAILURES

Robert Fulton should not be considered the inventor of the steamboat, but rather the first to operate one that was successful commercially. In America, so it seems, no one is considered successful unless he or she is *financially* successful.

What Fulton did was take the devices of others and combine them into something that worked. His first love, however, was not science but art; he was already a well-known painter of miniature portraits. He was in England studying with the famous artist Benjamin West when James Watt began applying the new steam engines to mechanical problems. Fulton's interest quickly changed to that field.

It was not until Fulton crossed paths with Robert R. Livingston that the ideas spinning around in his head began to take shape. Livingston was a wealthy man, a former chancellor of the state of New York and a member of the five-man committee that drafted the Declaration of Independence. The two met in Paris in 1800, where Livingston had taken up his new duties as ambassador to France and where Fulton had gone to try to interest the Emperor Napoleon in a submarine he had designed. Fulton demonstrated that his boat would work by submerging it in the Seine River, moving about under water, and returning to the surface—but the emperor wasn't impressed. Neither was Livingston interested in a submarine, but he was deeply interested in harnessing the power of steam for surface vessels. The ambassador sought out the young artist and put up the money for Fulton's first venture into steamboating.

The first boat was a disaster; the hull was too weak, and in its trial run on the Seine it broke in two and both halves sank. A second boat worked, but it would make only three and a half miles an hour—too slow to be of any use.

Fulton learned that John Fitch had left some of his plans with the American consul in Paris; he borrowed the plans and kept them for months. Returning to the United States, he immediately began work on another steamship. But just before it was to be launched, a midnight raiding party of sailing-ship men, who were afraid this strange monster would put them out of business, virtually destroyed it. Still undaunted, and still with Livingston's backing, Fulton started over again. The final result was the famous *Clermont*, named after Livingston's vast estate, Clermont-on-the-Hudson. On August 17, 1807, the *Clermont* made the first of many trips along the Hudson River from New York City to Albany and back. Now the public was ready to accept the steamboat, and Robert Fulton profited handsomely from his "invention" for the remaining eight years of his life.

It is rarely mentioned that Fulton's submarine, the *Nautilus*, later proved a success when it sank a wooden ship with torpedoes also designed by the maker. Little known also are Fulton's other inventions: a method for raising and lowering canal boats to integrate them into a surface railroad system; a device for sawing marble; and machines for spinning flax and twisting hemp into rope. And during the War of 1812 Fulton constructed a huge floating fort to protect New York Harbor.

STEAMBOATING ON THE MISSISSIPPI

All right, said the public, steamboating on the Hudson River is a success, but the Hudson is broad and deep and you'll never convince us that a steamboat can navigate treacherous inland waterways like the Ohio and Mississippi rivers. Fulton and Livingston set out to prove the public wrong.

After getting from the Territory of Louisiana the exclusive right to operate steamboats on the Mississippi, the partners sent out Nicholas Roosevelt, a grand-uncle of Theodore Roosevelt, with orders to build a steamboat at Pittsburgh and sail her down to New Orleans. The job was done by the fall of 1811 and Roosevelt, his wife and servants, a pilot, and a crew of six left the future steel capital in their spanking new boat, which Roosevelt confidently dubbed the *New Orleans*. All along the Ohio, farmers dropped their plows and gawked at this fire-belching sea serpent, and when she blew off all her stored-up steam at Louisville in the middle of the night the sleeping citizens were sure a comet had dropped into the river. When they found out what had really happened, the town declared a holiday. At all the towns along the route, Roosevelt took the *New Orleans* on a short turn upriver to show the folks it could be done. The keelboatmen in particular swore it was impossible.

No one thought the ship would survive the great falls of the Ohio below Louisville, but she did—barely. At the same time, Mrs. Roosevelt survived the birth of a baby.

The *New Orleans* also survived an unforeseen disaster— one of major proportions, to say the least. As they reached the Mississippi, its muddy waters began to heave with huge waves and the river banks to crumble and fall into the turbulent waters. As they reached New Madrid, Missouri, they found the town's survivors straddling logs, trying to escape the great cracks that had opened up in the earth's crust. It was the New Madrid earthquake of 1811, a monumental disaster seldom recalled today. During it, rivers changed their courses, whole islands disappeared, and new lakes—such as Reelfoot Lake in Tennessee—sprang up where not even a puddle had existed before. One night the *New Orleans* tied up to a tree on an island, but when the crew awoke the next morning the entire island had disappeared.

When coal for the boiler gave out, the crew had to go ashore often and cut wood; as a result it was three and a half months before the *New Orleans* reached New Orleans. The ship had successfully navigated an uncharted river full of snags, rocks, and sandbars, and it had even survived an earthquake. Now there was no doubt that steamboats were a practicable means of transportation on the nation's larger inland rivers.

They've Been Working
on the Railroad

The railroad was not an invention but merely a putting together of two existing ideas: steam power and tracks. For centuries, people had used tracks to get things from one place to another, usually in wagons or carts pulled by some beast of burden. By the nineteenth century, miners had begun strapping their wooden rails with iron to keep them from wearing out so fast. There were several of these "rail-roads" in use in the United States, most of them connecting quarries with streams. Sooner or later someone was bound to think of putting rails and steam engines together.

The first appears to have been Richard Trevithick, an Englishman, who in 1801 ran a steam engine on the highway and in 1804 ran another on rails. In 1825 the British were marveling over George Stephenson's "Locomotion," a little engine that ran sixteen miles an hour on the Stockton and Darlington Railway. Four years later they were even more impressed with Stephenson's "Rocket," which blazed along at the unheard of speed of twenty-nine miles an hour—the first true, fire-breathing "Iron Horse."

In America, meanwhile, a number of railroads were in the planning stage, but all of them were to use horses. So far no one had listened to John Stevens, who had been proposing steam-operated railways since 1812. (Congress, however, had listened to his proposal that the government protect an inventor's rights, and had passed the Patent Law in 1790.) In 1825 Stevens demonstrated a one-cylinder steam-powered locomotive on the grounds of his estate in Hoboken, New Jersey, but the public regarded it as an amusing toy.

The Delaware and Hudson Canal Company bought an English locomotive, the *Stourbridge Lion*, and operated it in the coal country around Honesdale, Pennsylvania. But it proved too heavy for their track, and its wheels were so rigidly mounted it would run only on straight track or on a very gradual curve. It was a failure, but it got more people interested.

The first successful locomotive ran on the first successful railroad in America, the Baltimore and Ohio. The B & 0 was chartered in 1827 to try to compete with the Erie Canal, and the company broke ground on the Fourth of July, 1828. B & O directors were trying to decide whether to use horses or steam engines, and were about to agree with a prominent English engineer that the terrain was too twisting and hilly for a steam engine, when Peter Cooper informed them: "I will knock together an engine in six weeks that will pull carriages ten miles an hour." And knock one together he did, an engine that looked like a teakettle and was so small he called it *Tom Thumb*. Cooper linked his little engine to a car that looked more like a boat and took a group of beaver-hatted dignitaries on a spin down to Ellicott's Mills, thirteen miles from Baltimore, which was then the end of the line. It was the first trip on an American railroad with an American-built steam engine.

The stagecoach people were envious. They brought up a carriage pulled by one of their best horses and challenged Cooper to a race on a parallel track. Cooper, eager to prove his point, accepted the challenge and the race was on. The first mile or two, while *Tom Thumb* got up steam, the horse drew ahead, but as pressure mounted the little engine overtook the horse and chugged out in the lead. Just when he thought he had the race won, Cooper discovered that a belt operating the blower had slipped off its drum. Without the blower to force a draft through the furnace, pressure began to drop. Cooper repaired the damage, lacerating his hand in the process, but it was too late— the horse had pulled ahead and won the race. It did not matter, however, because *Tom Thumb*'s performance had convinced the directors that steam power was what they needed.

Not to be outdone, Charleston, South Carolina, eager to pull in all the trade from south and west of the state, inaugurated in January 1831 the South Carolina Canal and Railroad Company and put into service the *Best Friend of Charleston*, a locomotive that could pull four cars with up to fifty passengers at a speed of twenty-one miles an hour. But not for long. On June 17, 1831, a fireman who was annoyed at the hissing of the boiler tied the safety valve down and the boiler blew up.

A RIDE ON THE IRON HORSE

What was it like riding on one of these early trains? (They were called "trains," incidentally, because the word means "a moving file.") Take the first ride on the Mohawk and Hudson Line and find out:

> *The train consists of the locomotive, the* De Witt Clinton, *three passenger cars that are only slightly modified stagecoaches, and a flat car behind the engine carrying a barrel of water and a stack of wood. All are not much longer than a modern-day locomotive. There is no cab for the engineer—he stands on a small platform behind the engine. The conductor draws from his pocket a tin whistle and gives the signal that the train is about to start.*

> *The engineer opens wide the throttle, and the little* De Witt Clinton *(named after the governor of New York who got the Erie Canal built) starts with such a violent jerk the train almost jumps the rails. As the slack between the cars is taken up, each one slams into the one in front of it and sends passengers sprawling onto the floor.*

> *The whole countryside turns out to see the Iron Horse. Many drive as close to the track as they can get. When the engine comes snorting along with sparks and smoke shooting out of the smokestack many horses take fright, rear, and shy, and dash into a ditch. Others go galloping through the midst of the crowd, upsetting carriages and wagons and spreading terror.*

> *After a while the train has to make one of its frequent stops at one of the big tanks along the line to take on water. The engine stops so abruptly the passengers are spilled onto the floor again. At the next stop*

some passengers get out, tear rails from a fence, and wedge them between coaches to try to lessen the effects of the jerking.

Pine wood is used as fuel, causing great billows of acrid black smoke to sweep back on the passengers riding on top of the cars. A steady stream of sparks and pieces of half-burnt wood come down on them in a hot shower, burning holes in coats and bonnets. Those who brought umbrellas raise them for protection, but they catch fire and have to be thrown overboard. The clothing of one passenger after another catches fire and wild confusion results as each passenger beats on his neighbor trying to put out the flames.

In spite of ruined hats and umbrellas, holes burned in clothing, frightened horses and bruised flesh, everyone considers this first train ride a roaring success.

Some improvements had to be made in a hurry, to be sure. A couple of the earliest were the sandbox and the cowcatcher. The idea of a sandbox came up after a plague of grasshoppers swept over Pennsylvania, making the tracks slippery. At first, men were sent ahead to sweep off the tracks; then someone thought of putting boxes of sand on the engine, a fine trickle falling continuously on the tracks.

After engines had run over several hundred cows, a man with the wonderful name of Isaac Dripps invented a "cowcatcher." His first attempt was a crude one, just two iron bars thrusting out from the engine and slanting toward the track. This protected the engine, but impaled the cows. His second one was a simple horizontal bar similar to today's automobile bumper. It was effective enough and used for many years before the V-shaped cowcatcher of modern trains replaced it.

PLENTY WAGON, NO HORSE

The Civil War made the nation's need for a transcontinental railroad stand out in bold relief. Congress passed legislation allowing the Union Pacific Railroad to start laying track westward from Omaha and the Central Pacific to start eastward from Sacramento, with the two lines to meet . . .somewhere. For each mile of track laid, the railroads got twenty square miles of land—which they could sell to settlers along with generous subsidies.

Chinese laborers provided cheap labor for the Central Pacific while the Union Pacific used thousands of Irish, many of them newly arrived immigrants. Although some Native Americans attacked the railroad—which they called "plenty wagon, no horse"—others were eager to work on it. On one occasion Paiutes convinced the Chinese working beside them that the Nevada desert was full of snakes so large they could swallow a man in one gulp. Next day the foreman had to send horsemen down the track to bring back about 500 Chinese who had left during the night and were headed for the safety of Sacramento.

Since every mile completed meant more money in their coffers, the two railroads wasted no time laying down track. An English visitor described their technique:

A light car, drawn by a single horse, gallops up front with its load of rails. The men seize the end of the rail and start forward, the rest of the gang taking hold by twos until it is clear of the car. They come forward at a run. At the word of command the rail is dropped in place, right side up with care, while the same process goes on at the other side of the car. Less than thirty seconds to a rail for each gang, and so four rails go down to the minute!

The moment the car is empty it is tipped over on its side of the track to let the next loaded car pass it, and it is a sight to see it go flying back again for another load propelled by a horse at full gallop. Close behind the first gang come the spikers and bolters and a lively time they make of it. It is a grand Anvil Chorus that these sturdy sledges are playing across the plain. It is in triple time, three strokes to a spike. There are ten spikes to a rail, four hundred rails to a mile, eight hundred miles to San Francisco.

RACE TO THE FINISH

Not only were the railroads making money from generous subsidies, they were making even more through graft and unforgivable wastefulness. They sometimes avoided places where they would have to build expensive bridges or make cuts through mountains, and instead laid track in great snakelike curves around such areas. During the last winter of work—1868–1869—they ignored snow and ice and laid track over them when the snow and ice melted, rails and ties were left dangling in mid-air. After entering Utah, the two lines laid 400 miles of *parallel* track, each company blithely ignoring the fact that the other was duplicating what it was doing.

In addition, some officers of the Union Pacific, notably the vice-president and general manager, Thomas C. Durant, were silent partners in firms selling supplies and equipment to the railroads at exorbitant prices. They took a ten percent rake-off on many contracts they were empowered to let, received kickbacks from tie-cutting contractors and timber haulers, and persuaded construction supervisors to report double the amount of rock hauled in for fills.

Durant also formed a construction company, the Crédit Mobilier, to loot his own Union Pacific Company. He, as general manager of the U.P., hired himself, as the silent president of Credit Mobilier, to build the line at $50,000 a mile when the actual construction costs averaged about $30,000 a mile.

President Ulysses S. Grant ordered the two railroads to stop playing games and pick a spot to join rails. The place selected was Promontory Point, near Ogden, Utah. The Union Pacific had already won the race across the continent but had an easier time of it since much of its territory was flat prairie land. Now, as the two lines closed on Promontory Point, Charles Crocker, one of the directors of the Central Pacific, bet Durant the C.P. outfit could lay ten miles of track in a single day.

Durant accepted, thinking the task impossible, and both railroads declared a holiday on April 28—"Ten Mile Day." Crocker planned the undertaking like a military campaign. He laid out ten miles worth of ties and had rails, spikes, and bolts brought up at regular intervals by Chinese laborers on handcarts pulled by horses at breakneck speed. A hand-picked crew of eight burly Irishmen, all of them moving at full speed, made up the rail-carrying crew. No one stopped for anything except an occasional drink of water or tea from pails a detachment of Chinese carried on poles over their shoulders. By 1:30 P.M., six miles of track were down and Crocker called a halt for lunch. He offered to release any track-layer who felt he couldn't go on, but there were no takers. By 7 P.M., the end of a full twelve-hour workday, the foreman signaled victory: his crew had laid down ten miles and fifty-six feet of track, or as someone figured up later, 3,520 rails and 25,800 ties.

DRIVING (MAYBE) THE LAST SPIKE

The last spike was driven into the nation's first transcontinental railroad on May 10, 1869—seven years earlier than the original estimate. The last-spike ceremony was planned for May 8, but two events delayed it. The special train bringing Leland Stanford, president of the Central Pacific, and other C.P. officials was held up while workmen repaired tracks washed out by heavy rains in Weber Canyon. Also, when Thomas Durant's private car pulled into Piedmont, Wyoming, an armed mob of several hundred workers demanding overdue wages switched it onto a sidetrack and chained the wheels to the rails. Durant promptly arranged for the money to be telegraphed from the railroad's New York headquarters.

The air was electric with excitement at noon on May 10 as several hundred railroad officials and workmen, army troops and officers, a few civic leaders from towns along the line, government representatives, and a group of Mormons with a small band gathered around the gap in the tracks where the last tie and last spike would he put down. Champagne flowed freely as the crowd jockeyed for positions close enough to see the grand event. As the main purpose of the railroad at that time was to bring the West Coast closer to the rest of the country, the Central Pacific was doing the honors. Stanford had brought with him the last tie, made of highly polished California laurel with a silver plate bearing the names of the Central Pacific directors, and a golden spike fashioned out of $400 worth of gold by a San Francisco jeweler. At the tip of the spike was a gold nugget, which was broken off and later made into souvenir rings and watch-fobs for Stanford, Union Pacific President Oliver Ames, President Grant, and Secretary of State William H. Seward.

The silver-headed maul to be used to drive in the last spike was wired to a telegraph key so the final blows would activate every telegraph key in the country—all lines had been cleared for the purpose—in what was probably the nation's first "coast-to-coast broadcast." It did not quite work out that way, however.

As a crew of Chinese, decked out in fresh white frockcoats, prepared to lay the laurel tie, one of several photographers present shouted, "Now's the time—shoot them!" The Chinese knew very little English, but one word they knew well was "shoot"— they had been shot at by Indians. They dropped the tie as if it were red-hot and dashed for safety in the Promontory hills. To the frustration of officials and the drunken delight of most of the crowd, they were coaxed back to finish the job.

Preparations ready once again, the telegraph operator tapped out to his colleagues all over the country: "Keep quiet. When the last spike is driven we will say 'Done.' Don't break the circuit, but watch for the signals of the blows of the hammer." After the Reverend John Todd of Pittsfield, Massachusetts, led the invocation, the operator bulletined: "We have got done praying. The spike is about to be presented."

Then Stanford, noticeably nervous and inconvenienced by the dangling wires, brought the silver-headed maul over his head and swung. He missed the spike! The maul struck the rail, but the telegraph operator, not to be robbed of his grand moment, pretended it had hit its target and tapped out: "Dot. Dot. Dot. Done." Now it was Durant's turn. Noticeably nervous and inconvenienced by a throbbing headache brought on by too much champagne, he also missed! Again the telegraph operator faked the signal.

The two engines, the Central Pacific's *Jupiter* and the Union Pacific's *Number 119*, both polished within an inch of their lives and covered with cheering celebrants, moved across the gap and touched noses. This touched off more wild cheering and the downing of more champagne.

To save them from souvenir hunters, workmen removed the spike and ties and replaced them with the usual materials. Within the next few weeks souvenir hunters reduced the plain tie—and half a dozen more to splinters and made off with two rails. Today the golden spike is in the Stanford University museum. The San Francisco earthquake and fire of 1906 destroyed the last tie.

Chapter 9

Texas and the War with Mexico

Texas Personality Profiles

WILLIAM B. TRAVIS

WILLIAM BARRET TRAVIS, like most Texans, was a Southerner, having been born in South Carolina and raised in Alabama, where he studied law. (To become a lawyer in those days all one had to do was get a few books and "read for the law.") While teaching school on the side to earn a living, he fell in love with one of his pupils, Rosanna Cato, daughter of a prosperous farmer. About two years after he married her something happened—no one knows what—and Travis, like so many other footloose young men at the time, headed for Texas. There was a rumor that Travis didn't just leave, but fled the law after killing a man who had been trifling with his wife. Lon Tinkle, in *13 Days to Glory*, says Travis undertook to defend a black man who had found the dead body and been accused of the act. When the jury found the black man guilty—which Travis never thought would happen—the young lawyer went to the judge in his chambers and admitted he had done the deed.

"I know," the judge said. Then he told Travis he had three choices: he could keep his mouth shut and let the black man take the rap, as most white men in the South might have done; he could confess; or he could go to Texas.

In Texas he fell in love again, with young Rebecca Cummings, who promised to wait until Travis got a divorce. Travis kept putting it off until suddenly one day Rosanna turned up in Texas demanding he return with her or give her a divorce. Travis was not long in drawing up the papers, a settlement giving her the young daughter and him the small son.

By this time Travis was deep in land transactions and other financial dealings. He was ambitious in the extreme—the quest for fame and fortune seemed to consume his whole being. He was vain; he had written his autobiography by the time he was twenty-three! He was hot-tempered and had a flair for the dramatic and a way with words, as his "Victory or Death!" message bears testimony.

JIM BOWIE

Jim Bowie was already a frontier legend when he came to Texas. He grew up in the sugar-cane country of Louisiana, where as a daredevil youngster he broke wild mustangs and rode alligators. In the latter case, he learned how to seize the upper jaw and gouge the alligator's eyes so it could not see. When older, he and his brothers, John and Rezin, engaged in slave smuggling with pirate Jean Lafitte after devising an ingenious plan for doing so without breaking the law. After smuggling the slaves in, they reported their whereabouts—as the law required—to the sheriff, who rounded the slaves up and sold them at auction—also as the law required. Slaves were cheap on the auction block if they were runaways, and the Bowies bought their own smuggled slaves at a dollar a pound. The average slave weighed about 140 pounds, so they paid an average of $140 for each. Then they sold them on the general market for about $1,000 each. Jim made about $65,000 in this manner, and added another $20,000 or so by selling fraudulent land claims in Arkansas. He also accumulated a tidy sum in Louisiana by operating a sawmill and the state's first steam-operated sugar press. He was, by the standards of the day, a wealthy man.

The legends of his fighting prowess included the time he fought an opponent while they both gripped opposite ends of a handkerchief in their teeth, and the time he and his enemy fought on a log in the river while their trouser legs were nailed down side by side. His most famous exploit—known as the Sand Bar Duel—had him wounded and lying on the ground with no weapon other than his large knife, which was not yet celebrated. When his first attacker came at him with a sword cane, Bowie grasped the cane, pulled the man close, and plunged the blade of his knife through the man's abdomen to the backbone. A second attacker lunged at him using a cane as a club, but Bowie's knife quickly dispatched him as well. Bowie had the blade polished and set in an ivory handle mounted with silver, and he carried it in a silver-mounted scabbard.

Jim Bowie was a restless man, always wanting to be on the move, always looking for more land, more money, more adventures. Thus he came to Texas in pursuit of land and silver mines. In San Antonio he met and fell in love with Maria Ursula de Veramendi, the beautiful, cultured daughter of the vice-governor of Texas. The marriage contract was an unusual one; it was Bowie who had to bring the dowry, a pledge of $15,000. He listed his assets at almost a quarter of a million dollars and his age as thirty instead of thirty-five.

In 1832 Bowie's wife, their two children, and both his wife's parents were struck down by cholera. When he went to the Alamo he was grief-stricken, sick, and drinking heavily.

DAVY CROCKETT

Davy Crockett was a rebel all his life, beginning with the time he ran away from home because his father had put him in school. He was twelve at the time, and four days of book learnin' were all he could stand. He worked at odd jobs until he was fifteen, then returned to school after a young lady spurned his attentions because he was illiterate. Six months later he left again—and that was all the education this man who later signed his name to several books ever had. (The books were probably given orally to writers.)

Crockett gloried all his life in his legend, most of which he made up himself: stories of shooting forty-seven bears in a month and six bucks in a day, riding alligators for exercise, grinning a bear into retreat, and once aiming his famous rifle, "Old Betsy," up a tree only to have the 'coon come down and surrender. After campaigning with Andrew Jackson against the Creek Indians in 1812, Crockett came back to Tennessee and discovered his talents as a politician—that is, he found one could go a long way in frontier politics on reputation, amiability, and a glib tongue.

He won a seat in the Tennessee legislature and later two terms in the U.S. Congress. In Washington he ran afoul of his erstwhile chief and now President, Andrew Jackson. Davy did a lot of speechifying about a settler's right to free land on the frontier—which he knew would keep him in the good graces of his constituents—but Jackson and his advisers wanted that land sold for federal revenue. Jackson's influence helped get Davy defeated in the next election, and he told his constituents if that was the way they felt about him "they can go to hell—I'm going to Texas!"

Davy Crockett knew time was running out for him. He had been defeated; his salad days were gone forever; he was fifty years old—more than middle-aged in those days—and had nowhere to go. He probably looked upon death in the Alamo as a final, crowning touch to his days of glory—as indeed it proved to be.

SAM HOUSTON

Sam Houston's political career is unparalleled in American history. He was

1. A member of a state legislature (Texas).

2. A U.S. congressman (Tennessee).

3. A governor of two different states (Tennessee and Texas).

4. A U.S. senator (Texas).

5. A president of a foreign country (the Republic of Texas, serving two non-consecutive terms).

He would have been governor of a state outside the United States if he hadn't opposed secession and been forced out of office when Texas joined the Confederacy.

One might add still another title: honorary chief of the Cherokee Indian nation. Houston ran off to live among the Cherokee in Tennessee when he was fifteen, rather than clerk in a store. He lived with them for three years, then served with Andrew Jackson in the Creek Wars, and at the Battle of Horseshoe Bend suffered a wound that would bother him for the rest of his life. Afterwards he became an Indian agent and helped in the removal of the Cherokee from Tennessee to Arkansas. After "reading for the law," he was elected to Congress for two terms, then became governor of Tennessee. While governor he married pretty, sixteen-year-old Eliza Allen, but three months later—and as in the case of Travis no one knows exactly why—the marriage suddenly tore asunder and Houston resigned to go and live again among his Cherokee brothers in Arkansas. He was adopted into the tribe and for several years ran a trading station on their lands. It was here he got his famous nickname, the Raven, but it is little known that the Cherokee had another name for him, an Indian word meaning "Big Drunk."

His old friend and benefactor President Andrew Jackson sent him to Texas as his personal Indian agent, and while there he got caught up in the revolutionary movement. As commander-in-chief of the Texas "army" (it never numbered more than a few hundred men), Houston three times ordered the Alamo blown up, first by Colonel James Neill, in command at San Antonio; then by Jim Bowie, who changed his mind when he saw that the old mission was a natural fort; and last by William B. Travis, who saw the whole thing as symbolic.

SANTA ANNA

Antonio López de Santa Anna intended to end up on the right side no matter what. While a young officer in the Spanish Imperial Army he was promoted for beating a bunch of rebels; the same afternoon the rebels promoted him even higher when he joined their ranks. Fighting under rebel leader Augustin Iturbi, the dashing twenty-eight-year-old colonel won the hand of Iturbi's sixty-year-old sister—and suddenly became a brigadier general. When Iturbi became emperor, General Santa Anna swore eternal fealty to him, then shortly afterward helped launch a successful rebellion against him.

Santa Anna was mixed up in one revolution or another over several years until he himself emerged on top in 1832. "My whole ambition is restricted to beating my sword into a plowshare," he said, and he promised his people he would die before seeing the Constitution of 1824, which established the Mexican Republic, trampled underfoot. No sooner was he safely in the saddle than he beat his plowshare back into a sword and dashed about the countryside brutally suppressing every attempt to restrict his authority.

He was a mountain of vanity. Bigger than the average Mexican, he pranced around on a horse with golden trappings, his epaulets dripping with silver, a $7,000 sword buckled to his waist. Even while campaigning he used monogrammed china, crystal decanters, and a silver chamber pot.

But Santa Anna could be a capable, imaginative leader. His men loved and respected him, and many would follow his great booming voice anywhere. Unfortunately, his army, although brilliantly costumed and equipped, was sadly lacking in some respects—marksmanship, for instance. Some of his men were afraid of guns, some closed their eyes when firing. What's more, they still used the smoothbore musket that was highly inaccurate even at close range. With the military behind him, Santa Anna was in and out of power four times. In one case, he used a lost leg to elicit sympathy. He had the leg, lost in repelling the French at Veracruz, buried with full military honors—twenty-one gun salute and all—and had a monument erected over it.

Santa Anna died with his boots off, in bed, the only early Mexican leader who did not go down before a firing squad sooner or later. He had lost half of his country's territory: that taken by the United States after the Mexican War amounted to 765,540 square miles, leaving modern Mexico's 760,372 square miles.

"G.T.T."

"G.T.T."—you could find it scribbled on the doors and walls of many a home along the southern frontier in the 1820s and 1830s: the inhabitants had "Gone To Texas." They were brought there by the lure of fresh lands and the possibility of gold or silver strikes. (Almost everyone, it seems, thought there were silver mines in Texas.) Others, however, felt like General Philip Sheridan, who said, "If I owned hell and Texas, I would rent out Texas and live in hell." Some were more graphic, like the author of this song of the day:

> *Oh, the devil in hell, they say he was chained,*
> *And there for a thousand years he remained.*
> *He neither complained, nor did he groan,*
> *But decided to start up a hell of his own,*
> *Where he could torment the souls of men*
> *Without being shut up in a prison pen.*
>
> *He asked the good Lord if He had any sand*
> *Left over from making this great land.*
> *The Lord answered, "Yes, I have plenty of sand*
> *Away down south on the Rio Grande.*
> *But the truth is, old fellow, the stuff is so poor*
> *I doubt 'twill do for a hell anymore."*
>
> *The devil went down and looked over the truck*
> *And he said if it came as a gift he was stuck.*
> *But after thinking it over and testing it well,*
> *He decided the place was too dry for a hell.*
> *So the Lord, just to get the stuff off of his hands,*
> *Promised the devil he'd water the land.*
>
> *He had some old water that was of no use,*
> *A regular old bog hole that stunk like the deuce.*
> *So the deal it was closed and the deed it was given,*
> *The Lord went home to his place up in heaven.*
> *The devil then said, "I have all that is needed*
> *To make a good hell"—and, by gosh, he succeeded.*

> *He scattered tarantulas on all the roads,*
> *Put thorns on the cactus and horns on the toads.*
> *He added a foot to the jackrabbit's ears*
> *And lengthened the horns of the Texas steers.*
> *He put thorns and stickers in all the trees*
> *And into the sand he stirred sandburs and fleas.*
>
> *He sprinkled the ground with million of ants,*
> *So the man that would sit must wear soles on his pants.*
> *The heat in the summer's a hundred and ten,*
> *Too hot for the devil and too hot for men.*
> *The wild boar snarls in the black chaparral,*
> *It's a hell of a place that he has for a hell.*

The Mexicans were not fond of having Americans settle their northern provinces, but the government needed someone to settle there. The Americans, although they had to become Mexican citizens, remained Americans. They did not like having to become Catholics, which the law also required, but resigned themselves to a convenient form of the religion designed for them by the Irish-Mexican clergyman Padre Miguel Muldoon. They were known among their Mexican compatriots as "Muldoon Catholics." The "Texians" as they were called, despised the republican constitution of 1824, which denied religious freedom and the right of trial by jury. They detested the presence of Mexican troops in their midst, many of whom were ex-convicts.

REMEMBER THE ALAMO!

It is hard to say how many men were in the Alamo at the time of its fall. Every book gives a slightly different number, but it is certain there were no more than 200. Most historians settle on a figure between 180 and 186. In the beginning there was a dispute between Bowie and Travis over leadership. Travis was in command of the handful of "regulars" there, and being the type of man he was, he assumed he had charge of all the men. Bowie had been sent by Houston, who had told *him* to take charge. In the end, the two men decided to let the defenders themselves elect their leader, and Bowie won almost unanimously. Travis was chagrined, but it did not matter, for it was not long before Bowie, already seriously ill and sometimes half-drunk, fell from the parapet and splintered several ribs into his lungs. Travis took over while Bowie repaired to a cot in a room of the chapel, where he remained until the end, already half dead.

In the early days of the thirteen-day siege, while waiting for all his army to come up from the south, Santa Anna tried to wear his opponents out with constant noise at night: horses galloping about, arms and artillery clattering, even a serenading by one of several brass bands he had on hand. For the first few days there were bombardments and desultory firing by both sides, with occasional casualties. A Mexican soldier later wrote these words about one Texian who fascinated him

> *A tall man, with flowing hair, was seen firing from the same place*
> *on the parapet during the entire siege. He wore a buckskin suit and a cap*
> *all of a pattern entirely different from those worn by his comrades. This*

> *man would kneel or lie down behind the low parapet, rest his long gun and fire, and we all learned to keep at a good distance when he was seen to make ready to shoot. He rarely missed his mark, and when he fired he always rose to his feet and calmly reloaded his gun seemingly indifferent to the shots fired at him by our men. He had a strong, resonant voice and often railed at us, but as we did not understand English we could not comprehend the import of his words further than that they were defiant. This man I later learned was known as "Kwockey."*

As for Travis drawing a line in the sand and inviting all those who would stay with him and fight to the death to step across, there is no reliable evidence that it happened. It certainly would be in character for the drama-loving Travis to draw such a line—and there is little doubt he did make a speech to that effect. The line was mentioned by two people who were there, but not at first. Mrs. Almeron Dickinson, wife of the artillery officer, mentioned the line in one of her later accounts, one that obviously was embellished somewhat by over-eager newsmen. Her first, unvarnished account did not mention it. The one man who took the opportunity to escape, Moses Louis Rose, told his story to a family who sheltered him for a time. When the story appeared in print for the first time, the line was mentioned—but that was not until 1873.

At dawn of the final day, the Texians in the Alamo heard the blood-chilling strains of the *deguello*—the traditional "no-quarter" bugle call whose name comes from the Spanish verb *degollar*, "to slit the throat." The Mexicans charged the fort with their ladders, climbing over and crushing one another in a mad rush to get over the ramparts where they had been told to use their bayonets, showing no mercy to anyone. Crockett and his Tennesseans battled with a wild fury that awed the attackers. Sergeant Felix Nunez remembered Crockett this way:

> *This man apparently had a charmed life. Of the many soldiers who took deliberate aim at him and fired, not one ever hit him. On the contrary, he never missed a shot. He killed at least eight of our men, besides wounding several others . . . A lieutenant who had come in over the wall. . .sprang at him and dealt him a deadly blow with his sword, just above the right eye, which felled him to the ground, and in an instant he was pierced with not less than twenty bayonets.*

Travis was one of the first to die, his body slumped over the cannon he tried to defend. There was only one wound in his body, a nice, clean hole in the head. (Some have tried to claim, in view of this unusual fact, that Travis committed suicide.) He was only twenty-seven years old.

Jim Bowie died as he had lived—fighting to the last gasp. He had been left on his cot in the chapel baptistry, his famous knife and a brace of pistols by his side. No one knows, but it can be assumed he took at least three Mexicans with him. Stories that he died in a delirium just before the attack have been generally discredited.

When it was over, Santa Anna poked through the rubble, asking to be shown the bodies of Travis, Crockett, and Bowie. Apparently he hesitated at first, then ordered these three bodies to be burned with the rest. His soldiers even killed a stray cat because it was an "American" cat. Although 500 to 600 of his own men lay dead or wounded, Santa Anna called the whole matter a "small affair."

THE MEXICAN WAR

President James K. Polk was narrow minded, stubborn, and bigoted. To him Whigs, abolitionists, and even many of his own Democratic colleagues were villains not to be trusted. All of this made fighting a war with Mexico more difficult than it should have been.

Polk wanted to acquire from Mexico its rich province of California and to settle the boundary dispute that cropped up when the United States annexed the Texas Republic in 1845. He tried to negotiate the boundary problem and offered to buy California. When the Mexican government refused—in fact, wouldn't even receive Polk's emissary—the President decided war was the only way to settle the matter.

He sent an army under General Zachary Taylor to the Rio Grande, but still on what the United States considered its territory, hoping the Mexicans would take the bait. "We were sent to provoke a fight, but it was essential Mexico should commence it," wrote Ulysses S. Grant, a young lieutenant in Taylor's command. The Mexicans took the bait, sending a patrol across the river—into what Mexico considered *its* territory and firing at a troop of American dragoons. "You may now consider hostilities commenced," Taylor wired Polk.

ROUGH AND READY

Once the war was under way, Polk wanted to control it from the White House. He was angered when General Winfield Scott, the Army's ranking officer, insisted on drilling the troops before taking them into the field: Polk wanted quick victories. They could be small ones, but they had to come soon.

Polk also wanted to control both Scott and Taylor, each of whom began to shape up as a formidable Whig candidate in the next election. The President wanted to win the war, but only if it was won by the Democratic Party. For this reason he had refused to appoint Scott to head the campaign—Scott was a big Whig. Instead he had appointed Taylor, who at the time the war began seemed to have no political ambitions.

Taylor was a plodding, taciturn man who unaccountably became known to the nation as "Old Rough and Ready." The nickname came from a soldier's letter home that was widely printed in the newspapers. The "Rough" part came from his unsoldierly appearance: he usually wore no insignia or gold braid and was often seen in a Mexican sombrero. The "Ready" referred to the fact that Taylor never backed away from a fight. The soldier's epithet was not entirely accurate, however, for his troops more often called their general "Old Zach." Taylor, who came up through the ranks, was loved by his men and commanded the respect of a lot of West Pointers.

Taylor's first two battles, Resaca de la Palma and Palo Alto, revealed the tactic that would mark all his engagements: fighting with artillery in line with—or even ahead of—the infantry. When he was able to do this he always won. It was a lesson well learned by young Ulysses S. Grant, who would put the lesson to good use in another war. (It was not a lesson learned by another young officer, Captain Robert E. Lee.) Mexican artillery, on the other hand, was so feeble the balls came rolling in slowly enough for the Americans to jump out of their way.

At Taylor's third battle, General William Worth's Texans gave birth to a cry that would become a legend in the Civil War. It started as a deep bass and rose to an ear-shattering crescendo—and it would become known as the "Rebel yell." Taylor might have ended resistance in northern Mexico with this battle of Monterrey (the Mexican spelling to avoid confusing it with Monterey, California), but instead gave the opposing general conditions that allowed the Mexican army to retire from the city with their weapons.

SANTA'S BACK IN TOWN

Nevertheless, the newspapers decided enough men were killed in the battle of Monterrey to toast it as a big victory, and now Old Rough and Ready was being boosted for the presidency. Even children sang:

> *Old Zach's at Monterrey,*
> *Bring out your Santa Anner;*
> *For every time we raise a gun,*
> *Down goes a Mexicanner.*

For sure enough old "Santa Anner" was back in town. After one of his periodic exiles he, with help from the United States, was again in charge in Mexico City. Polk had seen that the wily dictator had enough money to overthrow the existing government and establish himself in power again. Santa Anna had promised to halt the war and agreed to cede California and New Mexico (then including Arizona) to the U.S. and to set Texas' southern boundary at the Rio Grande. But as soon as he was safely ensconced in the Imperial Palace, he said "Sorry, amigos" and reneged on the deal.

Santa Anna personally took the field against Old Zach at Buena Vista, a battle some historians think Taylor needlessly engaged in to add more luster to his campaign for the presidency. Santa Anna's minions put up a stiff front, but after two days of fighting, Taylor's 6,000 had whipped the 17,000 Mexicans. It now appeared certain Old Zach would be elected, as one of his supporters at home put it, "by spontaneous combustion."

Old Fuss Ends the Fuss

Shortly before the battle of Buena Vista, Taylor's ranks had been seriously depleted when President Polk ordered some of his men to join General Winfield Scott's forces in a campaign to take Mexico City. Taylor was looking too promising as a Whig candidate in 1848, and Polk had decided to divert the nation's attention from him by opening a second front. Scott was known as "Old Fuss and Feathers" because of his fondness for fancy uniforms. ("He wore all the uniform the law allowed," wrote Grant) and his attachment to military pomp and circumstance.

Even though he was personally vain in the extreme—he often spoke of himself in the third person—Scott was a brilliant soldier, and he scored one triumph after another on his way to the Mexican capital. The people of Mexico City applauded when the American army paraded through its streets, and they were so impressed with Old Fuss and Feathers they asked him to stay on as their dictator.

Polk thought Scott had grown too big for his britches and replaced him with a Democratic general. Such was the end of one of America's most political wars. Over thirty years later Grant wrote in his *Memoirs* that the Mexican War was "one of the most unjust ever waged by a stronger against a weaker nation. It was an instance of a republic following the bad example of European monarchies in not considering justice in their desire to acquire additional territory."

Chapter 10

The Way West

The Overland Trail

OFF TO SEE THE ELEPHANT

"**O**FF TO SEE THE ELEPHANT" was a popular expression in the middle decades of the nineteenth century. It meant going out and finding what life was all about, and was applied particularly to those who "westered."

Those who went west to see the elephant got there in all sorts of ways: not only by "prairie schooner" (any large covered wagon), but in horse-drawn carts or drays, by horseback or muleback, by pushing wheelbarrows, and on foot. One lean Scotsman packed all his belongings in a wheelbarrow and rolled it over the plains at a clip of twenty-five to thirty-five miles a day, and the entire outfit of two Missourians was one elderly cow.

Of necessity, wagon trains were organized on a military basis. The emigrants elected officers and a council whose word was law. The council hired an experienced plainsman as "pilot." Each wagon had to carry flour, beans, rice, sugar, coffee, a ten-gallon water keg, and at least 150 pounds of bacon. Mules pulled some wagons, but more often it was two or three yoke of oxen. Horses were saved for riding, although just as many men walked as rode.

Many drivers put bells on the harnesses so their merry jingling would help break the monotony of the seemingly endless plains. If a wagon had problems—if it got stuck in the mud, for instance—and had to have help, it was customary for the driver to turn his bells over to his rescuer. It was something of an embarrassment to arrive at the final destination without bells, which led to today's expression, "I'll be there with bells on."

Toward evening the pilot rode ahead and marked a circle about a hundred yards in diameter as a camp site, and the travelers chained their wagons around the perimeter for the night. Occasionally, Native Americans killed a guard or stole an animal, but the fierce attacks of massed warriors against wagon trains came much later.

While the men got things ready for the night, the women and children went about preparing supper. Getting a fire started was a major accomplishment with only flint and steel to use, and sometimes the only fuel available was buffalo chips (dung). Everyone turned in early because the captains, men elected to be in charge of a group, or division of wagons, would have them up by four in the morning. The division that led the train the day before would bring up the rear the next day—eating the dust of all the other divisions.

Things were not always peaceful in a wagon train. People are people wherever they are, and there was arguing and fighting, both between families and within families. One family feuded so vehemently they cut their wagon in half and arrived in Oregon pulling two carts.

DANGERS AND DEATH

Independence, Missouri, was the principal "jumping-off place" for the overland trek. From there wagon trains followed the Platte River, said to be "a thousand miles long and an inch deep," to the Sweetwater River and on to South Pass, the gateway to the Far West. Beyond South Pass those going to Oregon headed northwest along the Snake River; those bound for California took either of two routes southwest. (See map.)

Overlanders taking the more southerly route to California had to contend with Death Valley, where many died of thirst or starvation or went insane. One man lay down saying, "I'm just going to take a little nap," and never woke up. One woman set fire to their wagon trying to get her husband to turn back.

Those on the northerly route faced the horrors of the Humboldt Sink, a treacherous forty-mile stretch of desert where the Humboldt River sank into the bowels of the earth. One overlander described the experience this way:

> *I traveled till I struck the Sink,*
> *Where outlet can't be found.*
> *The Lord got through late Saturday night—*
> *He'd finished all around;*
> *But He would not work on Sunday,*
> *So he run it in the ground.*

Death most often pursued the emigrants, however, in the form of cholera, a severe gastrointestinal disease caused by bacteria contaminating their water supply.

A surprisingly large number died as a result of accidents, most of them stemming from carelessness in handling firearms. In one company a canvas wagon cover brushed against a rifle, causing the gun to go off and kill a passerby. One man was shot while holding a trunk cover over his head for a friend to practice what was obviously inexpert marksmanship. A teenage member of a Missouri caravan thought it would be fun to put on a white sheet and sneak upon a guard in the middle of the night; the sentry, after hailing him several times, shot the youth in the arm and side.

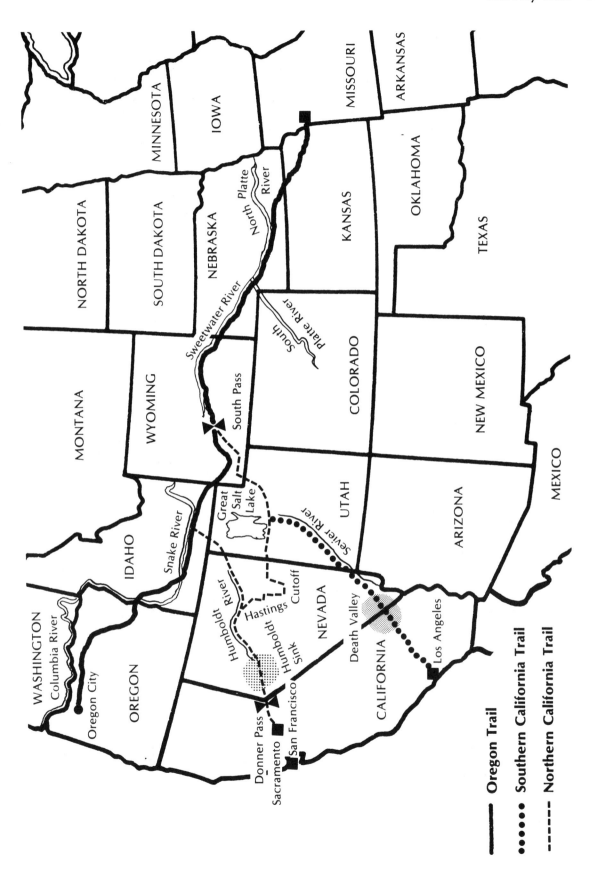

Oregon Trail

Southern California Trail

Northern California Trail

THE DONNER TRAGEDY

It was of the utmost importance that a wagon train leave in May, just after the grass came up for the animals to forage on, and to cross the mountains before the winter snows began in October. If it didn't, trouble and possible tragedy could be expected. The Donner party did not observe these rules, and the result was the westward movement's starkest tragedy.

The party, led by sixty-three-year-old George Donner, gathered in Springfield, Missouri, in July 1846, to head for California. July was too late to start, but the party's fate might still have been avoided had it not taken the unwise advice of one Lansford Hastings. Hastings was an opportunist who hoped to bring so many people to California owing him personal debts that he could one day seize their land and found an empire—or at least be the first governor of the state of California. Hastings' advice was to take a cutoff he guaranteed would save 350 to 400 miles.

The cutoff not only did not save time, but put them far behind other groups on the trail, those who had resisted Hastings' blandishments. The party reached the Sierra Nevada Mountains after the fall snows had begun and found themselves trapped. They had a few cattle with them and those were eaten first; then came the oxen, the horses, and finally the dogs.

Then came the people. The party had thought of drawing lots to find out who would be killed and eaten, but decided to wait until someone died. The first to go was a Mexican herdsman, followed by three Americans, one of them a fourteen-year-old boy. The others stripped the flesh from the bodies, roasted what they could eat, and dried the rest to take with them.

Before the forty-seven survivors were rescued by search parties from John Sutter's fort near Sacramento, thirty-five others had been devoured by their comrades. In one case a man ate five other men who had died in one of the cabins the group had built. One woman ate her own daughter. Another woman watched while others cut out her husband's heart and liver, broiled them over coals, and ate them.

The Mormon Odyssey

"Mormon" is a nickname derived from the ancient prophet Mormon who, according to the church, set down the story of his people in the *Book of Mormon*. The book tells of two tribes, the good Nephites and the wicked Lamanites, who migrated here from Israel presumably during Old Testament times. In a tremendous armageddon in the fifth century A.D. the Lamanites destroyed the Nephites, except for Mormon and his son Moroni. Members of the church call themselves "Saints" after the real name of their faith, the Church of Jesus Christ of the Latter-Day Saints. They do not claim, as commonly thought, that the Lamanites (who are now called Indians) or the Nephites are descendants of the Ten Lost Tribes of Israel. The church's official history gives the Mormon story this way:

> *As a boy, Joseph Smith was troubled by so many religious doctrines and asked God to show him the true way. While praying he was suddenly "seized upon by some power which entirely overcame me, and had such an astonishing influence over me as to bind my tongue so that I could not speak." Darkness gathered about him and he feared he would be struck dead. Then there appeared above him "a pillar of light exactly over my head, above the brightness of the sun, which descended gradually until it fell upon me." When the light had enveloped him he saw "two Personages whose brightness and glory defy all description, standing before me in the air. One of them spake unto me, calling me by name and said, pointing to the other, 'This is my beloved son, hear him!' "*

> *Young Joseph asked the "Personages" which religion was right, which church he should join, and he was told none of them—"All their creeds are an abomination in His sight." About three years later, while Joseph was praying in bed, there appeared to him an angel who said his name was Moroni, and that he had been sent to tell Joseph of the great work the young man was to do in the name of the Lord. In a later appearance Moroni directed him to dig up from a hill certain gold plates upon which Mormon had written an account of the former inhabitants of this continent, and which also contained "the fullness of the everlasting gospel." In the hill also were two instruments, the* Urim *and* Thummim, *with which he could translate the ancient writings. The gold plates vanished, but the translations became the* Book of Mormon. *From this point history takes up the story.*

LOOKING FOR ZION

After converting many in upstate New York, Smith decided to found a new Zion in the West. He took his converts first to Ohio, then to Missouri and finally to Illinois where he bought a deserted village and named it Nauvoo ("The Beautiful"). Here the Mormons' serious troubles began, for the "gentiles" learned what for a long time they had suspected—the Saints were practicing polygamy. Smith reportedly had a revelation in which God told him single women could not attain salvation, making it necessary for Mormon men to marry several wives. A monogamous society could not tolerate this situation, and it was not long before Smith and his brother Hyrum were in jail—charged with destroying the printing press of a Mormon splinter group that had publicly attacked Smith and the practice of polygamy. A mob stormed the jail and killed both of them.

The new leader, Brigham Young, believed the Mormons should move farther west, and in 1846 one of the great migrations of American history began. Young told his flock that it would be revealed to him where they should settle. The Saints were astonished when, as they beheld the desolate basin of the Great Salt Lake, their leader said, "This is the place." Through hard work, thrift, and some ingenious irrigation techniques, they made the desert bloom as much as it could; and everyone has heard of the "miracle" that brought great flocks of seagulls inland to eat the grasshoppers threatening to destroy the Mormons' first crops.

The hapless Saints found themselves with a problem again: when they left Illinois the Salt Lake region was Mexican, but no sooner had they settled in than Mexico ceded the territory to the United States as a result of the Mexican War. When Congress refused to admit the territory to the Union as a state, Brigham Young set up the state of Deseret, which included not only present Utah, but all or parts of Nevada, Arizona, and California. ("Deseret" means honeybee, an important Mormon symbol.) This extra-legal union could not be allowed, and it was not until 1896 that Congress admitted the present state of Utah—after the Mormons agreed to give up polygamy.

Brigham Young, like Joseph Smith before him, had twenty-seven or twenty-eight wives (no one seems to know for sure), and from these unions sprang fifty-six off-spring— enough to start a colony of their own. Young married as many as eight women in one year, one of them only sixteen years old. He once married twice in the same day, and in another case wed two sisters. Wife number nineteen divorced him and sued for $200,000. Young said he would be happy to make that sort of settlement— it would mean the courts would have to consider plural marriages legal. The case was dropped.

PARADISE FOR A PRICE

Many of those who went west to see the elephant used the Mormon colony as a "halfway house." Here they could repair, rest, and recuperate in preparation for the final leg of their journey. Some spent all of the cold months there and were known as "winter Mormons."

The Saints did not like outsiders in their territory, but accepted them once they realized the emigrants could be a good source of revenue. Mormons ventured far out on the trail to sell chickens, eggs, milk, butter, and vegetables, and luring travelers into the settlement became an established policy. Everything was not sweetness and light, however, as there was often trouble between the Saints and their temporary guests. The travelers resented the two percent property tax levied by their hosts, no matter how short a time they sojourned in the colony. Some wrote home that because of a minor infraction of Mormon law they were made to serve on crews building public works, and even to wear a ball and chain. Others reported being fined for expressing a derogatory view of Mormonism. One overlander, while drunk, shot a dog belonging to a Mormon and was fined $80; he had to sell his mother's team to get the money.

"It cost nothing to get in," wrote one emigrant of the Salt Lake paradise, "but a great deal to get out."

Gold!

When James Marshall found traces of gold in the tailrace of a mill he was building on the grand California ranch of John Sutter, he and his boss tried to keep the news a secret; Sutter did not want his lands trampled under the feet of frenzied gold-seekers. Before long, however, the discovery was the best-known secret in the world, and within a year there was an outbreak of "yellow fever" all over the face of the globe.

American gold-seekers got to California in one of three ways: (1) the overland routes described in the beginning of this chapter; (2) by ship around South America; (3) by ship to Panama, crossing the isthmus and a ship up the Pacific coast.

For those taking a ship all the way, the passage around Cape Horn, the tip of South America, was the worst part. The passage was always stormy and might take up to thirty days to complete. Great waves lashed the ship unmercifully, sending water across decks and down the hatches. There was no place of safety—a passenger had to resign himself to being wet. The only way to get any sleep was to lash oneself to the berth. Formal meals were suspended, everyone being served cafeteria style and taking his plate to whatever calm place he could find, if any.

The food was bad anyway, consisting mainly of salt meat, fish, rice, beans, and hardtack, all of which might have to be shared with the bugs and worms. None of this was sure to stay down, for seasickness, whether rounding the Horn or not, was a major problem. The "Californians," as they termed themselves, did not speak of vomiting or throwing up; getting rid of what was in the stomach was called "casting up accounts." A passenger on the *Pacific* may have set a gold rush record by "casting up" twenty-seven days in a row, while a passenger aboard the *Sweden* cast up his false teeth with his accounts.

THE ROUTE OF HIGH SOCIETY

Because of its higher cost, the Panama route attracted a better clientele: it was the way of bankers, lawyers, stockbrokers, and riverboat gamblers who soon separated some of their well-heeled shipmates from their bulging bankrolls. It was not uncommon on the Isthmus to find a stockbroker trying to sell his belongings in order to get money for the trip back home.

After arriving on the east coast of Panama and journeying over the Isthmus a traveler might have to wait for weeks before getting passage up the west coast. Ships were so crowded that their owners, as a New Yorker wrote, "appear[ed] to have taken the exact measurements of each man and filled the vessel accordingly." Some were on the Isthmus so long they set up housekeeping, even forming little American communities that celebrated national holidays, held lodge meetings and Sunday church services, and passed resolutions condemning the gouging habits of Panamanians who charged them, for example, only fifty cents for a chicken, but two dollars for a pot to cook it in.

Of the three paths to El Dorado, the Cape Horn route, despite some hazard, was much the safest. Thousands died along the overland trails and in the jungles of Panama, where cholera, malaria, and yellow fever took their toll. The best estimate is that no more than fifty to a hundred died on the all-water route.

HARD WORK AND NO PAY DIRT

The first gold discoveries were placer deposits in stream beds where the metal was distributed through the soil as dust; not many sizeable nuggets were found. But that did not prevent wild tales of incredibly rich strikes. One tale claimed the Indians in the Sacramento area used golden fishhooks and arrowheads. Another said that a man had lassoed on the river bottom a gold rock so big it took him three days to haul it in. The notion that gold could be picked up off the ground at one's leisure was so prevalent a French company arrived in California bearing rakes to gather in the bountiful harvest; their wives brought embroidered silk stools on which to sit while they plucked the nuggets with silver tongs. Gold-frenzied souls, as one observer said, "dashed around the countryside like a thousand hogs let loose in a forest would root up nuts." Even Notre Dame University sent out an expedition.

Digging for gold turned out to be hard, oftentimes back-breaking labor—and even then the prospector might find little, if any, "pay dirt." Miserable living conditions made matters worse, and the miners lamented their misfortunes in the names they gave their camps: Two-Bit Gulch, Dirty Socks, Grizzly Flats, Hangtown, Nary Red, Delirium Tremens, Dead Broke, Shirt-Tail Canyon, Louse Town, Hell's Delight, and Puke Ravine.

The denizens of such illustrious places did not fare any better. A few were the Scurvy Kid, Ben Long Ears, Nellie the Pig, Senator Few Clothes and Dog Tooth Harry.

The miners had their own names for everything: burros were "Rocky Mountain canaries," cow chips "prairie pancakes," whiskey "Taos lightning," pancakes "saddle blankets," beans "Mexican strawberries," and when one slept on a "Tucson bed" he lay down on the floor on his stomach and covered himself with his back.

QUICK JUSTICE AND A READY TONGUE

Some would-be millionaires did not live long enough to become rich. They died in barroom brawls, were shot to death for slipping an extra ace into the deck, or received a "suspended sentence" (hanging) for jumping a claim or stealing a horse. An accidental shooting death in a saloon caused hardly a ripple: "Some of the players got up to have a look at the body," wrote one miner of such a mishap, "and returned to their game quite unconcernedly." Even after a semblance of law and order came to a mining community, its citizens still often preferred the rough-and-ready justice of a vigilante group. One miner wrote home that in his camp when a row between two men broke out "it only requires one minute for the injured party to shoot the offender, two minutes for somebody else to stab the shooter, and three minutes for the whole crowd to hang the stabber."

Mining towns practiced the usual diversions of a raw frontier community. "Gambling, drinking and houses of ill fame are the chief amusements of the country," a youthful forty-niner wrote home to his parents. Vile language reached new heights of sophistication. A Presbyterian clergyman calculated that if they were joined together in one mighty blast "all the imprecations and oaths uttered in California in a month would cause a peal of thunder whose reverberations would make Perdition tremble to its lowest depths."

A LONELY LIFE

In their remoteness from home, and in the absence of women and a civilized social life, prospectors devoted themselves to their work and their fellow miners, their "pards." One pard wrote a poem about this strong bond.

> *I'd comrades then who loved me well,*
> *A jovial, saucy crew;*
> *A few hard cases I'll admit*
> *Though they were brave and true.*
> *Whate'er the pinch they'd never flinch,*
> *Would never fret or whine—*
> *Like good old bricks they stood the kicks*
> *In the days of '49.*

For many a lonely miner his only pard was his trusty mule, about whom he would sing:

> *My sweetheart's a mule in the mine,*
> *I drive her with only one line.*
> *On the dashboard I sit,*
> *And tobacco I spit*
> *All over my sweetheart's behind.*

The miner's only way of keeping touch with home was the mail, the volume of which was staggering. Some steamships arrived with as many as 45,000 letters and countless boxes of newspapers. Clerks in the San Francisco and Sacramento post offices might have to lock themselves in for two days in order to sort the letters, ignoring the mobs pounding on the doors. When the doors at last opened, the line of eager prospectors stretched for a mile or more. Some picked up spending money by selling their place in line for as much as $25. Other enterprising miners made even more by collecting letters at the post office and delivering them to camps at $2 or $2.50 each.

A LADY'S LUCK

The women did come, eventually. Many of the early ones were of "loose character and morals," but even they were treated with a deference generally reserved for the wealthy and beautiful. One lady wrote home that men had traveled forty miles just to look at her, "and I was never called a handsome woman, even in my best days and even by my most ardent admirers."

Many women who took miners as husbands found they had to endure loneliness, menial labor, and a wretched atmosphere greatly lacking in the social graces. All the males would talk about were mining and money. A wife asked one of her husband's visitors if he had read James Fenimore Cooper's new book *The Last of the Mohicans*. The gentleman said he had missed that one, but he had been "very much pleased with the First."

The home life of many new California wives was drudgery, pure and simple. A woman who ran a mining camp boarding house described the way she lived to her family back in Maine. The house was a single room with a cloth divider down the middle. Ten boarders slept on one side, she and her husband on the other. The beds were plain cots without pillows or sheets. She felt isolated both physically and socially. "Not that I am homesick, but it is nothing but gold, gold—no social feelings." The good news was that she was clearing $75 a week.

SAN FRANCISCO, HERE THEY CAME

San Francisco became a city almost overnight, and showed all the marks of premature birth: violence, the extravagances of the *nouveau riche*, bad roads, high prices for everything. Prices in 1850 ran like this:

Rent for a small room	$50 a month
Revolver	$100
Lady's hat	$10 (they sold for $20 a dozen in New Orleans)
Can of sardines	$16
Pound of bread	$2
Pound of butter	$6
Bottle of ale	$8
Pair of socks	$1.50

The city's dirt streets became quagmires when it rained, particularly so during the uncommonly heavy rains in the winter of 1849-1850. One eccentric, having found a decent half-mile stretch of road, drove back and forth over it all day; he said it was the only good piece of road he had found since leaving Sacramento and he intended "to get the good out of it." Another, after seeing his horse nearly drown in a boggy road, erected this sign:

> *This place is not crossible,*
> *Not even horsible.*

Another pilgrim, after falling into the same bog and struggling out, added:

> *This place is not passable,*
> *Not even jackassable.*

WHAT PRICE GOLD?

Most of those who went to the gold fields eventually realized that the real wealth of California lay not in the mines, but in soil and sunshine. They settled down to become farmers or merchants catering to those who still thought they were going to become overnight millionaires. The early comers virtually ruined John Sutter's agrarian empire, and a long court battle to establish the legality of his original land grants drained him of what was left of his fortune. Repeated requests to Congress for federal aid—on the grounds that Sutter had contributed greatly to the development of California—went unheeded and he died broke in 1880.

The California legislature granted James Marshall a pension of $200 a month, but rescinded it upon hearing reports that he spent most of it on drink. Shortly before his death in 1885 the legislature rejected a new appeal for aid, but later spent $9,000 to erect a monument to him.

Chapter 11

The Civil War

Some Facts and Figures

WHAT'S IN A NAME?

AT SOME TIME OR ANOTHER the Civil War has been called by at least thirty other names. Some of the more common ones:

> The War for Southern Independence
> The War for States' Rights
> The War of Secession
> The Great Rebellion
> The War Against Slavery
> The War for the Union
> The War of the North and South
> The War of the Blue and Gray
> Mr. Lincoln's War

Officially, it was the War of the Rebellion because the United States government considered the Confederate States in rebellion against the government and the Constitution. The name was unacceptable to the Confederacy because it thought secession was constitutional. "Civil War" was also unacceptable because it implied a conflict between two factions within the same country, and the Confederate States considered themselves an independent nation. Alexander Stephens, vice-president of the Confederacy, gave it the name "War Between the States" in his history of the Confederacy written after the war. The name has been adopted by many as a compromise.

THE TOLL IN LIVES

An accurate accounting of the lives lost in the Civil War is not likely ever to be taken; there are, especially on the Confederate side, too many lost or incomplete records. This war was, of course, different from any other of the nation's wars because every soldier killed was an American soldier.

Authorities say at least 618,000 men died, but the number was more likely to be around 700,000. Most of these, however, did not die in battle. More than twice as many soldiers were lost to disease than killed by enemy bullets. Many soldiers who would otherwise have recovered from their wounds died in hospitals that were pathetically ill equipped, especially in the South. Other causes of death were accidents, drowning, murder, suicide, sunstroke, and executions for desertion.

Some have called the Civil War the "last great war between gentlemen," but these "gentlemen" were killing one another in incredible numbers. At Petersburg a Maine regiment lost 700 lives in seven minutes—and it only had 900 men. At Gettysburg, the 1st Minnesota lost eighty-two percent of its men; at Antietam, the 3rd North Carolina lost ninety percent; and again at Gettysburg, Company F of the 6th North Carolina lost a hundred percent. During the Wilderness Campaign the Union forces lost almost as many men as the Confederates had.

The war's last survivor, Walter Williams, a Confederate in the Texas forces, died in Houston on December 19, 1959, at the age of 117.

COLORFUL CAMEOS

There were two Abraham Lincolns. The other was Private Abraham Lincoln of Company F, 1st Virginia Cavalry. He deserted and was never heard of again.

———

The "most shot-at man in the war" was Thaddeus Lowe, a pioneer balloonist whose balloon *Intrepid* made many observation flights over Confederate lines for the Union Army.

———

William Fuller, engineer of the locomotive *General*, looked out the window of a restaurant where he was having breakfast at Kennesaw, Georgia, and saw his train disappearing down the track. A band of Union spies had boarded the train and were balling the jack for Chattanooga, then the objective of a fierce Union campaign.

Fuller decided nobody was going to steal his train—especially before breakfast— and jumped on a handcart and lit out in hot pursuit. Up the track a ways he found an engine on a siding and commandeered it. It didn't matter that the engine was turned in the wrong direction: Fuller steamed off down the track, speeding over bridges the spies had set afire and around sharp turns in reverse!

Finally the *General* ran out of steam and the Yankees ran off into the woods. All were later caught and most of them were hanged.

————

General Joseph E. Johnston, senior officer of the Confederate Army, was forced to surrender to General William T. Sherman near the end of the war. After the war, while serving as a pallbearer at Sherman's funeral, Johnston caught pneumonia; he died soon afterwards.

————

One night early in the war Julia Ward Howe, wife of a Washington civil service official, watched from her hotel room as a dispirited Union column marched through the streets. Disturbed by this reminder that the war was going badly for the North, she went to bed deeply depressed. In the middle of the night she arose, went to a writing desk and scribbled some words hastily. Next morning, dimly aware of being up in the night, she went to the desk and found she had written a short poem. It was so good she changed only a few words.

Mrs. Howe sold the poem to the *Atlantic Monthly* for four dollars. Before long the entire North was singing its stirring stanzas to the tune of "John Brown's Body." Its new name was "Battle Hymn of the Republic."

————

Nathan Bedford Forrest, the Confederate cavalry general, had twenty-nine horses shot from under him during the war.

————

Thomas J. "Stonewall" Jackson seemed to be a hypochondriac; he reported himself the victim of all sorts of curious maladies. He had a chronically upset stomach, for which he sucked lemons. He would not eat pepper, claiming it made his left leg weak. He sometimes ducked his head in a bucket of cold water, thinking it was good for his eyestrain.

He often thought himself "off balance" and would go about holding up first one arm then the other in an attempt to reestablish "proper equilibrium."

————

Robert E. Lee had a pet chicken that laid an egg for him every morning. Even after the shattering defeat at Gettysburg, he would not leave the field until the chicken had been found.

————

A Scottish immigrant named Wilmer McLean lived on a farm near the village of Manassas, Virginia, until the day an artillery shell dropped down his chimney and exploded in a pot of stew. It was one of the first shots of the battle of Bull Run, which raged in his cornfields the rest of the day.

Unhappy at this turn of events, McLean packed up and moved away to the community of Appomattox Court House. When Lee and Grant were looking for a suitable place to discuss surrender terms, McLean offered his home. Despite the fact that most of his furniture was broken up and carried off by souvenir hunters, McLean for the rest of his life was proud of telling folks the Civil War started in his backyard and ended up in his front room.

A Soldier's Life

The Civil War soldier spent most of his time doing the same things today's soldier does: drilling, polishing, digging, and waiting for something to happen. When not drilling or working, he played cards—favorites were euchre and cribbage—chess, or "chequers," made pipes, and wrote letters. Most soldiers smoked pipes and they would spend days, perhaps weeks, carving intricate ones of wood, bone, horn, or hoof. Probably the favorite off-duty activity was writing home to parents, wives, or girlfriends. It was a writing age anyway, but the postmaster general encouraged writing by ordering all soldiers' letters carried free of charge. All that had to be done was to write "soldier's letter" on the envelope. One soldier, dramatizing the fact he had back pay coming, wrote: "Postmaster, please put it through; I've nary a cent, but six months due."

One of the worst parts of camp life was having to live with certain little visitors—lice and bedbugs. Soldiers tried to get rid of the little visitors by boiling their clothes in the big mess kettles, using salt water. That would usually work, but only temporarily, because there were too many soldiers who took little interest in bodily cleanliness; before long the vermin would return. This fact gave rise to the popular story about the scroungy soldier who, when he finally took a bath, found a number of shirts and socks he thought he had lost. There were usually a couple of men in each company who were willing to do the unit's wash for pay, and there probably was one who would cut hair, whether he knew how or not.

TRAVELING ON THE STOMACH

Napoleon's maxim that an army travels on its stomach was as true during the Civil War as it was during any other war. The Union soldiers were always better fed than the Confederates, a fact that could be observed even in death. The Confederate dead were white-faced and lean, as in life; the Union boys turned black and their bodies became bloated. More than a few times a Rebel attack carried the day because the half-starved Confederates wanted what was in the blue-clad boys' haversacks. During one charge a sergeant yelled, "Let's get 'em boys—they've got cheese!"

After the battle of Shiloh, Grant's army was hard hit by diarrhea caused by sorry food. Lack of food, in fact, may have been the immediate cause of Lee's surrender. Grant's forces had cut off supplies expected to arrive by railroad, leaving the Confederates with nothing to eat except corn stolen from the horses' rations.

The chief item in the soldier's diet—as it has been since time immemorial—was that tough, unleavened biscuit known as "hardtack." The soldier found it more digestible if he crumbled it in coffee or soup or fried it in pork fat. In the field the main items in the soldier's diet were salt pork, which he broiled or ate raw between hardtack; salt beef, known as "salted horse"; and occasionally ham or bacon, although these were too often black and smelly. To eat these delicacies a soldier was afforded a knife, fork, spoon, tin plate, and tin dipper. These he would clean, if at all, with leaves or straw. When they became too black to tolerate any longer, he would run the knife, fork, and spoon in and out of the ground and rinse them off.

The soldier could get a measure of relief from such a monotonous diet by visiting the sutler's tent. The sutler was a trader licensed by the government to follow the armies and sell food items and dry goods such as boots, hats, and suspenders. His prices, however, were outrageous and his food was not necessarily better than the mess hall's chow— just different. This fact occasioned one customer to say of his pies, "They are moist and indigestible below, tough and indestructible above, with untold horrors in between."

DISCIPLINE AND DESERTION

Since "Joshua fit de battle of Jericho" there has been little change in the enlisted man's view of his superiors: he always resents the privileges an officer has that he doesn't. This Civil War song sums up the attitude perfectly:

> *Whiskey is good medicine,*
> *It helps the great and small,*
> *But when you're in the army,*
> *Headquarters gets it all.*
> *They drink it by the barrel,*
> *They drink it by the yard,*
> *But if a private touches it,*
> *They put him under guard.*
>
> *CHORUS*
> *How do you like the army,*
> *The rootin', tootin' army,*
> *The high-falutin' army,*
> *Where a soldier is a mule?*
> *Oh, how do you like the army,*
> *The rootin', tootin' army,*
> *The high-falutin' army,*
> *Where the big brass buttons rule?*
>
> *The generals eat the chickens*
> *Till they cackle in their sleep.*
> *The colonels and the captains*
> *Eat all the cows and sheep.*
> *When the soldiers get so hungry*
> *They steal a mangy pig,*

The biggest dump in Dixie
They're sure to have to dig.

[CHORUS]

And when we take a city,
They put us all on duty.
The general and his officers
Go in to judge the beauty.
The general gets the choicest,
The majors get the pickin's
The captains get the servants,
And the privates get the dickens.

[CHORUS]

It wasn't as bad as in the Revolutionary War, but in this conflict there were thousands of officers, including generals, who were totally incompetent. It was especially true in the Union Army, where the ranks were filled with "political generals" who got commissions because they had influence in high places. Many were completely ignorant of military life.

Some enlisted men were troublemakers in any case, but most were unlikely to obey the orders of an inept officer and often they didn't. Others were not inclined to obey anyone. Punishments for such as these ranged from having to bury a dead horse for failing to salute a superior officer, to execution by firing squad for desertion. Cowards were drummed out of camp at bayonet point and were subject to the death penalty if they returned. Other punishments, major and minor, were

1. Having half the head shaved.

2. Walking guard duty with a haversack full of rocks.

3. Sitting on a high platform in any kind of weather.

4. Being tied up by the thumbs, feet on ground, arms extended.

5. Being tied up with arms and legs together and some object tied in the mouth. (Called being "bucked and gagged.")

6. Standing all day in the "sweat box," a structure about seven feet tall and eighteen inches square.

7. Wearing all day the "wooden overcoat," a barrel with the bottom end knocked out and a hole big enough for the head cut in the top.

8. Being lashed all day to the spare wheel on the rear of the gun carriage if an artilleryman.

9. Carrying a loaded saddlebag all day if a cavalryman.

The longer the war went on, the higher the desertion rate rose. When a deserter was to be executed, his entire regiment lined up in a quadrangle, while the doomed man sat on the edge of his coffin in front of the open grave. Twelve men picked at random made up the firing squad, with six in reserve in case some of the twelve fainted or could not bring themselves to pull the trigger. Two or three muskets had powder but no ball, so that in each man's mind there was the possibility that he was not the one who carried out the sentence.

Lincoln Looks for a General

In all wars, it seems, opposing nations think they can put an end to the whole nasty business if they can take the other side's capital. One of many unique aspects of the Civil War was the fact the two capitals were just across the Potomac River from each other, not more than a hundred miles apart. The South intended to fight a defensive war, wishing only to protect her borders while waiting for the United States to recognize her independence. In the North the immediate cry was "On to Richmond!" as strategists thought they could take the Confederate capital in a matter of weeks and the war would be over almost before it started. Cooler heads believed it would not be that easy, but the hotheads prevailed.

For four bloody years Lincoln's pet army, the Army of the Potomac, hammered away at Richmond—while the war was being won elsewhere. And for three of those years Lincoln tried one general after another, looking for one capable of carrying out the task.

The first army that headed down to Richmond was commanded by General Irvin McDowell. The soldiers were only in for a three-month hitch, so they needed to get on down to Richmond before their enlistment ran out. McDowell pleaded for a little time to at least show the boys how to shoot, but the public clamored for a quick victory and Lincoln, yielding to the pressure, ordered McDowell to get going. "You are green," he told the general, "but so are they." As it turned out, the Yankee boys were a bit greener— or a bit more scared—than the Rebs. When the bullets started whistling around their ears at Bull Run Creek, they lit out for home— right through the middle of the Washington bigwigs and their ladies who had come out on this summer Sunday to watch the battle. The disorganized and totally demoralized army limped into the capital for two days, while Washington women set up soup kitchens to feed them or took them into their homes.

Almost 1,500 Union soldiers were killed or wounded at Bull Run and about the same number were missing. One who was not missing was Congressman Alfred Ely of New York, who was captured and sent to Libby Prison in Richmond. Not killed, wounded, or captured were the members of two volunteer regiments; their enlistments ran out the day of the battle, so they turned around and left the field.

MCCLELLAN AND POPE

After the Bull Run disaster Lincoln appointed General George B. McClellan to take over the Army of the Potomac, whip it into shape, and take Richmond with it. "Little Mac" was a brilliant organizer and trainer of troops. His problem was that after all the training he did not want to take his brilliant army out and get it messed up by fighting.

McClellan transported his army to the peninsula between the James and York Rivers and moved slowly on Richmond. At Yorktown he found the Confederates heavily entrenched, so he spent weeks digging in and hauling up big guns—and all the time sending to Washington for reinforcements. Finally he moved on Yorktown and took it easily: there was no one there to fight. The Confederates had watched him continue to stack the cards in his favor—then pulled up stakes and left. The Confederates knew they were outnumbered three to one, so they played it smart.

"Tardy George," as a derisive Northern song was now calling him, moved cautiously up the peninsula and came so close to Richmond the gold and archives of the Confederate government were loaded on railroad cars ready to move. Tardy George didn't strike, but Robert E. Lee did, pushing the Army of the Potomac slowly back down the peninsula until it boarded ships and returned home.

McClellan's excuse was—guess what—he was outnumbered. And he needed more equipment. And more cannon. And more time. And he began writing Lincoln long letters on how to run the government. A favorite joke in the North was that Lincoln asked Little Mac for more detailed reports of the fighting, and the general, piqued, wired back: "Have captured two cows. What disposition shall I make of them?" Lincoln replied: "Milk 'em, George."

Now Lincoln gave the command to General John Pope, a dashing soldier who bragged that out West where he had been serving they had seen nothing but the backs of the enemy. When Lincoln asked him where his headquarters were, General Pope told him, "Sir, my headquarters are in the saddle," after which Lincoln told friends, "General Pope's headquarters are where his hindquarters ought to be."

Pope got to see the enemy's front side for a change, and he didn't like what he saw: Lee in front of him and Stonewall Jackson behind him. The two Confederates began cutting his army to pieces at Second Bull Run, and Pope decided to run himself, back to Washington, in a repeat performance of the year earlier. A desperate President went to his advisers saying, "What shall I do? Pope is licked and McClellan has the diarrhoea [sic]."

MCCLELLAN AND BURNSIDE

Diarrhea or not, Lincoln put McClellan back in command and prayed. The soldiers, who loved him, hugged the general's horse as he rode in. This time McClellan had better luck—up to a point. Lee decided on an invasion of Maryland, but some careless Confederate officer lost his plans for the campaign. A Union soldier found them wrapped around three cigars. So when Lee entered Maryland, McClellan knew what he was up to and met him at Antietam Creek. The battle was more or less a draw, but Little Mac, ever cautious because he just knew he was outnumbered, failed to follow as Lee retreated into Virginia. McClellan had 93,000 troops to Lee's 40,000, but he stayed on the battlefield resting on his laurels. Lincoln was furious when he heard the news, along with an intelligence report that Lee could probably have been destroyed with 10,000 fresh troops. McClellan had kept 30,000 men in reserve, none of them ever firing a shot.

McClellan was out again—to get ready to run against Lincoln in the next election—and General Ambrose Burnside was in. Burnside did not want the job, and did not think himself capable of commanding so many men. With press, pulpit, and public screaming for a victory, the new leader made a stupid, reckless frontal attack on Lee's heavy fortifications near Fredericksburg, Virginia. It had rained heavily and some of the men got stuck in the mud; 7,000 others were killed or wounded. Burnside drew off and planned another attack, but more rain and mud made it impossible. A Union soldier made up this new version of a bedtime prayer:

> *Now I lay me down to sleep*
> *In mud that's many fathoms deep;*
> *If I'm not here when you awake,*
> *Just hunt me up with an oyster rake.*

Burnside sported a particularly ornate growth of sidewhiskers, as they were called then. His chief contribution to history was a new name for such growth—"sideburns."[1]

A RIGHT HOOK FOR HOOKER

Next it was the turn of Joseph "Fighting Joe" Hooker, an energetic but headstrong commander. "Our enemy," he declared, "must either ingloriously fly or come from behind his defenses and give us battle on our own ground, where certain destruction awaits him." Destruction came about all right, but not quite in the manner Fighting Joe expected. Lee daringly divided his force, which was less than half of Hooker's, and sent Stonewall Jackson to strike the Union flank. The strategy was successful, and Hooker's army was badly beaten at Chancellorsville, Virginia, in what would prove to be Lee's most brilliant battle. Baffled by his opponents, Hooker called a council of war and asked his generals for a vote on what to do. Four voted to stay and fight, the other two voted to retreat. Hooker retreated.

Lee now decided on a bold stroke. He would take his ragged Confederates, now grown contemptuous of a foe they had beaten so many times, and invade the North, hoping to throw panic into the Yankees and perhaps win recognition abroad. Thus he led his troops across Maryland and into Pennsylvania. As the Southern boys marched through Chambersburg, Pennsylvania, some of the women of the town taunted them. One wrapped herself in the American flag and jeered, "Come and take it if you can." A woman with a fierce look in her eye roared, "Look at Pharoah's army marching to the sea." When one sang "The Star-Spangled Banner," Lee took off his hat and bowed in the saddle. Watching the cool and impressive Southern leader go by, one woman murmured, "Oh, I wish he was ours."

MEADE WINS . . . AND FAILS

Meanwhile, General George G. Meade had been told he was now in charge of the Army of the Potomac. Meade knew Lee was somewhere in Pennsylvania, north of Washington, and took his army off in that general direction. Neither general intended to fight at Gettysburg, but firing commenced when a Union patrol encountered a Confederate force that had gone to that village looking for a shoe factory.

For three days Meade's men and Lee's men were locked in furious combat, but when the charge of General George Pickett's men against the Union center failed, the Confederates knew the cause was lost and retired from the field. It was the bloodiest battle in modern warfare up to that time. One blue-clad boy and one gray-clad boy were found with their bloody fingers still fastened in each other. A cow lane was filled with thirty dead horses. A tree had 250 bullets in it. Like McClellan at Antietam, Meade did not pursue the retreating Confederates: if he had, he probably could have crushed Lee's army—which had a ten-mile-long wagon train of wounded—and brought about an end to the war before long. The North was jubilant over the victory, but Abraham Lincoln was angry. What did this new general mean by reporting: "We have driven the invader from our soil"? *All* the United States was "our soil," and its two parts might have been reunited sooner if he had followed up the victory.

"USELESS" GRANT BECOMES USEFUL

The same day Lee retreated from the field at Gettysburg—July 4, 1863—Vicksburg, Mississippi was falling to a scroungy-looking warrior named Ulysses S. Grant.[2] Soon Lincoln was thinking of making this man the new commander of all Union armies. The thought met stiff opposition, for it was rumored that the general drank too much and was, in fact, drunk at the Battle of Shiloh.

And it was true that during his earlier career Grant had been something of a tippler, but he was no drunkard. The drinking stories grew out of his unhappy experiences when he was stationed on the West Coast after the Mexican War, where he drank too much because he was lonely for his wife and child and because his monotonous duties did not challenge him. When his commanding officer reprimanded him for his drinking habits, Grant wrote out a resignation leaving the date blank to be filled in by his commander when whiskey got the better of him again. It did and Grant quit the Army.

As a civilian he tried working in his father's harness shop, farming land left by his wife's father (with two slaves, by the way), and selling real estate, but he wasn't successful at any of them. People had begun to call him "Useless" Grant. When the war broke out, he got a colonel's commission because of his experience and the fact that he was a West Point graduate.

Some thought Grant so unsoldierly in appearance he could not be a good leader of men. He seemed always to have a scruffy look, as if he had just gotten out of bed, and quickly at that. His hair appeared to need combing and his uniform pressing. One eye was lower than the other, which gave his face a sort of lopsided look. Then there was that ever-present cigar that seemed as much a part of his face as his nose.

The story is probably apocryphal that when Lincoln's advisers told him not to appoint a man with such a reputation for drinking, the President replied, "Find out what brand he drinks and send some of it to my other generals." (Or something like that.) It is known that he said, "I can't spare this man: he fights."

Fight Grant did, but many on both sides called him "butcher" for sacrificing in his long drive on Richmond almost as many men as Lee had.

The Strange Case of Jefferson Davis

When Union troops captured Jefferson Davis at the end of the Civil War, he presented the United States government with a problem. Many Union officials had hoped the Confederate president would escape to Europe so the government could avoid the considerable dilemma of what to do with him. He could not, as a popular song suggested, be hung from a sour apple tree. Public clamor demanded that he be tried, but tried for what? The only charge seemed to be treason, but had he done anything treasonable? Was secession a treasonable act? There was nothing in the Constitution about the matter and there were no legal precedents on which to base the charge. If the trial did not establish that leaving the Union was a treasonable act, then where would the government be? And if he were tried, who would do the trying—a U.S. court or a military tribunal? Frankly, the United States did not know what to do with him, and the situation was downright embarrassing.

Davis could have solved the problem by asking, as General Lee and other high-ranking Confederates did, for a pardon, but he was too proud a man for that. Such a request was the same as admitting guilt, and neither then nor at any time later in his life would he admit he had done anything wrong.

While the U.S. government pondered these vexing questions Davis, like a captured Crusader awaiting ransom, languished in a cell at Fortress Monroe. This military post was off the tip of the Virginia peninsula between the York and James rivers and was indeed like a medieval fortress, with high stone walls and what amounted to a moat. For the first several days—after he had thrown his first meal into the face of his guard—he was kept in chains. His tiny room was whitewashed, and that together with the single light that burned incessantly almost cost him the sight of one eye. The ever-burning light was there so his "silent friends"—the guards in an outer room—could see him at all times. They had been ordered never to take their eyes off him and never to speak to him. Davis once remarked to John J. Craven, the prison doctor and for a long time his only friend: "To have a human eye riveted upon you in every moment of waking or sleeping, sitting, walking or lying down, is a refinement of torture on anything the Camanches [sic] or Spanish Inquisition ever dreamed."

His quarters were dank and forbidding, and the tide in the moat created a "malarial poison." Mold gathered on his shoes and on the crumbs he scattered about for his sole companion, a mouse. Prison rules at first were stark: no visitors, no mail, no exercise, and no eating utensils except a spoon (suicide was his jailers' paramount fear).

LIFE BECOMES LIVABLE

In later months Dr. Craven, citing medical reasons, brought a measure of relief into the prisoner's life. The monotonous meals were replaced with a more liberal diet, and a knife and fork were provided. Newspapers, though censored, and a few books were allowed. The guards were told to stop pacing all night and, best of all, the prisoner was permitted an hour's walk daily on the ramparts, but accompanied always by the officer of the day and four armed guards. A crowd of the morbidly curious gathered outside the walls each day to watch.

Eventually Davis was moved to more spacious quarters in Carroll Hall, "spacious" meaning two rooms, a cot, a small table, and two cane-bottomed chairs. There were still bars on the doors and windows, and the guards still stood vigil outside, but the entire atmosphere was different. His family was allowed to come and were given several rooms and a kitchen in another part of the hall.

Jefferson Davis was in this place two years. He repeatedly asked for—and was repeatedly denied—a trial. No grounds for the denials were ever given. Finally, on May 14, 1867, he was released on a bond signed by some of the most prominent men in America. Two of them, ironically, were Gerrit Smith and Horace Greeley, ardent abolitionists both.

President Andrew Johnson pardoned Davis in 1868, and Congress was at last generous enough to restore his citizenship in 1978.

Chapter 12

Follies, Frauds, and Fortunes

Andrew Johnson's Impeachment

FIRST OF ALL, it should be made clear that an official who is impeached is charged with and tried for "high crimes and misdemeanors" while in office. The official does not have to be found guilty and removed from office, as is generally believed.

President Andrew Johnson's impeachment resulted from his opposition to the plans of the radical element in the Republican Party. They wanted to treat the South as conquered territory, control the legislatures of the Southern states and establish Republican ascendancy there and in the whole nation. More important was the fact that if the Radicals had succeeded they would have destroyed constitutional government by making the legislative branch supreme over the executive branch, the President becoming little more than chairman of a cabinet that was responsible to Congress.

The two branches had been at each other's throats for two years, snarling and bristling. Andy Johnson, or "Andy Veto" as his critics called him, had vetoed bill after bill that he considered unconstitutional, or too hard on the South, or that interfered too much with executive authority. Congress, dominated by its Radical members, repassed most of them over the President's veto.

Andrew Johnson had come up the hard way, not even being able to read and write until his schoolteacher wife taught him. Now he had become a professional common man. He was always ready for a fight; if his back was to the wall, all the better. His pugnacious personality did not help his cause. Too often he met situations calling for tact and diplomacy with stubbornness and arrogance, which turned many moderates in Congress from him to the Radicals.

STANTON SENT PACKING

There would have been no impeachment if Johnson had removed Secretary of War Edwin Stanton before the Radicals rammed through the Tenure of Office Act of 1867. The act stated that no official whose appointment required Senate approval could be removed by the President without the Senate's approval for that act also. Now the only way Johnson could fire Stanton, who outwardly upheld the administration, but acted secretly as a Radical spy, was to break the law and make himself impeachable.

In August 1867, Johnson sent Stanton a curt note: "Public considerations of a high character restrain me to say that your resignation as Secretary of War will be accepted." Stanton refused to resign, even when Johnson appointed the most popular man in the country, Ulysses S. Grant, to replace him. When in February 1868, the President told the Secretary to pack his bags and get out, the Radicals went wild. Thaddeus Stevens, the aging Radical leader, exulted: "Now we've got Johnson and we're going to hang him!"

The House of Representatives, suspending all other business, passed a resolution of impeachment and sent it to the Senate. But in its haste to get rid of the "dead dog in the White House" it forgot to draw up formal charges. Returning to its designing board, the House detailed eleven articles of impeachment, most of them blatant nonsense.

THE TRIAL: A RADICAL DEPARTURE

The trial, which lasted from March 5 to May 16, 1868, was a mockery of justice. Johnson's three lawyers, who had volunteered their services free of charge, asked the Senate for forty days to prepare their case—and were granted ten. So sure of success were the Radicals that Ben Wade, the Radical President *pro-tempore* of the Senate—and, because there was no Vice-President, next in line for the presidency—had already drawn up his cabinet. The prosecution's "managers," as they termed themselves, brought into testimony all sorts of irrelevant and ridiculous charges. They claimed the President was a drunkard who kept a private harem, and they made the monstrous charge that he had been party to the assassination of his predecessor. When the defense tried to show that Johnson intended to test the constitutionality of the Tenure of Office Act before he fired Stanton, it was not allowed to do so.

As voting time approached, the Radicals began counting heads. The twelve Democrats in the Senate could be expected to vote for acquittal. Of the forty-two Republican members, the Radicals could lose only six and still be assured of the thirty-six votes needed to convict. At a party caucus, to their dismay, they learned six Republican senators did not think the evidence convincing. However, if no more of the party faithful defected they were still assured of a victory. But one senator refused to commit himself. He was Edmund G. Ross of Kansas, and everything hinged on his decision.

ROSS RUINS THE RADICALS

Ross had been wrestling with his conscience throughout the trial. It appeared obvious to him that all the charges were trumped up, but he knew if he voted for acquittal his young political career would be over—the Radicals would see to that.

When the Chief Justice reached his name during the roll call, Ross later recalled, "I almost literally looked down into my open grave." "Mr. Senator Ross, how say you?"

intoned the Chief Justice's deep voice. "Is the respondent Andrew Johnson guilty or not guilty?"

The gallery was hushed, every voice in the chamber still, every eye fixed on one face. The situation was so overpowering, Ross's "Not guilty" failed to be heard by senators on the other side of the chamber and had to be repeated. The second time the words came loud and clear: "NOT GUILTY!"

Almost immediately Ross fell into his "open grave." His constituency made it clear he would not be reelected. Newspapers called him a "poor, pitiful wretch" and a "miserable poltroon and traitor." A Kansas legislator told him: "The rope with which Judas Iscariot hanged himself has been lost, but Jim Lane's pistol is at your service."

Twenty years later Congress repealed the Tenure of Office Act and fifty-eight years later, to clear the record, the Supreme Court declared it unconstitutional.

As for Andrew Johnson, he served out the remaining few months of his (or rather Lincoln's) term and went home to Tennessee to become a private citizen for the first time in twenty-five years. In 1875 he returned to Washington in triumph as a senator, but showed no rancor towards his former enemies. Five months later, as he was being talked up for President again, he died of a heart attack. Johnson had always thought of himself as first and foremost a supporter of the Constitution and had asked that a copy of that document be buried with him. He was laid to rest with a copy of the Constitution as his pillow, while his body was wrapped in the American flag.

The Scandalous Grant Administration

One thing made Ulysses S. Grant President of the United States: the notion then prevailing, as to some extent it has in recent times, that good generals make good presidents. He was the great hero of the day—the "cloud-sent man," a poet called him—and he was unbeatable. Little did his admirers know he would go down in history as one of this nation's worst presidents.

Grant could have had the nomination of either party, but he chose to run as a Republican. He had voted only one time in his life, for James Buchanan, a Democrat, in 1856. As far as the voters were concerned his political naïveté was a point in his favor, but once the great warrior was in office his total lack of experience proved disastrous.

Grant's main problem was loyalty. He was fiercely loyal to his friends, especially old comrades-in-arms, and he expected them to be totally loyal to him in return. Such personal dedication was often the sole requirement for a job in his administration. For example, four former generals in his Army of the Potomac were on the new President's staff—and even the White House butler was a former mess sergeant. With one or two notable exceptions, Grant chose his cabinet the same way.

As Grant took office the nation was entering the industrial age, and although the country was growing by leaps and bounds in physical might, it was at the same time sinking to a new moral low. Waste, extravagance, speculation, and graft were rampant, but what was worse, the public as a whole showed a callous disinterest in such sharp practices. It was that disregard that allowed the government to fall into the hands of incompetents and crooks.

NO GUILTY MAN ESCAPES?

The worst scandal of the Grant administration smelled of liquor. Oddly enough, the Whiskey Ring (actually Rings) was exposed through the persistent efforts of Grant's new Secretary of the Treasury Benjamin Bristow, who had been appointed to replace a secretary accused of tax fraud. Bristow discovered that for a long time distillers in some cities had been cheating the government of tax money by filing false reports, forging revenue stamps, and bribing collectors. Since the crooked path led even into the Treasury Department's offices, Bristow organized a new unit of special agents and in May 1875, staged sudden raids on thirty-two distilleries in Milwaukee, Chicago, and St. Louis. In all those cities he found numerous politicians with their hands in the till, but the Whiskey Ring in St. Louis put all the others in the shade. Here a supervisor of internal revenue himself had his hand in the government's pocket, and the ring's operations had grown so large an experienced manager had to be brought in to handle its far-flung activities.

Among those taking payoffs in this scheme, to Grant's chagrin, was the President's personal secretary, Orville Babcock (an old army buddy). His loot, Bristow's investigators learned, came in strange ways: a cigar box with thousand dollar bills in it, a letter with money inside, a gift of large diamonds, paid-up hotel bills.

Bristow and the Attorney General called on the President and laid out their case. "Let no guilty man escape!" was Grant's much-publicized reply. "If Babcock is guilty there is no man who wants him so proven [more] than I do," he added. Privately, Babcock told his boss Bristow was just trying to further his own political ambitions.

Babcock was tried twice, first by a military court, then by a civil one. At the first trial Grant made sure several generals favorably disposed toward Babcock were on the review board. At the civil trial he sent in a sworn affidavit stating that the accused was a man of the highest integrity who would never think of doing such a thing. Babcock was acquitted in both instances.

Grant tried to dismiss his overzealous Secretary of the Treasury, but when the press got wind of his intentions he changed his mind.

LOYALTY UNDER FIRE

There were a host of minor scandals that tarnished Grant's image because of his stubborn loyalty to the accused. When his brother-in-law (there was a whole battalion of in-laws on the public payroll) was reported guilty of misconduct as collector of customs at New Orleans, Grant's response was to appoint him to another term. When a contractor friend was accused of spending twice as much as necessary to improve streets and parks in the District of Columbia, Grant replied by making him governor of the District. When Congress condemned the Assistant Secretary of the Treasury for allowing some collectors to keep part of the proceeds, Grant accepted his resignation only to turn around and appoint him to the Court of Claims.

Secretary of War W. W. Belknap was selling to the highest bidder the right to sell supplies on Indian reservations. He needed the money to support his extravagant wife in high society. When she died, Belknap continued the practice in order to pay for the social ambitions of his second wife, his first wife's sister. Grant accepted Belknap's resignation "with great regret."

The "Election" of 1876

The election of 1876 has the unique but dubious distinction of being the only election in American history in which one candidate won (probably) and another took office. It was also an election "stolen" by both political parties.

Rutherford B. Hayes, three-time governor of Ohio and a Civil War general with an undistinguished record (a "grade B hero," the Democrats said), was the Republican candidate. The Democrats put forward Samuel J. Tilden, former governor of New York, who had won fame in helping bring down the reign of the notorious Boss Tweed.

The chief issue in the campaign should have been Grant's record, but it wasn't. Had the Republicans chosen to defend the record, Tilden undoubtedly would have been an easy winner. Instead the G.O.P. put Hayes forward as a reform candidate, and because Tilden's fame rested largely on reform as well, there was little to argue about.

As election time neared, the odds seemed to favor Tilden, and as the first returns came in, he was clearly out in front. Then the backstage scene-shifters of the Republican Party went to work. Early on the morning after the election they discovered that although Tilden led in the popular vote, the electoral vote was so close Hayes could win if the Republicans carried South Carolina, Florida, and Louisiana, three states where carpetbag rule still flourished.

FRAUD AND COUNTERFRAUD

The three states represented nineteen electoral votes. Quickly telegrams went out to the Republican Party organizations in those states, all of them reading: "Hayes is elected if we carry your three states. Can you hold?" Then Zachariah Chandler, Republican National Committee head, announced to the country: "Hayes has 185 electoral votes and is elected."

The actual count was Tilden 184, Hayes 166, doubtful nineteen. Tilden needed only one of the nineteen doubtful votes to win; if Hayes could get all of them he would win by one vote.

There is no doubt that both parties had cheated in the three disputed states. The Democrats intimidated blacks, scaring them away from the polls or voiding their ballots with one flimsy excuse or another. The Republicans bribed officials or assured them of government patronage. Even more connivance began as both parties sent "visiting statesmen" to the three states, allegedly to make sure the counting was properly done, but really to pressure local boards into seeing that their party's ballots were made the official ones.

The key state was Florida. The Democrats probably won in all three, but it is possible that in an election free of trickery and intimidation the black majority in Louisiana and South Carolina could have given those states to the Republicans. But in Florida a white majority and an undisputed Democratic government would undoubtedly have given that state's eight electoral votes to the Democrats, and Tilden would have won by seven electoral votes.

A COMPROMISING SITUATION

As it was, Congress was faced with two sets of returns from each of the three states, which left the legislators in a quandary. The Constitution states that electoral returns shall be opened by the president of the Senate in the presence of both houses of Congress, but does not say *who* shall count them. The president of the Senate was a Republican; if he counted them the Hayes ballots would be accepted. The speaker of the House was a Democrat; if he counted them the Tilden ballots would be accepted.

Congress hammered out a compromise, setting up a special electoral commission of five senators, five congressmen, and five Supreme Court justices. The commission was evenly divided among Democrats and Republicans, except for the fifteenth member, an independent justice. The independent had Democratic leanings, but in the end it didn't matter. Before the commission met, the justice left the high court to take a seat in the Senate, having just been elected to that position by the Illinois legislature, as was still the custom. The only justices left were Republicans, which left the commission with eight Republicans and seven Democrats.

THE "GREAT SWAP"

In February 1877, Congress began the roll call of states. When it reached Florida, the first of the disputed states, its returns were submitted to the commission sitting in a nearby chamber. After long discussion the committee voted to accept the Hayes returns, by a vote of eight to seven. When Louisiana's returns were accepted by the same eight-to-seven vote, the Democrats saw the handwriting on the wall and vowed to filibuster "until hell freezes over." Worse, there were mutterings of armed revolt, and Grant reviewed the troops. Someone fired a shot through the window while the Hayes family sat at dinner. Some Democratic newspaper editors were urging their readers to march on Washington crying "Tilden or blood!"

As the March 4 inauguration date (later changed to January 20) came closer, Democratic and Republican leaders met in a hotel room and worked out the Compromise of 1877, known in some quarters as the "Great Swap." If the Democrats agreed to accept Hayes as the winner, the new administration would see that the remaining federal troops were removed from the South, that Southerners were awarded a substantial number of federal offices—including a cabinet position—and that long-overdue government support for internal improvements in the South would be forthcoming. (There were a number of important railroad men in attendance and it could be no coincidence that chief among the internal improvements was government aid to railroads.)

The Democrats surrendered and Hayes received the remaining electoral votes, by the same eight-to-seven decision. The issue was settled only three days before someone had to take over the country, and since March 4 was on a Sunday the country would be without a president for twenty-four hours. To be on the safe side, Hayes was sworn in privately on March 3 and the public ceremony was held on March 5.

"RUTHERFRAUD" PROVES HIS METTLE

Hayes considered himself duly elected, but his administration operated under a cloud and the Democratic press never missed an opportunity to refer to him as "Rutherfraud" or "Old Eight to Seven." Surprisingly—to many, at least—Hayes turned out to be a competent chief executive who impressed the nation as a man of integrity and intelligence. He selected a top-flight cabinet, including a former Confederate general. Only a few weeks after taking office he boldly withdrew federal troops protecting carpetbag governments in parts of the South, despite vehement denunciations by carpetbag officials and vindictive Republicans. It was a courageous act that officially ended reconstruction.

Hayes and his wife Lucy were temperance advocates and soon banned liquor in the White House. His years in office became the "cold water administration" and his wife was popularly referred to as "Lemonade Lucy." He announced early that he would not run for a second term.

Age of the Moguls

The word "trust" came into being when John D. Rockefeller's lawyer, Samuel C.T. Dodd, persuaded the owners of forty oil companies to put their stock into the hands of a group of trustees who could operate all the companies as a unit, charging what they pleased and forcing out any competitors. The trustees, of course, would be headed by Rockefeller.

Before long there were sugar trusts, beef trusts, rubber trusts, and many others, but when the public outcry against this kind of cutthroat consolidation rose, the federal government felt compelled to move. The Sherman Act and other antitrust legislation followed, but a Supreme Court sympathetic to big business interpreted these laws narrowly for many years. It did not matter, however, for before long the money magicians came up with a successor to the trust.

In 1889 the governor of New Jersey asked the state's lawyers to find ways of fattening the state's pocketbook. The lawyers said a neat way to do that would be for the New Jersey legislature to pass laws allowing companies incorporated in the state to hold the stock of other corporations, a practice that until then had generally been held illegal. The legislature obliged and soon there was a great rush of companies to incorporate in New Jersey. The state made a lot of money out of corporation fees—while instituting a new age of American capitalism.

No longer did companies have to form a trust to combine themselves and stifle competition. Now it was only necessary for their New Jersey company to buy the stock of their various companies and thereby control the operation of all of them. The "holding company" had been born.

By such financial shenanigans, it was not difficult for a businessman to become a big businessman and for a big businessman to become a giant corporation. Some became rich almost overnight; here are a few of the better-known ones.

CORNELIUS VANDERBILT

The first of the great moguls, Vanderbilt showed later ones how to get things done—and how to live after things got done. Almost before he was old enough to shave he went into business for himself. With $100 borrowed from his mother he bought a barge and ferried people and goods around New York Harbor. Business was good enough to allow him to buy two more barges, then when the War of 1812 came along he was able to make a great deal of money. By the age of twenty-three he was a rich young roughneck already known as "Commodore," partly because of his little fleet, partly because of his gorgeous profanity.

Vanderbilt fought Robert Fulton's monopoly of the steamboat trade along the New York and New Jersey coasts all the way to the Supreme Court and won. Then he started a steamship line of his own, cutting out competition by cutting fares to the marrow.

After amassing a fortune in steamships, he built another by branching out into railroads.

The Commodore trusted no one, and kept all his accounts in his head. When competitors tried to horn in on some of his properties while he was in Europe, he wrote them:

> *Gentlemen:*
>
> *You have undertaken to cheat me. I will not sue you, for law takes too long. I will ruin you.*
>
> *Sincerely Yours, Cornelius Van Derbilt [sic]*

In a similar emergency on another occasion his famous words were: "What do I care about the law? Hain't I got the power?"

Vanderbilt treated his family with not a great deal more respect than he showed his business competitors. When his wife refused to move from Staten Island to New York he sent her to a sanitarium for a few months of "reflection." He was brutally indifferent to his nine children, the eldest, William Henry, being confined to a Staten Island farm until he was middle-aged.

The style of living set by this patriarch of the parvenues was best reflected in the homes he built. In the mid-1880s there were no less than seven palatial Vanderbilt houses within a seven-block area on Fifth Avenue. Most were the traditional brownstones—although the interiors were princely—but one was a limestone castle and another a Louis XIV mansion.

He died in 1877 worth at least $105 million.

DANIEL DREW

"I got to be a millionaire afore I knowed it hardly," old Uncle Dan'l was fond of telling anybody who would listen. Daniel Drew started out in the cattle business by using money he had been paid for going into the Army during the War of 1812 as a substitute for someone else (a common practice at the time). On the way to market he fed his beef cattle all the salt that could be forced down them, then just before reaching the market he allowed them to drink their fill. Since cattle were bought live-weight, the water added several tons to the aggregate weight of the herd. When Drew later went into another kind of stock market, "watered stock" came to mean a certificate sold in excess of what a company was worth, a practice Daniel Drew found amusing.

With the money from his cattle enterprises he bought an old tub of a boat and offered to carry passengers on the Hudson River for almost nothing. This forced Commodore Vanderbilt, whose monopoly of Hudson River traffic was threatened, to buy him off at a fat price.

This was when Uncle Dan'l migrated to Wall Street and became a legend—a dirty, ugly, almost illiterate legend. Though worth millions, he always wore an old drover's hat and carried an umbrella every day, rain or shine. Like Vanderbilt, he kept in his unkempt head how many "sheers" of this or that stock he owned and all his other dealings and misdealings.

Between stock quotations he spouted Bible quotations. After being knocked silly by a bolt of lightning he had become quite a pious man—or pretended to be—when it was to his advantage. When things didn't go right, he figured it was because he had somehow sinned. At such times he would hole up alone for three or four days in some obscure hotel and there, lying in bed smothered with blankets and with all the windows shut, he would exorcise the spirits of evil from his body with spirits of another sort.

JOHN D. ROCKEFELLER

John D. Rockefeller— "Old John D."— craved order the way an alcoholic craves liquor. With his Standard Oil Company trust he wiped out the competition because, as he told the courts, having so many oil companies strewn about the country was disorderly. By consolidation he meant to tidy up the business—and he was sincere in that belief.

When the Sherman Antitrust Act ordered Standard Oil to break up into thirty-eight different companies, nobody at headquarters fretted about it. Taking advantage of New Jersey's new law, Standard merely switched from a trust to a holding company, and its capital jumped overnight from $10 million to $110 million. The same men controlled all the companies, only individually instead of collectively.

By 1877, Rockefeller had gained control of ninety-five percent of the oil refineries in America. "Sell all the oil that is sold in your district" was the hard-boiled order that went out to his agents. Spies and secret rebates also helped matters.

John D., like Daniel Drew, was a pious man, but in Rockefeller's case the piety was genuine. All his life he was a dedicated Baptist and taught a Sunday school class for many years. When he said "God gave me my money," he meant it.

Shortly after the turn of the century, the popularity of the automobile began to multiply Rockefeller's millions faster than he could give them away. Unlike most of the other men of great wealth of the period, John D. preferred to live rather simply, even frugally. The home he used at his Pocantico Hills estate near Tarrytown, New York, was a modest one compared to those of the other moguls, and he drove the same car for fifteen years. Nevertheless, Pocantico Hills had seventy-four other buildings, a garage that would accommodate fifty cars, seventy miles of paved roads, a private golf course, and 1,000 to 1,500 employees, depending on the season. He also maintained homes in New York, Cleveland, and Ormond Beach, Florida.

In his sixties (he lived to be ninety-eight) Old John D. was stricken with alopecia, a disease of the nervous system that caused the loss of his hair, eyebrows, mustache, and beard. For the remainder of his life he appeared in public in a skull cap. He was in poor health all of those years, living mainly on milk and Graham crackers.

ANDREW CARNEGIE

Simply put, Andrew Carnegie turned steel into gold, and did it so well that by 1900 he was making a profit of $25 million a year— and with no income tax to pay. That was a time when the average American worker was bringing in $500 a year.

Carnegie (he insisted it be pronounced Car*ne*gie) came to the United States from Scotland as a $1.20-a-week bobbin boy, but mounted the ladder of success so swiftly he scorched the rungs. He quickly went from telegraphy to railroads to the iron-bridge industry and finally into the just-burgeoning steel business. His spectacular success was due to tough-fisted methods, the picking of first-rate associates, and the systematic cultivation of important people.

His worst mistake was to order the manager of his Homestead plant to hire no union workers, and then to go off on a vacation in Scotland. While he was away, hell broke loose at Homestead, and the manager had to call in 300 Pinkerton guards to try to stop the rioting. When the smoke cleared, 14 men were dead, 163 seriously hurt. The public cursed Carnegie for allowing such a thing to happen and for not being there when it did.

By the 1900s, the little (five feet four inches, 130 pounds) Scotsman had wearied of "steeling" and offered to sell his holdings to the great banker J. P. Morgan. The banker was eager to buy, but not at Carnegie's price of nearly $500 million. When the Scot threatened to go into the steel tubing business, which Morgan had plunged into heavily, the banker changed his mind.

Though not to the extent Rockefeller did, Carnegie eschewed extravagant living. His house on Fifth Avenue in New York, though large, was not palatial. His yacht was not in a class with those of other moguls. On Skibo Castle in Scotland, though, he lavished millions. The estate eventually reached 32,000 acres and had up to 300 tenants. Guests were awakened in the mornings by the Carnegie bagpiper skirling beneath the bedroom windows and ate their breakfast to the music of the Carnegie organist.

Afraid of being "disgraced" by dying with so much money, Carnegie worked hard at giving it away. Starved for books in his youth, he gave millions to libraries, eventually building or contributing to 2,800 of them. As a music lover, he bought hundreds of organs for churches, but he was not interested in religion, and to the churches themselves he didn't even give the time of day.

J. P. MORGAN

The name J. P. Morgan became so synonymous with the management of enormous sums of money that today any banker or top executive portrayed in films, TV shows, or cartoons is likely to go by his initials. In the 1950s a singer who called herself "Jaye P." Morgan won a measure of popularity partly by capitalizing on the magic name.

Pierpont Morgan (as he was generally known in his lifetime) was indubitably the greatest financial organizer the country has ever seen, but he did not, like so many speculators of his time, plunge into a deal to make a quick profit and then split. He stayed with any corporation he invested in, and he refused to lend money to anyone who had even the mere hint of a shady reputation.

Even the federal government recognized Morgan's preeminence in the field. Once when the nation's gold reserves were dwindling, President Grover Cleveland sent Morgan an urgent appeal and the Great Moneychanger tided the country over with a few loans. The government so often asked his advice on fiscal matters that some accused the Secretary of the Treasury of being an errand boy for the House of Morgan.

The financial wizard reached the pinnacle of his long career when he bought out Carnegie's holdings, added a few other companies picked up here and there, dumped some water into the stock and called the mixture the United States Steel Corporation. It was the world's largest industrial organization, with a capital of well over a billion dollars—more than the total wealth of the country when Morgan was born.

J. P. Morgan was a big, fleshy man with shaggy brows, a walrus mustache, and a nose that looked like an upside-down ice cream cone. It was the prominent proboscis that worried Mrs. Dwight Morrow when her husband was invited to join the Morgan firm. Mrs. Morrow had asked the great man to tea, and she was afraid her little daughter Anne (who would become Mrs. Charles Lindbergh) would make some innocent disparagement of their benefactor's snout. She carefully instructed Anne to do no more than curtsy politely, say "Good afternoon, sir," and skedaddle on out of the room.

When the moment of introduction came, a tense Mrs. Morrow held her breath while Anne went through her paces, performing to the letter of her instructions. Sighing with relief, Mrs. Morrow turned to her guest and asked, "Mr. Morgan, do you take nose in your tea?"

Chapter 13

The Wild West

Good Guys and Bad Guys

FIRST LET US DEFINE a few terms and dispel some of the legends about the men of the Old West who lived by the gun.

Gunfighter meant anyone skilled in the use of a revolver, but usually referred to someone on the side of the law.

Gunman also referred to anyone handy with pistols, but usually meant an outlaw. (Outlaws were more often called desperadoes.)

Marshal could mean a United States marshal or a town marshal. A U.S. marshal was appointed by the president and his jurisdiction extended over a large territory. The local peace commission chose a town marshal, whose authority ended at the city limits.

Sheriff meant the same as it does now: an officer who was responsible for law enforcement in a county and was elected by the people thereof.

Boot Hill was a cemetery in Dodge City, but became a synonym for any place where a man "died with his boots on." Epitaphs in many a Boot Hill bore testimony to the grim humor of the Wild West: "Killed by Lightening [sic]"; "Died of Lead Poisoning"; "Too Many Irons in the Fire" (for a cattle rustler).

Most of the West's "shootouts" were recorded in Hollywood rather than in the annals of the day. There were few such occurrences because every man had too much respect for Samuel Colt's invention—even if he had none for the person behind it—to take the risk. When there was a shootout it probably was between men who had had a long-standing grievance, not who had just come from an argument in a saloon.

More killings took place at night than in the daytime. For every shooting in which the victim got an even break, there were four cold-blooded murders. More corpses were buried with a hole in the back than in the front. Even when the victim was shot in the chest, he may have been tricked into turning around by a man who "had the drop" on him.

No man squaring off against another would try the fancy shooting seen in movies and TV shows—not unless he hankered for a permanent resting place in Boot Hill. "Fanning" during a gunfight, say the pistol experts, is patently ridiculous. It would have been too hard to do with a gun that weighed over three pounds.

There was often no clear division between "good guys" and "bad guys." When a town hired a "shootist" to clean the place up, it had to take his morals too, good or bad. Many town marshals, including the celebrated Wyatt Earp, took a cut of the earnings of some saloons and gambling halls in return for extra "protection." Others moonlighted as faro and monte dealers. A man who served as a marshal in one town might turn up in the next as a gambler, horse thief, or murderer.

WILD TALES OF WILD BILL

When the cowboy, just paid off after his long, dusty cattle drive, took up "hurrah-ing" a town as his national sport, he also gave rise to a new kind of American folk hero: the town-taming marshal. The first of the famous ones was "Wild Bill" Hickok, who held sway in the first of the famous cow towns, Abilene. Some of his legend Hickok invented himself, and much of the rest was invented for him by open-mouthed and closed-eyed biographers. No one can tell where the legend ends and the man begins

James Butler Hickok is known to have served with Jim Lane's Free State forces, a guerrilla band, during the border warfare in Kansas just before the Civil War and to have been a scout with Union forces in the war. According to the man himself, as he claimed in later years, he once picked off fifty Rebels with fifty shots, undoubtedly with some sort of miraculous rifle. As a civilian, according to his own accounts, he tangled with a grizzly bear and won, and he once killed two gunmen at the same time by shooting over the left shoulder at the one behind him while outdrawing the one in front of him with his second pistol.

His legend really began with the slaying of Dave McCanles and his gang of desperadoes, horse thieves, and murderers. Hickok boasted of getting six of the desperadoes with six shots and cutting down four others with his trusty Bowie knife. After this mayhem he walked away with eleven buckshot wounds and thirteen stab wounds.

Actually the "gang" consisted of Dave McCanles, his twelve-year-old son Monroe, and two friends. They were not desperadoes, but ordinary citizens who had sought out Wild Bill on a matter of debts, or perhaps over a girl, as Hickok was believed to have been interested in the same woman McCanles was. All the men are believed to have been unarmed. According to Monroe, Hickok shot his father from behind a curtain, then wounded one of the friends. This friend was finished off by a companion of Hickok's, who bashed in his head with a hoe. The third "desperado" fled into the underbrush before being felled with a shotgun blast, but it is not clear who fired the gun.

There is no doubt that Wild Bill Hickok was a crack shot and because of this was feared by many. After a stint as a lawman at Fort Riley and Hays City, both in Kansas, his reputation was firmly established and Abilene hired him as town marshal. There he divided his time between keeping the peace and playing cards at the Alamo Saloon, which he made his headquarters. He did not tame Abilene; it had already been tamed by Tom Smith, one of the truly great lawmen of the Old West. Smith had been shot in the back.

Hickok lasted only eight months. He was fired after accidentally shooting one of his deputies during a scrape with some of the local gambling element.

From then on it was downhill for Wild Bill. He migrated to Deadwood, Dakota Territory, when gold was discovered there, and while playing cards in a saloon he was shot in the back of the head. The young fellow who plugged him, Jack McCall, claimed Hickok had killed his brother in Hays City, but that isn't believed to be true. Wild Bill was holding aces and eights, ever since known as "dead man's hand."

WYATT EARP AND FRIENDS

In the person of Wyatt Earp the legend and the man come closer together. Earp kept the peace, apparently quite well, in Wichita and Dodge City, but he was never more than a deputy marshal. Wherever he worked, he was often assisted by Bartholomew "Bat" Masterson and John H. "Doc" Holliday.

While working in Dodge City Earp, like many lawmen of the day, worked the gaming tables also. The Long Branch Saloon was his favorite hangout. After cleaning up Dodge once, he left for the Black Hills gold rush, hoping to make enough from prospecting to retire from the gunfighting trade. Pickings were lean, however, and he returned to Dodge after receiving an urgent message from the mayor: the cowboy element was getting rowdy again.

The cowboys reacted violently when they heard Earp was back, and word went out there was $1,000 for anyone who put the marshal out of the way permanently. But Earp seemed to lead a charmed life. Two attempts on his life failed because of poor marksmanship—cowboys were notoriously bad shots. Another would-be assassin failed to hit the marshal after emptying his six-shooter at him at close range. Although the cowboy's mount bucked frantically, Earp brought the man down with his third shot.

SHOOTOUT AT THE O.K. CORRAL

The classic confrontation, and the best documented one in western history, took place in Tombstone, Territory of Arizona, in 1881. The town was only about ten months old and wild and woolly. Wyatt and his brother Virgil were plying their trade there, Virgil as town marshal and Wyatt as his assistant. Morgan Earp—who was also an assistant from time to time—and Jim Earp were also there, although Jim, who had a bad arm, played no part in the West's best-known shootout.

Tension had been building up for some time between the Earps and a band of wild cowboys who were also occasional cattle rustlers, led by two sets of brothers, Ike and

Billy Clanton and Tom and Frank McLaury (also spelled "McLowery"). The sheriff of Cochise County, Johnny Behan, sided with the cowboys because he needed the cowboy vote and because Wyatt Earp had been courting the girl he wanted.

Matters came to a climax on October 26 when Virgil, Wyatt, Morgan, and Earp-admirer Doc Holliday approached the O.K. Corral with the intention of disarming the Clanton and McLaury brothers and a friend, Billy Claiborne. The cowhands had no intention of being disarmed, and six-guns began to blaze. When the smoke cleared thirty seconds later, Tom and Frank McLaury and Billy Clanton lay dead; Ike Clanton and Billy Claiborne had fled; Morgan was wounded in the shoulder, Virgil in the leg, and a bullet had creased Holliday's back. Wyatt's luck held: he had not been touched.

The cowboys had fired seventeen times, only three bullets finding a mark. The Earps and Holliday had also fired seventeen times, hitting Tom McLaury twice, Frank McLaury three times, and Billy Clanton, who was only a teenager, six times.

Within the next five months mysterious assailants fired buckshots at Virgil, hitting him in the left arm and rendering it useless for the rest of his life, and killed Morgan with two bullets into his spine while he was bending over playing pool. Three hired guns who had been seen in town on those nights, and who were known to have been associated with Ike Clanton, were later found dead.

Wyatt Earp lived until 1929, when he died in bed in Los Angeles. His luck had held to the last: unlike most gunfighters, he died in bed with his boots off.

DOC THE DEADLY DENTIST

Doc Holliday idolized Wyatt Earp and devoted his life to him. He hooked up with the marshal in Dodge City and later followed him to Tombstone. He too was destined to die with his boots off.

Doc's father was killed in the Civil War, but the family somehow got enough money to send the boy to the Baltimore College of Dentistry. Doc hated Negroes, and when a former slave insisted on sharing a swimming hole with him he killed the black man and wounded two others. He fled to Texas where he hung out his shingle, "J.H. Holliday, Dentist." There is much doubt that he ever finished dental school.

Doc's greatest love was gambling. He had not been long in Texas before he killed a man who accused him of cheating at cards. Just a few months later he killed a soldier, and with a posse at his heels he rode 800 miles to Denver, where he proceeded to carve up a man with a knife. The man lived to tell the tale, and Holliday lit out again, this time for Dodge City.

Doc was a small, frail fellow, always dressed in a coat and tie and always carrying a blue handkerchief into which he periodically coughed blood. He was slowly dying of tuberculosis, or "consumption," as they were still calling it. He also carried a nickel-plated six-shooter, a Bowie knife tied around his neck, and often a shotgun under a long frock coat. He died in a Colorado sanitarium in 1885 at the age of thirty-five.

THE MASTERFUL MASTERSONS

Three Mastersons were in the lawman's trade at one time or another—Bat, Ed, and Jim. Bat was sheriff of Ford County, of which Dodge City was the seat, for a time. For part of that time, Ed was chief deputy on the city force. When Ed was killed, Jim took his place.

Bat was always the dandy. When he first arrived in Dodge he wore a sombrero with a rattlesnake band, silver-mounted pistols and gold-plated spurs. He had the edge on any opponent, the wits said, because such finery would blind them. After being elected sheriff he abandoned this fancy garb, but was always neatly decked out in a black business suit and bowler hat. For some time he used a cane because of an old wound, but now he carried a gold-headed one purely for ornament. He was only twenty-three when elected to his post.

When a fickle public voted Bat out, he drifted. He was in succession a gambler at Leadville, Colorado, a marshal in Trinidad, Colorado, and both in Creede, Colorado. Eventually he gave up law enforcement and became a promoter of prize fights, but he fell on bad luck and started drinking heavily. Finally he realized western heroes were bigger attractions in the East than in the West and moved to New York City, where he became well known as a sports writer.

Bat's luster as a frontier lawman never completely wore off—people continued to ask for his autograph. On one occasion, a man asked to buy one of his old "peacemakers." Bat had none of his old pistols, but he told the fellow to meet him at the same spot the next day. In the meantime, he bought an old gun in a pawn shop, carved a few niches in the handle and sold it to the worshipful admirer for $100.

JESSE JAMES AND COMPANY

Jesse James was the first of the West's notorious badmen. He and his brother Frank, along with their cousins the Youngers, raised bank and train robbery to an art.

Jesse and Frank were products of the Missouri-Kansas border warfare during the Civil War. Frank, four years older than Jesse, learned his wicked ways riding with the irregular troops of William Clarke Quantrill. That outfit was infamous for the sacking of Lawrence, Kansas, in which the raiders shot every man and boy in sight—about 150—and burned the town to the ground. Despite legend, Jesse probably wasn't there. More likely, he joined the band later, in time to take part in the killing of seventy-five Union soldiers in Centralia, Missouri. He was only fifteen or sixteen years old at the time, but he had tasted blood and seemed to relish it.

Coming in to surrender after Appomattox, holding a white flag, Jesse was shot by Union soldiers and almost died. While he had been gone the Federals had raided his farm home, held his mother and little brother prisoner for a time and tried to hang his stepfather. All these events surely helped push Jesse into a life of crime afterwards.

The career of the James Younger gang ran on for some ten years, from their first bank robbery in Liberty, Missouri, in 1866, to the disastrous raid on Northfield, Minnesota, in 1876. Northfield citizens, refusing to be intimidated by the fiercest band of desperados in the West, came on the run when they were alerted that the First National Bank was being robbed. Armed with revolvers, rifles, pitchforks, and rocks, the sturdy citizenry killed three of the gang and captured all three Younger brothers.

The James brothers lay low for two years before emerging again with a new gang. But things were never the same during the three more years the brothers were at large. For the first ten years their friends and neighbors in southern Missouri had been proud of "the boys." They had refused to help lawmen who came snooping around the James's Clay County home, especially after detectives of the Pinkerton Agency tossed a fire-bomb into the family farmhouse, killing the youngest James boy and blowing off the right arm of Jesse's mother. But as the 1880s dawned, the political climate had changed, and the brothers found themselves the objects of an intensive man-hunt started by a new governor who had vowed to bring them to justice.

When the governor persuaded the railroads to offer a $10,000 reward for the boys, Bob Ford, a new member of the gang, shot Jesse in the back while the outlaw was hanging a picture in the St. Joseph home where he was living as "John Howard." His tombstone read: "Murdered by a coward whose name is not worthy to appear here," words that were soon echoed in a song the refrain of which went:

> *The dirty little coward*
> *That shot Johnny Howard.*

Frank James surrendered personally to the governor. On the way back to Clay County for his trial he was mobbed and cheered at every train stop. The trial had to be moved from the Clay County courthouse to the opera house in Gallatin to accommodate the overflow crowd. He was acquitted of the murder of a conductor and passenger during a train holdup because the railroad's star witness was too scared to say anything.

Frank, a quiet man who loved Shakespeare and Francis Bacon, lived out his days peacefully, sometimes picking up extra cash selling souvenir pebbles from his brother's grave.

Big Bad Billy

Billy the Kid was an ungainly, buck-toothed youngster probably born in the slums of New York City. It isn't known whether his father was William Bonney or Patrick McCarty. He and his mother moved to Indiana, where Billy acquired a stepfather,

William Antrim. After the family moved to New Mexico Territory, Billy at various times called himself by all three last names.

Legend insists the Kid killed a man for every year of his life—twenty-one victims—but the figure was probably closer to ten, and some of those were ambushed. The first victim was a barroom bully whom Billy dispatched by jumping on his back and stabbing him with a pen knife. It isn't known how old the Kid was at the time, but he couldn't have been over sixteen.

In 1876 Billy involved himself in the so-called Lincoln County War, a bitter bloodbath between two rival factions in New Mexico's rapidly developing cattle industry. During the "war" he may have killed as many as five men, one of them Lincoln County Sheriff William Brady.

When the struggle ended, the Kid made a deal with the new territorial governor, Lew Wallace, to submit to a false arrest and give evidence against others involved in the fighting. The district attorney defied Wallace's orders and clapped Billy in jail, from which he escaped by wriggling out of his handcuffs. (He had large wrists and unusually small hands, which stood him in good stead more than once.)

The outlaw returned to his first love, stealing horses, and during that time made friends with a bartender named Pat Garrett. Shortly afterwards, Garrett was elected sheriff of Lincoln County, and his first duty was to bring in his erstwhile friend. Garrett tracked his prey down and, after killing two other rustlers by mistake, took Billy to jail. The courts sentenced the young outlaw to death, but once more he escaped by slipping out of his handcuffs, this time while going with his guard to the outside privy. The Kid killed the guard, apparently with the guard's own gun, then went back to the jail and shot the other jailer.

Garrett was out of town at the time, but when he returned he tracked Billy to the home of a friend, Pete Maxwell. The Kid was coming back into the darkened house after having cut himself a piece of meat for supper out back. He could see nothing, but seemed to sense someone else in the room. "Who is it? Who is it?" he asked of the darkness. Those were Billy the Kid's last words, for two explosions from Garrett's Colt snuffed out his brief life.

WES HARDIN: TEXAS TERROR

In the 1870s John Wesley Hardin, son of a Methodist preacher and named for the founder of the Methodist Church, inspired such terror in Texas that little children shouted to their playmates, "Wes Hardin will get ya if ya don't watch out!"

Wes Hardin claimed to have killed forty-four men—not counting Mexicans. At age fifteen he fled Texas after killing a black man, which probably would have brought a death sentence under a Reconstruction government such as Texas had. By the time he was sixteen he had gunned down three more men, all shot in ambushes. Two years later he drifted into Abilene where he killed a man who had pounded on the bar and shouted, "I don't like Texans!" He got out of town in a hurry before Marshal Hickok had time to hear about it.

Not long afterwards, Hardin reappeared in Abilene only to promptly get into trouble and flee once more. This time he shot a man whose snoring bothered him in a hotel. To escape Hickok's wrath this time, he crawled onto the roof and jumped into a haystack, where he spent the remainder of the night before high-tailing it out of town. He later claimed he was afraid Hickok would kill him while he was defenseless just to add to his reputation.

A few years later Wes had to flee Texas for the umpteenth time after murdering a deputy sheriff who he claimed was his thirty-ninth victim. He hid out in Florida for a time, but after Pinkerton men discovered his whereabouts he headed for Mexico. Intercepted at the Florida line, and after killing two pursuers, he made it to Alabama. There he was captured by Texas Rangers when his gun caught in his suspenders.

After serving fifteen years of a twenty-five-year sentence for second-degree murder, Hardin turned up in El Paso where, as usual, he got into trouble almost immediately. He threatened a lawman who had arrested his lady love for carrying a gun, but this was one lawman who was not to be tampered with. John Selman was his name, and he walked up behind the outlaw in a saloon and shot him dead. A court acquitted Selman on the grounds he had rid the state of Texas of a major menace.

Boots and Saddles

During the years from the end of the Civil War to 1890, the United States Army was almost constantly at war with the Native American tribes of the Plains or the desert Southwest. In the first twelve years of that period alone—from the Sand Creek, Colorado, massacre in 1864 to the Custer massacre in 1876—there were more than 200 pitched battles.

All the fighting was not, as Hollywood would have you believe, between dashing cavalrymen and colorfully costumed Indians riding spirited ponies. Many battles were fought on foot, some of them from entrenchments. There were as many infantrymen as horsemen—perhaps more—and artillery also played a major role in many engagements. Native Americans were especially fearful of howitzers and might run away at the mere sight of one. The artilleryman was as proud of his cannon as the cavalryman was of his mount—and took as good care of it.

Many black men filled the ranks, lots of them newly freed slaves who could not find work. The all-black 10th Cavalry was one of the finest regiments in the service, but, like every black unit, it was still commanded by white officers. Because the black troopers had thick curly hair, the Indians called them "buffalo soldiers."

LIFE ON THE PLAINS

There was little romance about Army life in the West. An isolated military post—and all of them were isolated—was incredibly boring and lonely, especially without women. A soldier-poet wrote:

> *In this fort we are like Adam*
> *'Ere he had obtained his madam.*
> *Butter, cheese and women's eyes*
> *Would make this place a paradise.*

Women in a fort were mostly officers' wives. If there were any wives of enlisted men, they lived in barracks outside the regular quadrangle, a place known as "Sudsville" because the women often took in washing to supplement their husbands' meager paychecks.

Men had to create their own entertainment. Major sources of amusement were dances, drinking, plays (for officers only), drinking, horse racing, drinking, gambling, drinking, fighting, and drinking. Alcohol helped alleviate the boredom, and on some posts it became such a problem it had to be strictly curtailed. But a thirsty soldier could usually get a pint or two from an unscrupulous sutler who brought in several gallons for "personal consumption" and sold it under the table at outrageous prices. Many men, like U.S. Grant in an earlier time, developed such a drinking problem they were forced to resign.

Summer on the plains—with temperatures of 110 degrees or higher—was bad enough, but winter—with temperatures of 30 to 40 degrees below zero—was an agony of survival. The Army issued "greatcoats"—heavy woolen overcoats—and fur caps that pulled down over the ears, but many soldiers bought buffalo robes from the Indians to wear in the day and sleep in at night. They also wrapped their food ration in the robes or it would freeze solid.

Officers, many of whom were jealous of one another and jockeyed for positions in their commander's favor, were particularly vulnerable to quarrels and all sorts of back-stabbing. Some of General George A. Custer's men despised their leader, claiming he was too much of a glory-hound. One, Captain Frederick Benteen, told the newspapers Custer's book, *My Life on the Plains*, should have been called *My Lie on the Plains* because the general had stretched the truth so far. Custer vowed to horsewhip his insubordinate subordinate, but thought better of it.

The Indian Wars

The Indian wars began in 1864 when the militia of Colonel J.M. Chivington, a church elder, massacred about 600 Cheyennes and Arapahos at Sand Creek, Colorado. The tribes were peaceful, having been assured they would not be harmed if they gave up their weapons. Chivington's men harmed them all to death and took their scalps to Denver to display between performances at a theater.

Chief Red Cloud of the Sioux avenged the death of his Sand Creek brothers by wiping out about a hundred soldiers in the Fetterman Massacre. Captain William J. Fetterman was a young fire-eater who had boasted he could walk through the whole Sioux nation with eighty men.

After this the Indians were less successful for a time, thanks particularly to the Army's new Springfield repeating rifle. The Indians were amazed at this "gun you load in the morning and fire all day."

"CHIEF YELLOW HAIR"

George Armstrong Custer graduated at the bottom of his West Point class, but during the Civil War some commanders were so impressed with his reckless courage he was quickly jumped from lieutenant to major general. At twenty-three he was the youngest general in the history of the United States Army.

After the war he joined the 7th Cavalry at Fort Riley, Kansas, but was disappointed because the fighting wasn't to his taste. He found the Native Americans, unlike his Confederate foes, would not stand still and would not obey the rules of the game. He hadn't been on the Plains long before he was accused of leaving his post without orders, shooting deserters, making unnecessary forced marches, and abandoning some of his men during a skirmish with Indians.

One bitterly cold dawn the 7th Cavalry swept into a Cheyenne camp on the Washita River in Kansas and destroyed it, killing indiscriminately. Of 103 Cheyennes who lay dead only 11 were warriors—the rest were women and children. Afterwards Custer ordered all the lodges burned and about 700 ponies shot.

THE LAST STAND

In 1876 Custer and his entire command of about 266 men were wiped out by the Sioux at the battle of the Little Big Horn in Montana. Ignoring instructions to wait for two other columns, the former "Boy General" plunged into the Little Big Horn valley in hot pursuit of an Indian trail his scouts had picked up. Dividing his force into three parts, he sent Captain Benteen in one direction and Major Marcus A. Reno in another. Reno ran into an overwhelming force of Sioux and retreated in a very disorganized fashion. Benteen's scouting expedition was uneventful.

Meanwhile, Custer had discovered a Sioux village and headed for it in his usual reckless manner. It proved to be several times larger than he had guessed, and soon he was engaged in a fight to the death.

We don't know much of what happened. It appeared later that the cavalrymen had shot their horses and used them as a barricade against the Sioux attack, and the position of some troopers seemed to indicate they had hastily formed themselves into companies. Those killed included two of Custer's brothers, Tom and Boston; a brother-in-law; and a nephew.

The pictures of the massacre—especially the famous barroom painting by the noted American artist Bud Weiser—are inaccurate. Certainly Custer was not standing alone in the middle of a circle of dead comrades; he may have been, for all we know, among the first to die. He was not wearing his famous long locks, all the company having been ordered to cut their hair short for the expedition. The Sioux did not scalp him, apparently out of respect.[1]

BURY MY HEART AT WOUNDED KNEE

Symbolically as well as actually, Native American resistance to the white man's encroachments ended in 1890 in the bitter cold of a South Dakota winter. The 7th Cavalry was escorting some 350 Sioux to a reservation when a scuffle erupted. Someone fired a shot, and the soldiers answered with a blistering fusillade. The Sioux fought back as best they could under the circumstances—even their dogs charged the troopers. When the madness ended, almost 300 Sioux lay dead, some of them chased down as far as three miles away.

The Sioux dead were left on the field for several days; when a burial party arrived it found the bodies frozen into grotesque shapes. The soldiers buried the bodies in one long trench.

Chapter 14

Technology Takes Over

Bell and the Telephone

THE WORLD IN THE LAST hundred years has been undergoing a revolution. It is a revolution in science and technology, and the leader has been the United States of America.

Alexander Graham Bell's telephone; Thomas A. Edison's incredible number of inventions and improvements on inventions; the automobile; and manned flight—all of these have changed not only the face of America, but the very fabric of life in this country. The technological revolution has even changed the way we think: there has come a feeling that nothing is impossible.

It is fitting that this revolution began in America's centennial year, with a device that changed forever the way we communicate with one another.

Alexander Graham Bell was more—much more—than just the inventor of the telephone. His interests were wide ranging. Here are some examples:

Bell invented a device to locate bullets or other metal objects in the body. The device's immediate purpose was to find the assassin's bullets in the body of President James A. Garfield; it failed because doctors did not remove the steel springs in Garfield's bed.

Bell perfected an electric probe that was used in surgery for some years before X-rays came into use.

He published a paper describing a machine that would serve the same purpose as the modern iron lung.

He advocated a method of locating icebergs by detecting their echoes, and he experimented with condensing fresh water from vapor in the air, to be used by men adrift at sea.

He designed houses to make the best use of natural air-conditioning.

He directed experiments in sheep-breeding, trying to develop ewes that would bear more than one lamb at a time.

He developed the basic method of making phonograph records on wax disks.

And all his life Bell was interested in flight. He personally conducted experiments with man-flown kites, and he helped finance the nation's first experiments with flying machines conducted by Samuel P. Langley.

THE BELL BOY

Graham Bell, as he was called, grew up in the footsteps of his father, who enjoyed a wide reputation as the author of textbooks on proper speech. Bell, Sr. also invented a system of symbols for indicating the action of the tongue, lips, and throat during speech. He intended the system as a key to pronouncing words in all languages, but it soon became apparent that it could be used to help the deaf speak.

Young Graham early became interested in ways of transmitting sound. As older boys, he and his brothers made a model skull and a dog "talk." They fitted the skull with a reproduction of human vocal apparatus and used a bellows to work it. Their model wailed "Ma-ma" in such a life-like manner neighbors rushed out of their homes to search for the child in distress. They trained a terrier, a particularly loud-mouthed breed of dog anyway, to growl steadily while they manipulated its vocal cords to produce sounds that were surprisingly like words. At the height of its career the terrier could say "Ow-ah-oo-ga-ma-ma" ("How are you, Grandmother?").

ELEMENTARY, MY DEAR WATSON

By age twenty-one Bell had decided to make teaching the deaf his life's work and had taken a job in a school for the deaf in Boston. Soon he became deeply interested in the idea that sound might be sent from one point to another over a wire, an interest that came about by accident.

He had read a book by the German scientist Hermann von Helmholtz, but in trying to read the book in German had misinterpreted what Helmholtz was trying to say. The scientist described how he had made tuning forks vibrate with an electrical current, but Bell thought he had managed to "telegraph" sounds from one fork to another. He soon realized his mistake, but the idea of "telegraphing" sounds would not leave him. He decided to try some experiments, but first he had to learn something about electricity. That need led him to the door of an electrical shop run by the man who would become his partner in the great adventure: Thomas A. Watson.

The partners called the device they eventually constructed the "harmonic telegraph." The idea was that pressure on a telegraph key would send current from a battery through an electromagnet, which in turn would cause tuning forks to vibrate. Tuning forks proved unsatisfactory and they substituted steel organ reeds.

After three years of experimentation and frustration, the great "break"—a literal break—came on June 2, 1875. Bell, on one end of the line, and Watson, in another room on the other, were tuning the reeds when the assistant found one of his reeds was screwed down too tightly. He tried to pluck it free, and suddenly Bell heard a *twaang-g-g!* Bell came running and shouted, "Watson, what did you do? Don't touch anything. Let me see."

The two men plucked reeds for an hour or more, like two children with an amazing new toy. Next day the primitive instrument transmitted the sound of Bell's voice— not words, but recognizable sounds. After further experiments Bell applied for a patent and received it on March 7, 1876.

Three days later intelligible words were heard over the new invention for the first time. The circumstances are well known. Bell accidentally spilled battery acid on his clothes and called out, "Mr. Watson, come here. I want you!"

Rushing down the hall, Watson cried, "Mr. Bell, I heard you—distinctly!"

Bell continued to improve his epoch-making invention and began setting up telephone lines in the United States, Canada, and England. By the early 1880s he had stopped taking an active part in the telephone business, except to defend his patent rights in numerous lawsuits. Many others claimed to have anticipated his discoveries, and some of the suits reached the Supreme Court, which upheld Bell's rights in every case.[1]

THE EDISON EFFECT

No man, perhaps, changed America more than Thomas Alva Edison, an unkempt, unwashed, and unschooled genius who spat on the floor. A detailed list of his contributions to the technological progress of this country would fill the remainder of this book.

He was never "Tom" Edison, except in books and motion pictures. His family called him Alva and his friends called him "Al." Because he was a sickly child his mother kept him home from school and taught him herself. His formal education amounted to three months in a Port Huron, Michigan, grammar school.

Ill health prevented him from doing many of the chores at home too, but Alva didn't mind: he loathed any kind of work except thinking. Once when his father told him to plant six acres of turnips, he finished the job in two and a half hours by spacing the turnips fourteen feet apart.

In his youth he also developed a loathing for cleanliness, one which stuck with him all his days. Never in his life did he take more than one bath a week. He loved to chew tobacco, and oftentimes the juice dribbled down his chin. Asked why he spat on the floor instead of in a spittoon, he answered, "No chance of missing."

All of Edison's inventions were of a practical nature, intended to make money. If there was no market for a product, he wasn't interested in it. "A scientist busies himself with theory," he explained. "He is absolutely impractical. An inventor is essentially practical. Anything that won't sell I don't want to invent. Its sale is proof of utility, and utility is success." Asked what he thought of Einstein's theory of relativity, he admitted, "I don't know what I think about it. I don't understand it."

While working on the incandescent light bulb, Edison made his only purely scientific discovery, the "Edison effect" of a one-way current between separated electrodes in an evacuated tube. Considering the discovery of no commercial value, he left to others the development of the electron tube that led eventually to the invention of radio.

INSPIRATION AND PERSPIRATION

"Nature will reveal itself if we only look," said the Wizard of Menlo Park. "But nothing will work by itself—you have to make the damn thing work."

Work Edison did. Sometimes he ate and slept in the laboratory for days on end. His method was to keep trying until he found something that worked. In the search for a workable filament for the light bulb, he tested 6,000 kinds of vegetable growth, not to mention thousands of other items, from bamboo to monkey hair. "Genius," he said, "is one percent inspiration and ninety-nine percent perspiration."

It is said that the great inventor never slept, but of course he did. He took frequent catnaps—twenty minutes was enough to refresh him completely—and could sleep anywhere, anytime. His helpers often found him in a closet, curled up on a stack of newspapers like a cat. He could even sleep on a laboratory table.

Edison's hearing problem—he was virtually deaf by early manhood—was an aid in sleeping and contributed to his phenomenal work output by cutting out noise and other distractions. He claimed to be glad he was deaf. "Deafness has been of great advantage to me, as my business is thinking. I don't think it would help my nerves or give me much pleasure to have my hearing restored. Now everything is quiet and my nerves are perfect and I am satisfied." He said he was not disappointed when someone else invented a hearing aid before he did. He used the device for special occasions such as attending the opera, one of his favorite pastimes.

THE WIZARD'S WORK

It could scarcely be said that anyone ever invented anything entirely alone. There are always many ideas going around, ideas that are eventually picked up and meshed into one big idea that results in an "invention." Edison was an expert at meshing ideas—and therein, in large part, lay his "genius."

The only invention that was entirely Edison's own, in concept and execution, was the phonograph. Like so many of his other inventions, however, the phonograph grew out of experiments he was making for some other purpose. Edison started his working life as a telegraph operator, and it was while developing the quadruplex telegraph—which could send several messages at once—that he got the idea for the "gramophone." He wondered why sound vibrations couldn't be engraved on a rotating disk and then be turned back into sound. (His deaf ears couldn't pick up vibrations, but he had ways of "hearing" them, such as putting his teeth against a piano.) He of course found that it could be done, and the phonograph was an immediate success. But he was disappointed when entertainment became the chief use of his invention.

All Edison's inventions were basic ones in the fields of light, sound, and power generation. He received his first patent in 1869, when he was twenty-one, for an electric vote-counter, but no one was interested in it. Next he brought out a stock-ticker, which became an overnight necessity in every brokerage house in the country. In quick succession came the quadruplex telegraph, the carbon transmitter that made the telephone practical for wide use, the phonograph, and the light bulb.

The carbon transmitter led to the microphone, and the light bulb led to the wide and efficient use of electricity from a central generating station. He also designed an electric railway system and made important improvements in motors and dynamos. Later he devoted time to developing an improved storage battery, a magnetic method of separating iron ore, and the manufacture of cement.

Edison is sometimes thought of as the inventor of the motion picture camera, but credit for that has to go to a lot of men. The movie camera, however, grew out of his "kinetoscope," a machine that created the illusion of moving pictures by rapidly rotating a shutter over the lens.

PATENTS, PATENTS, PATENTS

The amount of work turned out by Edison was incredible: he was issued 1,093 patents. Here are the technologies he made major contributions to and the number of patents issued for each:

Electric light and power	389
Phonograph	195
Telegraph	150
Storage battery and related	141
Ore separation	62
Telephone	34
Railroad	25
Motion pictures	9
Automobile	8
Mimeograph	5
Typewriter	3

The Horseless Carriage

Americans did not invent the automobile: German and French mechanics were making them before any American ran a successful one on the street. However, European cars in the early days were handmade and very expensive. It was the ever-practical American who put the world on wheels by building cars one did not have to be a millionaire to afford.

Some early experimenters tried running cars on laughing gas or building ones that wound up like a toy. Some tried cars with two motors in case one conked out, or with six or eight wheels for better traction on muddy or nonexistent roads. For a time the automobile was considered a dangerous weapon. Some cities banned it from the streets or imposed a speed limit of three miles an hour. In some places the car had to be preceded by a man waving a red flag, or the driver was required to fire off a Roman candle every two miles.

The early driver had to take out an "engineer's" license, wear a linen "duster" and goggles, and buy gas in a hardware store.

SUING SELDEN

The first American patent for a gasoline-powered automobile went to George B. Selden, a lawyer. Selden applied for the patent in 1879, received it in 1895 and, by filing periodic amendments alleging further improvements, he intended to keep it in force indefinitely.

Selden's car existed only on paper—he made no attempt to build one. His plan was to collect a royalty on every car produced by others, and for a period of years he did exactly that. Not until 1911, after a court case that lasted eight years, did Henry Ford finally break Selden's stranglehold on the burgeoning auto industry. During the litigation, much to his chagrin, Selden was forced to make a car—the only one he ever built—to show the court.

HAYNES WAS THE FIRST

A "horseless carriage" on view in the Smithsonian Institution is believed to be the oldest American automobile. Elwood Haynes built it in 1893-1894.

Haynes was superintendent of a natural-gas company in Kokomo, Indiana. He began experimenting with gas-run carriages because he was tired of losing so much time bouncing around his territory in a horse-drawn buggy. His friend Elmer Apperson, owner of a machine shop, built a body for him and on the Fourth of July, 1894, the first Haynes-Apperson automobile belched its way into Kokomo at the spanking speed of six miles an hour. The partners continued to build autos for some years before dropping out of the auto race.

THE DURYEA BROTHERS

Charles Duryea is considered by some to have been the Father of the Automobile. Charles was a remarkable technician, both in theory and in practice. At seventeen he built a bicycle without ever having seen one, and in his high school graduation thesis predicted that in the near future a flying machine would cross the Atlantic Ocean in half a day.

With his brother Frank, Charles built a vehicle that looked like a trim buggy with wooden-spoked wheels, rubber tires, and a water-cooled engine hidden in the rear. It would do eighteen miles an hour. In 1895, the brothers founded the Duryea Motor Company and in 1896 produced thirteen cars, a remarkable number for the times. That same year they sold the first car in America.

Frank soon retired from the automobile field and Charles's fortunes went steadily downhill until he sank into total obscurity.

THE OLDS IS OLD

Ransom E. Olds built a car earlier than any of those mentioned, but it was a steam carriage. In advertising his steamer Olds wrote: "It never kicks or bites, never tires on long trips and never sweats in hot weather. It does not require care in the stable and only eats while on the road."

He started the Olds Motor Works in 1899 and was the first automobile maker to use the assembly line and standard parts. For the first few years the plant's production was phenomenal, and the Olds firm became the first to sell an American car abroad—in India, of all places.

Olds did more than any other to center the automobile industry in Detroit, and he dreamed that his mass-production methods would make the automobile available to the average person. The dream died when his financial backers, who thought only the rich would ever buy cars, insisted on big, expensive models and forced Olds out of the company.

THE "DIVINE TINKERER"

It was Henry Ford who made Olds's dream come true. Ford was a born tinkerer (some have called him the "Divine Tinkerer") with an uncanny aptitude for repairing things and keeping them running. His first job was as a journeyman mechanic in Detroit, where he installed and repaired steam and gasoline engines. The year 1896— a halcyon year for the automobile industry—found him chief engineer for Detroit's Edison Electric Company.

The same year marked the entrance of his famous "quadricycle," a vehicle made from parts of old steam carriages, bicycles, motorcycles, buggies, and odd bits of scrap metal. He fussed over this contraption for a long time, often making life difficult for Mrs. Ford as he tested the gasoline engine fastened to the kitchen sink. People laughed at this first "Ford," but Henry took encouragement when Thomas Edison, whom the Tinkerer worshipped, told him, "You've got it, boy. Keep at it."

MODEL-T MANIA

Even though he had the backing of several wealthy men, Ford's first two attempts to produce cars failed. After he opened the Ford Motor Company in 1903 he still met with no success for the first five years. He was looking for the "universal car," one that could be bought by anyone and driven anywhere. He found it— and so did the nation—in the Model T.

In 1908, the Tinkerer announced that from then on the Ford Motor Company would produce only the Model T and that the customer "can have any color that he likes as long as it is black." This "Tin Lizzie" was to change profoundly the society and culture of the United States and in fact became a veritable symbol of American democracy. Dealers proved its viability to an incredulous public by such stunts as having it climb the steps of the Tennessee state capitol or chug through the streets of Payne, Ohio, loaded with fifty boys weighing a total of 3,492 pounds.

Although it could go anywhere and do anything, the Tin Lizzie was almost always in need of repairs, which the owners had to learn to make themselves. The Ford owner, the saying went, swore by his car and at it. Some anonymous owner, probably after a bout of repairing and swearing, wrote the "Ford's Prayer":

> *My Ford is my headache, it falleth apart.*
> *It maketh me to lie down on hard road beds*
> *   beneath it.*
> *It restoreth my hangover.*
> *It leadeth me to strange places I cannot find*
> *   on my road map.*
> *Yea, though I pusheth it miles to the nearest*
> *   gas station, I shall fear no evil,*
> *For it is worth a hundred dollars at the*
> *   used car lot.*
> *The springs they pincheth me.*
> *It prepareth a blowout before me in the*
> *   presence of speeding autos.*
> *The radiator runneth over.*
> *Surely policemen and traffic shall follow it*
> *   all the days of its life,*
> *And it shall sell in the second-hand market*
> *   for more than I paid for it twelve years ago.*

WHAT HATH THE AUTO WROUGHT?

The automobile changed American society from top to bottom. The whole face of America changed, as governments were forced to build more and better roads. It made the country's magnificent natural wonders available to almost anyone. It began not only the mechanization of American society, but its urbanization as well. Dozens of auxiliary industries sprang up to make products to be used by auto manufacturers. By the 1950s one out of every seven Americans worked in a business directly or indirectly related to the automobile industry.

But even before the auto was out of swaddling clothes, traffic accidents began mounting at an alarming rate. After the eruption of Mount Pelée on Martinique in 1902 killed 50,000 people, the humor magazine *Life* printed this joke:

Attendant: Another large party has just arrived, sir.
St. Peter: Volcanoes or automobiles?

Perhaps the best commentary on the dangers of American highways, then and now, occurred in 1910 when the state of New York erected a roadside marker beside the spot where the nation's first traffic fatality took place. Not long afterwards a car ran over the marker.

Conquest of the Skies

In England at the beginning of the twentieth century a popular limerick ran:

There was a young man of Park Lane
Who constructed a new aeroplane;
It flew, so we heard,
Like a beautiful bird;
His tombstone was pretty but plain.

The first American to build an "aeroplane" was Samuel P. Langley, director of the Smithsonian Institution. Using a catapult mechanism, Langley launched his twenty-six-pound plane from atop a houseboat in the Potomac River. On its maiden flight the little plane shot out over the river then took a nose dive into the water. The launching mechanism had not worked properly.

After minor repairs the machine was ready for another try. As it left its catapult cradle this time, there was a rending crash as the entire tail section was torn asunder. The plane dropped backwards into the river. Had this plane been launched properly, many have said, it would have flown—and Samuel P. Langley would be remembered as the inventor of the airplane.

Glenn Curtiss, another pioneer aviator, successfully flew Langley's plane eleven years later, but it is generally accepted that Curtiss revamped the structure and control system and that the flight was in fact a shameful attempt to discredit the Wright brothers.

THE WRIGHTS RUSH IN

It was fear that Langley would beat them to the post that caused the Wright brothers to rush their first attempts at manned flight. They had been experimenting with gliders for years, and probably would have continued to for some time had they not heard of the professor's abysmal failures on the Potomac.

For their glider experiments, Orville and Wilbur Wright chose Kitty Hawk, North Carolina, because the area had the kind of steady winds they needed as well as sand dunes and low hills. Here they labored, off and on for three years, making one glider flight after another. Convinced all existing aeronautical information was wrong, they built the world's first wind tunnel.

By December 1903, the experimenters had a 600-pound glider powered by a 125-pound automobile engine. The landing gear was a sled-like attachment, which is a strange choice since the brothers were bicycle builders. Bike wheels were introduced as undercarriage gear three years later by European flyers and why the Wrights did not think of using them first is still a mystery.

Their craft, called the *Kitty Hawk Flyer* (not just *Kitty Hawk*, as it is usually given), cost less than $1,000 and was to be launched by means of a pulley contraption from a sixty-foot monorail. On December 14 the brothers tossed a coin to see who would make what they hoped would be the first flight of a manned, heavier-than-air craft. Wilbur won.

A DUCK-SNARER FLIES

This first flight was a failure, the brothers decided. The wind wasn't right and the track wasn't straight downhill. The *Flyer* stalled, slid sideways, and touched down. It was in the air three and a half seconds and went 105 feet, statistics that did not meet the Wright's criteria for flight.

By December 17 the *Flyer* was ready for another run. Looking on were four local men, a boy named Johnny Moore, and Johnny's dog. Johnny was intrigued (perhaps the dog was, too) and asked what the machine was. "Why that's a duck-snarer," explained one of the men soberly. "You see, this man is going to go up in the air over a bay where there are hundreds of ducks . . . and drop a big net and snare every one of them. If you'll stick around, Johnny, you can have a few ducks to take home."

Whether Johnny was thrilled by the flight that followed, or merely disappointed because he went home with no ducks, was not recorded, but Orville took the ship up for twelve seconds, traveling 120 feet into the teeth of a twenty-seven-mile-an-hour wind. Both Orville and Wilbur made two flights that day, the final one covering 852 feet in fifty-nine seconds. The great dream of centuries—that human beings would fly through the air like birds—had come true at last. Less than three months earlier, the great astronomer and mathematician Simon Newcomb, in a magazine article, had said it was "unassailable logic" that human flight was impossible.

Only a handful of newspapers picked up the Associated Press story that later went out about this historic flight. They gave it only brief mention on a back page, and their accounts were full of gross exaggerations such as "flew three miles" and "had a six-bladed propeller." The Wrights decided then and there not to inform the press of their activities, a decision that would later lead to all sorts of charges and counter-charges among pioneer aviators over who did what first.

KITTY HAWK TO THE MOON

In 1904 the Wright brothers, with the *Wright Flyer II*, made 105 flights, the longest almost three miles. In October 1905, Wilbur flew a little over twenty-four miles and stayed aloft thirty-nine minutes. The few reports of this and other flights that leaked out were ignored by the newspapers—they didn't believe it.

But they believed it when Charles Lindbergh made the first solo flight over the Atlantic in 1927, and when two American astronauts walked on the moon in 1969. The moon walk came only fifty-six years after the Wright brothers launched their little plane from a hill in Kitty Hawk. And it was only a hundred years—a drop in the bucket, historically speaking— between Edison's vote-counter in 1869 and the walk on the moon in 1969. In such a short span of time American technology had proved that anything was possible.

Chapter 15

Teddy Roosevelt and the Spanish War

T.R.—The Man

FEW WOULD ARGUE WITH the proposition that Theodore Roosevelt was the dominant personality in the United States during the first two decades of this century. An English visitor summed up the feeling succinctly when he remarked: "I have seen the two greatest phenomena in America—Niagara Falls and Theodore Roosevelt."

Teddy Roosevelt's public life is well known, but what of his private side, his youth, and his nonpolitical endeavors?

"TEEDIE"

Roosevelt hated the nickname "Teddy," but as the whole world came to know him by it he had no choice but to accept it. Those who knew him well called him Ted, while those who didn't felt his wrath.

But as a boy he was "Teedie." He was always a scholarly lad who loved to read, a penchant that would follow him the rest of his days. His first love was nature—he was interested in "all curiosities and living things." This interest would later shape his attitude toward conservation, but as a boy it was a great trial to his elders.

In his bedroom Teedie developed the "Roosevelt Museum of Natural History," with wee creatures, dead and alive, stuffed into every nook and cranny. (As an eighth-grade student described it, "His drawers were always full of dead mice and birds.") The "museum" eventually had to be moved to an upstairs back hall, lest the chambermaid quit in disgust.

The Roosevelt household learned to beware of beasties at all times: they didn't put on a hat before checking for frogs; they didn't sit on a couch without looking under the cushions for field mice; they didn't pour from a pitcher without looking for snakes.

He was a puny lad, though—small, sickly, and suffering acutely at times from asthma. So he began going to a gymnasium for frequent workouts with weights and other body-building equipment. Soon his father fitted him out with a private gymnasium on the second-floor piazza, and in the years to come he developed the robust body that was an amazement to all: the bulging biceps, barrel chest, and thick neck straining to break out of its collar. Small hands and exceptionally tiny feet, however, told the observer this was a man-made, not a nature-made, body. Along with his physique he developed a love for "the strenuous life" that would be his trademark forever.

LITERARY LIFE

A friend who knew Teddy as a boy called him "the most studious little brute I ever knew." The "little brute" read voraciously in all fields, while receiving private tutoring in Latin, English, French, and German. A great love of reading followed him all his life—he would read anywhere, anytime: on the heaving deck of his yacht, waiting for a carriage at the door, between stops on the campaign trail. "Reading with me is a disease," he said, and for most of his adult life he read a book a day.

He not only was a speed reader, but his retention of what he had read was phenomenal. He would surprise an author by quoting at length from one of the writer's works, even passages the author had forgotten.

His range of reading was equally amazing. He studied everything from tropical flora to Italian naval history. He could declaim on German poetry, Hopi Indian songs, Greek drama, metaphysics, forestry, football techniques, and cowpunching.

Roosevelt published the first of his thirty-eight books at the age of eighteen. It was *The Summer Birds of the Adirondacks*, a scientific catalog that brought him notice in scholarly circles. This book was followed before long by *Notes On Some of the Birds of Oyster Bay*, which established him as one of the foremost young naturalists in the United States. *The Naval War of 1812*, published when he was twenty-three, is probably his most enduring work.

One of Teddy's literary endeavors, which has escaped the notice of most people, was a reform of the English language. Ever one to cut out the fat and get straight to the matter at hand, he advocated dropping the "u" in such words as "labour" and "rumour," and making words like "through" and "though" phonetically simpler by spelling them "thru" and "tho." The former suggestion was eventually adopted, but the latter suggestion horrified grammarians everywhere and inspired one of them to write this parody of the idea:

The Go-Gebtor

A merchant addressing a debtor
Remarked in the course of his lebtor
That he chose to suppose
A man knows what he ose
And the sooner he pays it the bebtor.

THE POLITICAL ANIMAL

Theodore Roosevelt loved politics and people. He was probably the fastest hand-shaker in American history, averaging fifty grips a minute. He insisted that everyone who was "sober, washed and free of bodily advertising" be allowed to shake the hand of the President of the United States. After wringing the hands of numerous dignitaries he would then seek out the hand of every aide, usher, and policeman in sight. Once, after shaking the hands of several important people in a car, he turned to their chauffeur and said, "I have not yet met this gentleman." Often after one of these handshaking binges, however, he would retire to the nearest washroom and disgustedly scrub himself clean.

Roosevelt could hate as well as he could love, and woe to the person who fell under the lash of his biting satire. Pulling himself up to his full height (he was only five feet eight inches tall, but seemed much bigger), he would pound his fist like a gavel, gnash his magnificent teeth, and spit out epithets that pierced his unfortunate victim like shrapnel. "He looks like a man biting ten-penny nails," said one observer.

Roosevelt loved power, and he loved and actively courted publicity for the power it brought him. As a twenty-four-year-old legislator in the New York State Assembly, he wore outrageous clothes and said outrageous things, partly for the publicity. As Rough Rider commander in the Spanish-American War, he made sure there was room for reporters wherever the regiment went and that they had battlefield observation posts to get good pictures. As Governor of New York, and especially as President, he planned many of his exploits for Sunday, knowing that Monday was a slow news day.

At whatever gathering he attended, T. R. had to be the star attraction. As his daughter Alice Roosevelt Longworth put it many years later, "He had to be the bride at every wedding, the baby at every christening, and the corpse at every funeral."

The "Splendid Little War" with Spain

CITIZEN HEARST FANS THE FLAMES

Even before the Spanish-American War broke out in 1889, William Randolph Hearst was already at war—with his chief rival, Joseph Pulitzer of the *New York World*. Hearst knew his *New York Journal* could win this war over circulation if he could fan the flames of revolt in Cuba into a full-scale war between the United States and Spain.

He had already sent to Cuba the famous reporter Richard Harding Davis and the noted artist Frederic Remington. But not much was going on in Cuba. Most of the fighting between Spain and her rebellious colony reported in the news was fiction concocted by bored journalists. When Remington found little action to paint, he asked to come home. Hearst cabled back: "Please remain. You furnish the pictures and I'll furnish the war."

When Davis found little action to write about, he elaborated on an account of how three young American women boarding a ship in Havana were stripped naked on the deck by Spanish policemen looking for secret messages. Readers were incensed when the story, along with a drawing by Remington, appeared on the *Journal*'s front page. This ploy backfired, however, when the women arrived in New York and explained that they had been searched by matrons in a room while the men waited outside.

Failing in this attempt to stir up war fever, Hearst hatched another plan. One of his reporters uncovered the saga of Evangelina Cosio y Cisneros, an eighteen-year-old Cuban beauty in jail for trying to free her father, who was in prison for revolutionary activities. In the *Journal* version of this story, this "Cuban Joan of Arc" had been thrown into prison for trying to defend herself against the lustful advances of a Spanish officer, and the paper hinted she would probably be sent to an African penal colony.

Hearst bled the story for all it was worth and soon had many American women up in arms over the matter. Petitions to the Queen Regent of Spain were signed by such illustrious females as Clara Barton and Julia Ward Howe.

After Hearst money bribed her guards, the young woman was brought to New York, outfitted at the swankiest shops, wined and dined at Delmonico's, and presented to screaming thousands in Madison Square. Before long, Señorita Cisneros's propaganda value wore thin, and Hearst began looking around for another way to get the war started. He didn't have long to wait.

THE "*MAINE*" CAUSE OF THE WAR

On the night of February 15, 1898, Captain Charles Sigsbee, skipper of the new battleship *Maine*, settled down in his cabin to write his wife a letter. The *Maine* was in Havana harbor on a "goodwill visit," and its officers had just been to a reception in their honor hosted by Spanish authorities ashore. Sigsbee glanced at his watch, saw it was 9:30, and began writing. He had scarcely put pen to paper when a tremendous explosion rocked the ship. The lights blinked out, then a second blast shook the *Maine*. The captain, half stunned and choking with the thickening smoke, stumbled on deck. Flames already engulfing the stricken vessel convinced him it was doomed. "Abandon ship!" he ordered.

A bugler sounded the call and surviving crewmen leaped overboard. All but three of the ship's lifeboats had been shattered by the explosions, but nearby Spanish ships quickly lowered boats to rescue those men floundering in the water. A launch from one of the Spanish ships picked up Sigsbee and took him to shore. The *Maine* sank in five minutes, settling into thirty feet of mud with only her superstructure showing above water.

Captain Sigsbee sent a hurried cable to Washington, ending it with the caution: "Public opinion should be suspended until further proof of the disaster's causes." But the only thing suspended in the Hearst press were the wires under the *Maine* in a front-page drawing below the screaming headlines "MINES!" The paper claimed the Spaniards had blown up the ship with some "infernal machine" and demanded war immediately.

To this day no one knows the cause of the explosion. A U.S. court of inquiry reported the cause as a submarine mine that touched off explosions in the ship's powder magazines. A Spanish investigation claimed it was all due to internal explosions, but the investigators were never allowed a close inspection. The American commission was unable to fix the blame. Many believe the Cubans themselves blew up the ship so they could get the Americans to win their revolution for them. (Or did Hearst himself have it done?)

The *Journal* reported that war was certain. In fact, it said, war was inevitable because the night before there had been two rings around the moon, the smaller standing for puny Spain, the larger one for the powerful United States!

WHO ARE THESE AMERICANS?

When the war began, neither nation knew much about the other, but Spain's ignorance of the United States was little short of incredible. One Spanish newspaper described us this way:

> *The country is not fit to live in. The climate is execrable. When it is not sleeting or snowing, the heat is almost unbearable. Avalanches are frequent at all times, and these threaten the principal cities. As for the people, besides the few whites engaged in business along the eastern coast, the remainder of the country is one vast plain, covered with Indians, called cowboys, and great herds of roaming cattle.*
>
> *Word has just been received here that the Indians are rising against the Yankees in Illinois, Ohio, and other places. The farmers are petitioning the government to protect them from the blood thirsty [sic] savages, who are burning and killing on every side. Troops are asked for at Colorado, in the state of Denver and at St. Louis in Missipa [sic].*

And later:

> *News is brought to us that Buffalo Bill, a notorious outlaw and leader of a band of half-breeds, has risen against the American government and is burning towns near his birthplace in New York.*

Another newspaper informed its readers that:

> *The average height among the Americans is five feet two inches, and they have never produced an athlete. This is due to their living almost entirely on vegetables, as they ship all their beef out of the country, so eager are they to make money. There is no doubt that one full-grown Spaniard can defeat any three men in America.*

WHAT DID DEWEY "DEW"?

The first fighting occurred not in Cuba, but thousands of miles away in Manila Bay, the Philippines. Before leaving his job as Undersecretary of the Navy to join up, Theodore Roosevelt picked out Spain's Asiatic fleet as the easiest touch and sent this order to Commodore George Dewey at Hong Kong:

> *Keep full of coal. In the event declaration of war Spain your duty will be . . . offensive operations in Philippine Islands.*

Roosevelt had no authority to do this, but the Secretary of the Navy had left early to go home and soak his corns. Dewey slipped into Manila Bay under cover of night and next morning, May 1, 1898, gave his nondescript but renowned order to his first officer, "You may fire when you are ready, Gridley." The American fleet raked the line of Spanish ships five times, and it was all over. Without losing a man, Dewey had turned Spain's Pacific fleet into scrap iron—and had done it on an empty stomach.

When the news reached home, Dewey became the grandest hero since Grant. He was promoted to admiral and his name was on everyone's lips. And they wrote poems about him, like this one:

> *Oh, dewey was the morning*
> *Upon the First of May,*
> *And Dewey was the admiral*
> *Down in Manila Bay.*
> *And dewey were the Regent's eyes,*
> *Them orbs of royal blue,*
> *And dew we feel discouraged?*
> *I dew not think we dew!*

Seventeen months later, after he had seen enough American troops landed at Manila to secure the islands, it was announced the grand admiral was coming home at last. It was the occasion for another burst of patriotic fervor—and for more verse:

> *Admiral George Dewey,*
> *Coming home they say.*
> *Bring out the pyrotechnics,*
> *Let's have a holiday.*
>
> *Shoot up colored rockets,*
> *Turn the searchlights high.*
> *See the name of Dewey*
> *Ablazing in the sky.*
>
> *Sank the Spanish navy,*
> *In a manner new.*
> *Honored grand Old Glory,*
> *Did it shipshape, too.*

The Soldier: How He Lived, How He Died

Americans rushed to share in the glory of a new war. Almost everyone—or so it seemed—wanted to get up a regiment and go wipe out the Spaniards in a few days. Buffalo Bill Cody promised that if the government would allow him to form a regiment of 30,000 Indian fighters, he would clear the Spaniards out of Cuba in sixty days. Nellie Bly wanted to get up a regiment of women. These and similar offers were all politely turned down.

The most famous regiment, of course, was the Rough Riders, who will be dealt with presently. Two other regiments that don't generally get their due were the 9th and 10th Cavalries, all black except for their officers. Both played a key role in defeating the Spanish in Cuba, just as they had done in conquering the Plains Indians—facts that are all too often ignored in history books of today, as they were in the newspapers of yesteryear.

Theodore Roosevelt, after fighting beside them in two battles, praised these black soldiers for their steadfastness and valor. A reporter for the *Santa Fe New Mexican* said of the 10th Cavalry:

> *The bravery and efficiency of the Negro soldier can be fairly appreciated by every man. . .who is in Cuba, and more so by the Rough Riders, who were in the battles of Las Guásimas and San Juan with them, than by any other regiment.*

> *We saw them make their great, fearless charges, and we cheered them too. . . Too much cannot be said of the Negro soldier[s], and words can never be found to express the praise due them.*

HOW THE COMMANDERS SHAPED UP

Commander of the American Expeditionary Force was Major General William Rufus Shafter—sixty-three years old, winner of the Congressional Medal of Honor in the Civil War, and enormously fat. No one—perhaps not even the general himself—seemed to know how fat he was. Estimates ranged from 300 to 400 pounds, and some let the matter go by saying he weighed in at one seventh of a ton.

Because of his bulk, Shafter rarely appeared at the front. When he appeared anywhere it was usually in a specially built buckboard with extra-strong springs. Occasionally he rode one of the larger mules, but as one soldier said, "He looks like he could carry the mule better than the mule could carry him." When he mounted his horse, a crowd gathered to watch.

Commanding the cavalry was Major General Joseph "Fighting Joe" Wheeler, an ex-Confederate well into his sixties. Wheeler was too old to be campaigning, and he knew it, but President William McKinley convinced him it was his patriotic duty. As one of the highest-ranking soldiers of the old Confederacy still living, the President said, he could help heal some of the wounds that still existed between the North and South.

Wheeler was the exact opposite of Shafter. He was not much over five feet and very frail. "He looks," said a soldier, "like a little boy dressed in his father's soldier suit, with a wig and false whiskers." His men respected him, though, and found him worthy of his nickname.

In the first fighting in Cuba, at Las Guásimas, the general proved a little too worthy of his nickname. The battle was unnecessary, the Spanish already having elected to retreat. Wheeler brought on the fight by out-flanking the American advance units in order to get his own brigade into action first. The move so surprised the Spanish (not to mention the Americans) that they got up out of their trenches and ran. Momentarily forgetting the time and place, Fighting Joe shouted, "Go get 'em, boys! We've got the damn Yankees on the run!"

GUNS AND SONS OF GUNS

Since the Spanish-American War lasted only 133 days, the American soldier got precious little training before embarking for Cuba. The infantryman's basic weapon was the .45 caliber Springfield rifle, which used the black powder of Civil War days. Such powder left a pall of smoke hanging over his position every time the soldier fired, and he soon learned that if he didn't move quickly, a Spanish artillery shell would come hurtling down on him. He undoubtedly found himself wishing he were in one of the select units, such as the Rough Riders, that were issued Krag-Jorgensens, a new Swedish-made rifle that fired a .30 caliber slug and used smokeless powder.

All American soldiers quickly learned to listen for—and to fear—the sound of the Spanish Mauser rifle. It made only a small popping sound—compared to the roar of a Krag—and went *z-z-z-z-eu* as it sped past. It was a deadly accurate weapon and its bullet, as tests showed, would sink nine inches deep in yellow pitch pine.

The Expeditionary Force also carried several experimental dynamite guns, a strange weapon that looked like a pile driver lying on its side. As the dynamite projectile was too delicate to be fired in the ordinary manner—it might explode in the barrel—the gun was fired by means of a compressed-air mechanism. There was no way to carry them into battle; they had to be fired from ships. The only way to aim the gun was to aim the ship, so naturally they were not very accurate. But when they did strike a target, they would blow off the whole side of a hill.

FEAR OF "FOREIGN DISEASES"

Worse enemies than the Spaniards were the tropical diseases and the great variety of creepy-crawly things—not to mention the heat and humidity. It rained every day, promptly at 3:00 P.M. One could spot the Army's line of march by the military paraphernalia strewn along it. The soldier's equipment was aggravating enough in dry weather; when the rains came he felt he had to get rid of some of it. Littering the jungle trails would be horse-collar blanket rolls, bulging haversacks, canteens, and perhaps even ammunition belts. A reporter wrote: "Many of the regulars are already walking about clad only in a cartridge belt or rifle and a chew of tobacco. The officers overlook these eccentricities, knowing that their men will go farther and fight better if left unhampered by burdensome regulations."[1]

Among the diseases, malaria and yellow fever were the chief culprits: more men died of these two maladies than from Mauser bullets. Back home the ladies heard about this problem and set about remedying it by making their heroes "abdominal protectors." These were long strips of red flannel about a foot wide, which the boys were to wear around their midsections to protect them from the dangerous night air of the tropics, and therefore from "foreign diseases."

THEY WERE WHAT THEY ATE

Intestinal disorders often began within a few days of landing, but much of the problem was caused by food—or the lack of it. The war was so short, supplies did not catch up with the army until it was over. For days on end some troops had nothing to eat except that old standard, hardtack, and sometimes a little sowbelly (fat salt pork), which was likely to be rancid. The men soaked hardtack in water until it swelled up to the size of a dog biscuit, then fried it in grease—if they had any grease.

They might trade hardtack to a Cuban rebel for mangoes, which they didn't much like and which probably aided their dysentery. Their stomachs became so bloated they had to let out their cartridge belts before they could buckle them. They had to lie down and rest on the way to and from the latrine.

There was nothing to drink with meals except water and coffee, and the way the soldiers often had to prepare the coffee made their dysentery worse. They took green and unroasted coffee straight from the plantations and fried it in mess kits, which left it charred on one side and green on the other. They then pounded it into bits with their bayonets, boiled it, and drank it. "At least it's hot," they said.

The soldiers complained as much about the shortage of tobacco as they did about the lack of food. Cigarettes were hard to come by, but plug tobacco usually was available in small quantities. The men made up for the lack by using the same quid twice: they chewed it, dried it out in the sun, then smoked it. Some men didn't mind passing the same chew from one to another!

THE CREEPY-CRAWLERS

Ominous rustlings in the brush did not necessarily mean a Spaniard was creeping up on you. It could mean the presence of any one of a number of snakes that thrive in tropical climes or of a giant land crab. The snake problem can be illustrated by the tale of a soldier who picked a spot beside a large rock as a resting place—it was the only bit of shade he could find. While sleeping he heard rustling noises near his head, but thinking they were caused by rabbits he ignored them. Discovering a hole there next morning, he poked a stick down it and out slithered a nine-foot boa constrictor!

The big land crab was a sort of armored spider, with a turret in the middle out of which protruded a pair of eyes on stems, like periscopes. It had five pairs of legs and at the end of each was a hideous foreclaw. Some of them, according to Teddy Roosevelt, were "as big as rabbits." At times they moved in vast hordes to the sea, while the men fought them off with sticks, gun butts, and even feet.

Speaking of feet, it wasn't wise to leave them sticking out from under a blanket during the night. Mosquitoes were as serious a threat to comfort in Cuba as in other tropical lands, and many a soldier woke up in the morning with feet so swollen from their bites he could not walk.

The Rough Riders

The most famous regiment in the war was the First United States Volunteer Cavalry commonly known as the "Rough Riders." At least that was the name that stuck after the press had tried out "Roosevelt's Rounders, "Roosevelt's Rough 'Uns," "Teddy's Terrors," "Teddy's Texas Tarantulas," and "Teddy's Cowboy Contingent." (Spanish newspapers, understandably confused, called them "Rough Rioters.")

Teddy Roosevelt, however, was not the commander of the Rough Riders until the closing weeks of the war. He was originally offered the command but turned it down because he felt it unseemly for a man with no military experience to lead a regiment into war. He accepted a job as second-in-command while insisting his good friend, Colonel Leonard Wood, be put in charge. Although a military doctor by profession, Wood was a fine soldier who had won the Congressional Medal of Honor for fighting Indians. The group was sometimes referred to as "Wood's Wild Westerners."

All such nicknames were misleading, for less than half the regiment were Westerners. Only 160 of 1,200 members were cowboys, although a few more were sheriffs, marshals, trappers, and Native Americans. Easterners included sports heroes such as Stanley Hollister, champion half-miler; Dudley Dean, said to be Harvard's greatest quarterback ever; and Bob Wren and Bill Larned, the nation's top tennis players. On the other hand, some Easterners were simple bookkeepers, accountants, and clerks. Seven members had previously deserted the Army, and two or three were running away from the law for other reasons.

There were two other regiments going by the name "Rough Riders," but neither of them got to Cuba. One spent the war in Camp Thomas, Georgia, the other in Jacksonville, Florida.

Oddly, this perhaps most famous of cavalry units never did any rough riding. For lack of space on the transport ships, all their horses except officers' mounts had to be left at the embarkation point, Tampa. The Rough Riders fought as infantry.

HOW THE ANIMALS FARED

After learning they had to leave their horses at home, the Rough Riders were again stunned to hear there was no transport ship available to them. Teddy Roosevelt, in his usual forthright manner, took care of that problem by hijacking a large transport intended for two other regiments. He simply took a steam launch out to the ship and commandeered it. There was a band on board, and the men whiled away the hours singing "The Star-Spangled Banner," "The Girl I Left Behind Me," "There'll Be a Hot Time in the Old Town Tonight," and their favorite, the children's song "The Animal Fair" ("We went to the animal fair, the birds and the beasts were there . . ." etc.).

The landing at Daiquirí was total confusion. The men apparently had no instructions on how to get equipment and animals ashore. (Besides the few cavalry mounts, there were artillery horses and pack mules.) They pushed many of the animals overboard, expecting them to swim ashore, but the animals didn't know which way to go; some of them swam out to sea and drowned. Among the victims was one of Roosevelt's two mounts, "Rain-in-the-Face." (The other was "Little Texas.") Teamsters saved some of the animals by rowing out and talking to them and patting them, then hauling them to shore with a tow rope. Buglers saved others by having the presence of mind to blow a retreat call, causing the cavalry horses to turn and swim in the right direction.

THE CHARGE (?) AT SAN JUAN HILL

After taking part in the fighting at Las Guásimas, the Rough Riders moved on down the jungle road to Santiago. Defending the approach to that city were two hills on San Juan Ridge—San Juan Hill and Kettle Hill. As orders came down to attack the two hills, more than 10,000 men poured out into the narrow jungle road, creating a monumental traffic jam.

The Rough Riders were ordered to join the attack on Kettle Hill, which disappointed Roosevelt: there was more glory in attacking San Juan Hill, the largest and most heavily fortified. His pique did not last long, for shortly he received word that he was now in command of the regiment—Colonel Wood had been moved up to command the whole division.

As the Rough Riders approached the slopes of San Juan Ridge they found troopers of the 9th Cavalry lying in the tall grass. "Why aren't you advancing?" asked Roosevelt.

"We have no orders," said a captain.

"Where is your colonel?"

The captain shrugged.

"Then I am the ranking officer here, and I order you to charge!" roared Teddy.

Still the captain hesitated, and the Rough Riders pushed on through and began not really a charge but a wild, free-swinging rush up Kettle Hill. Three other regiments, including the black 10th, caught the spirit of the moment and joined in. Teddy Roosevelt was at the head of his men. A soldier said after the war, "He never said, 'Go on!' He always said, 'Come on!' " Colonel Wood later wrote: "During the assault Colonel Roosevelt was the first to reach the trenches in his part of the line and killed one of the enemy with his own gun." The gun, given to him by an admirer, was from the wreck of the *Maine*.

The Rough Riders took Kettle Hill just in time to see their fellow soldiers rush San Juan Hill. T.R. then gave an order—or thought he did—for his troopers to follow him in taking part in that charge. Halfway to San Juan he looked back to find only five of his men behind him. Rushing back to Kettle Hill, he started to reprimand the others, but they said, "We didn't hear you. Lead on—we'll follow."

San Juan Hill was all but taken by the time the Rough Riders struggled up it, but by one of history's strange quirks they have become famous for their small role in that attack rather than for their courageous assault on Kettle Hill—something like the battle of Breed's Hill going down in history as the battle of Bunker Hill.

Chapter 16

World War I

Life in the Trenches

THE WORLD HAD NEVER SEEN—and doubtless will never see again—trenches like those on the Western Front. There were front-line trenches, communications trenches, reserve trenches—hundreds of miles of them, many bearing the names of hometown streets. Over and over they were built, demolished, and rebuilt. Thousands of men died in one charge after another for possession of a few feet of them. As a poet of the time put it:

> *Five hundred miles of Germans,*
> *Five hundred miles of French*
> *And Englishmen, Scotch and Irish men,*
> *All fighting for the trench;*
> *And when the trench is taken,*
> *And many thousands slain,*
> *The losers, with more slaughter,*
> *Retake the trench again.*

Soldiers slept in holes dug into the trench walls or on cots squeezed into small dugouts. Rats were a constant problem, and the men amused themselves by taking potshots at them as they crawled up the wooden supports. One officer told of hearing a scuffling sound on his bed one night; when he turned on his flashlight he found two rats on his blankets tussling for possession of a severed hand.

The rat story circulated among the soldiers as a good joke, for the men quickly grew accustomed to the casual presence of dead flesh, whether animal or human. In a British trench a dried-up hand of a German or Frenchman, which had been left jutting out from the wall, was shaken by the men when they went out to fight, for good luck.

The rats were there because of so much dead flesh lying about. Sometimes the trenches were piled high with dead bodies and the stench from them became intolerable. Sometimes soldiers risked their own lives by going into "no man's land," wearing gas masks because of the stench, to bury the enemy's dead. For the rest of the day everything they ate, drank, or touched smelled of rotted flesh.

Making matters worse was the fact that the winter of 1917-191fl was the coldest France had suffered in years, and flu made great inroads among the troops. Some of the American doughboys[1] were not always well supplied with proper clothes, especially shoes. What footwear they had was not always durable enough—the boys called them "tango shoes" and "hen's skins." General Billy Mitchell, head of the U.S. Air Service, said he saw "a division go by the other day with the men practically barefooted, many leaving blood marks in the snow."

THE SOLDIER: AN ENDANGERED SPECIES

To lessen the casualties from close-in fighting, each side unmercifully pounded the other's trenches with long-range artillery.[2] When a charge was coming up, the bombardment would first be aimed high to reach the enemy's artillery, then dropped down to destroy his trenches. Even uncontested sectors were bombarded steadily, just to be sure; the British called this "normal wastage." Soldiers learned which whine threatened them and which one didn't. They even learned to sleep during a bombardment, just as they learned to doze while working. A soldier filling a sandbag might look up to find the buddy holding it fast asleep.

The new machine guns killed the enemy faster than twenty men could. The machine-gunner, therefore, became an endangered species because the enemy was always after his hide most of all. A machine-gunner's life expectancy was said to be about thirty minutes.

The machine-gunner learned to live with such a grim statistic, and his outlook often became detached, even amused. For fun he would take cartridges out of the gunbelt at the proper intervals to make his gun rat-a-tat out some familiar tune, such as "shave-and-a-haircut, six bits." Those with water-cooled guns sprayed enemy lines indiscriminately to heat the water in them for tea or soup.

GOING "OVER THE TOP"

When America finally entered the war in 1917, the Army tried to get its men to the front as fast as possible. As a result, some doughboys arrived in the trenches with very little training; indeed, some learned to load their rifles at the front. These unfortunate soldiers were like the one in a popular song who said:

> *Goodbye, Maw! Goodbye, Paw!*
> *Goodbye, mule, with yer old heehaw!*
> *I may not know what this war's about,*
> *But you bet, by gosh, I'll soon find out!*

And find out the young man did—the first time he had to go "over the top" into no man's land. The attack would begin just before dawn, after the artillery finished its softening-up barrage. Loaded down with a rifle and perhaps a pistol, cartridge belt, canteen, trench knife, first-aid kit, and—if the weather was cold—an overcoat, he began his hellish run of 500 yards or so to the enemy's lines.

His first problem was the barbed wire, which might consist of as many as ten aprons of wire with barbs as thick as the thumb. (Soldiers joked that the war would last a hundred years: five of fighting, then ninety-five of winding up the barbed wire.) He cut his way through this, or stepped over it on the back of a dead comrade. Dodging shell holes—some of them big enough to put a house in—he jumped into the enemy's trench and took it, was killed, or was driven back by a counterattack.

In a passage revealing how war can blind a soldier to the humanity of his enemy—and even create a craving to kill—one doughboy wrote of his assault:

> *Oh, it was a dandy barrage, and we walked over behind it and took our objective without much opposition. I threw my grenades at a couple of Huns[3] in a bay and when they exploded (both Huns and grenades) I slid into a trench, and, according to plan, rebuilt the firing step. I prepared myself in case of counterattack. I did not get a chance to use my lovely bayonet.*

STRANGERS IN THE NIGHT

In the day the attacks went on; at night the patrols went out. Night was the time of greatest danger: a sudden snipping of barbed wire and someone died of a bayonet in the stomach; a bursting flare brought a burst of machine gun fire in the face; someone silently slid into a trench and a throat was cut.

Douglas MacArthur, who won his first star in this war commanding the Rainbow Division, made up of some of the best National Guard units from across the country, described what it was like crawling on his belly through no man's land under the cover of darkness:

> *The dead were so thick in spots we tumbled over them. There must have been 2,000 of those sprawled bodies. I identified six of the best German divisions. The stench was suffocating. Not a tree was standing. The moans and cries of wounded men sounded everywhere. Sniper bullets sung like the buzzing of an angry bee . . ."*

When a flare burst, MacArthur hit the dirt and saw, dead ahead, three Germans: a lieutenant pointing with outstretched arm, a sergeant crouching over a machine gun, and a corporal feeding a bandolier of cartridges into the weapon. He held his breath, waiting for the burst of fire that would take his life . . . but it didn't come. His aide got a grenade ready and turned on his flashlight to throw it—then they realized the truth. "They were dead—all dead—the lieutenant with shrapnel through his heart, the sergeant with his belly blown into his back, the corporal with his spine where his head should have been."

Two Heroes

CHER AMI—HEROIC PIGEON

Dogs and a few other animals often figure in stirring sagas of heroism and daring—but pigeons? Well, this little pigeon did not save the lives of one or two people, but of a whole battalion of soldiers.

The battalion, of the American 77th Infantry and commanded by Major Charles Whittlesey, had advanced farther into the Argonne Forest than other units of its division and was cut off and surrounded by Germans. But being surrounded was only half of Major Whittlesey's problem: his own artillery, never dreaming American troops were behind enemy lines, was pounding away at them. Several men had already been killed—the barrage had to be shut off and division headquarters notified of the battalion's predicament.

Whittlesey had seven carrier pigeons on hand (there had been more, but the men, tired of hardtack and tasteless coffee, had eaten the rest), and one by one he sent them out with a message. None of them got through. After the men had been cut off for five days their only hope was the last pigeon, a black-checkered runt named Cher Ami. The major attached a message to Cher Ami's little leg: "Our own artillery is dropping a heavy barrage directly on us. For heaven's sake, stop it!"

Cher Ami was a veteran of seven missions and had been under fire more than once, but this time he didn't seem concerned about his assignment. He flew only as far as the nearest tree and lighted. When the soldiers waved their helmets and shouted "Boo!" he merely moved to the next tree and preened his feathers. Sticks and stones thrown at him did no good. In desperation, and in danger of his own life, a soldier climbed the tree and shoved him off.

The little pigeon flew through a hail of bullets and shrapnel, but made it to his destination with the message intact. The paper dangled from a leg shattered by a bullet, and another shell had pierced his breastbone.

The Americans—ever afterwards to be known as the "Lost Battalion"—were rescued and Cher Ami became an instant hero. General John J. Pershing, commander of the American Expeditionary Force, recommended him for the Distinguished Service Cross and sent him home on the giant ship *Leviathan*, with a private stateroom and all the trimmings.

The little pigeon appeared in bond rallies and other patriotic gatherings before dying suddenly in the summer of 1918. You can see this fine feathered friend, stuffed, in the Smithsonian Institution.

SERGEANT YORK—HILLBILLY HERO

Sergeant Alvin C. York didn't believe in killing, but he did a better job of it than any other single American soldier in the war.

York was a deeply religious Tennessee mountaineer who could have stayed out of the war as a conscientious objector, but he decided it was his bounden duty as a patriotic American to go into the Army. Once York was in the Army, his religious sincerity so impressed his commanding officer he was given another chance to go home. Again York declined.

In basic training his fellow recruits marveled at young York's ability to hit the bullseye of a target almost every time. After arriving in France he picked off Germans in opposing trenches by first giving the turkey call he had learned in the Tennessee hills. Turkeys were unfamiliar birds to most Europeans, and when the Germans raised up to see what the strange noise was, York let them have it—right between the eyes.

His great moment of glory—although York did not think much of the feat—came on October 8, 1918, during the Meuse-Argonne campaign. He was a member of a patrol that, after surprising and capturing fifteen Germans, found itself pinned down by heavy machine-gun fire. Most of the men in the patrol were killed, leaving York, who was a corporal at the time, as the only noncommissioned officer. He found a protected position, and as the Germans charged he shot them down the way he used to shoot turkeys—picking off the last man first so his comrades would not know what was happening to them. When he had exhausted his rifle ammunition, he drew out his 45 pistol and killed more—twenty in all.

After the Germans discovered what was going on, York shouted that he would kill no more if they all surrendered. A major blew his whistle, and they all threw their hands up—except for one recalcitrant York had to "tetch off."

York herded the group back to American lines—carrying a gun in one hand and a grenade in the other—and when asked how many prisoners he had said, "Jesus, I don't know. I haven't had time to count 'em yet." There were 132.

General Pershing said he had never seen such fighting by an individual soldier before and awarded Sergeant York the Congressional Medal of Honor. When the war ended, York returned to his hillside farm in Tennessee, caring little for his fame. After twenty years he finally agreed to a movie about his exploits, but gave all the money to the poor and got into tax troubles.

The movie *Sergeant York*, starring Gary Cooper, came out just as we entered World War II and still comes around occasionally on the late show.

THE PROPAGANDA WAR

Once the United States entered World War I, it became essential to whip the nation into a fighting—and giving—spirit. That meant a war of words.

A week after Congress passed his war resolution President Wilson created the Committee on Public Information and appointed a young journalist named George Creel to head it. Its purpose was to end the differences of opinion among Americans and convince them of the rightness of the Allied cause. To carry out that purpose Creel used artists, writers, public speakers, and entertainers of all sorts.

A deluge of advertisements, pamphlets, posters, speeches, news articles, and movie reels rained down on the country. It became almost impossible to walk down an American street without being reminded that there was a war on and you were expected to play your part in it by buying Liberty Bonds, growing a Liberty Garden, saving fats, metal and rubber, and a host of other things. Everywhere signs exhorted the citizen to "BUY BONDS," "DO YOUR BIT," "WIN THE WAR," "BEAT BACK THE HUN," "CAN THE KAISER."

The Committee on Public Information had agents in every town. Post Office clerks tacked up its posters, Boy Scouts gave out its pamphlets, and "Four-Minute Men" delivered its speeches. The Four-Minute Men appeared on theater stages before the movie came on and in a four-minute speech asked the audience to buy savings stamps, conserve fuel, and eat less meat, wheat, and sugar. Children and housewives were asked to join the Food Administration Agency and to sign pledge cards promising to "live by your conscience" in helping the war effort in every way possible.

One spoke in those days of Liberty pups, not dachshunds (a German breed); liberty cabbage, not sauerkraut (a favorite German dish); liberty sausages, not frankfurters (food named after a German town). No one was supposed to catch a certain brand of measles, and anyone was unpatriotic who listened to the music of the three German B's—Beethoven, Bach, and Brahms.

HONEST, LOYAL . . . AND PERSUASIVE

Boys couldn't go to war, but they could share in the soldiers' glory by wearing the uniform of the Boy Scouts and helping carry on the home-front campaign. The Committee on Public Information told the Scouts they had been chosen as President Wilson's special messengers to counteract the German propaganda with American propaganda. The wartime Scout manual said:

> *As a democracy our country faces great danger—not so much from submarines, battleships and armies, because, thanks to our allies, our enemies have apparently little chance of reaching our shores. Our danger is from within . . .*

> *Our enemies have representatives everywhere; they tell lies; they misrepresent the truth; they deceive our own people; they are a real menace to our country . . .*
>
> *Here is where our service begins. We are to help spread the facts about America and America's part in the war. We are to fight lies with the truth . . .*
>
> *We are to help create public opinion "just as effective in helping to bring victory as ships and guns," to stir patriotism, the great force behind the ships and guns. Isn't that a challenge for every loyal Scout?*

The Scout's principal job was not to hand out information himself, but to persuade a dozen or so of his town's most influential adults to distribute pamphlets with such titles as "How the War Came to America" and "Why We Hate Germany." He was reminded to be always polite, to dress correctly, and to be spotlessly clean: "What you have to say will count more if you make a good impression."

IN THE SCHOOLS: TESTING LOYALTY

Schoolteachers, with their powerful influence over young minds, became key people in the dissemination of propaganda. Learning war aims and war ideals became a part of every child's education. Students were taught and tested on the Kaiser's crimes and how to "do your bit" in the war effort.

They were encouraged to buy "thrift stamps" at a quarter each, which would be used to fill a "thrift card." The card would then be exchanged for a Liberty Bond. They were asked to turn their backyards, and in many cases the schoolyard, into a vegetable garden, and those who did could proudly wear an armband showing they were members of the U.S.S.G.A.—the United States School Garden Army.

And for homework they wrote essays on how to take part in bringing on the victory. Here is part of one child's essay printed in a Raleigh, North Carolina, newspaper:

> *The young men of the country are Pershing's army. We must save every cent and buy thrift stamps—that is our battle. We will have to struggle against every kind of enemy from moving-picture shows to gum drops, but we will win. We will have to wear half-soled shoes and mended trousers and dresses, and let our hair grow six inches, but the Hun will lose. We will fight potato-bugs and weeds that we may cut down the grocery bill and buy War Savings Stamps with the difference. Of course, there are slackers in this army, and they may be readily distinguished. They are the guys who hang around the pool hall sucking early death through a cigarette, and the girls who spend all their money on costly apparel while the soldiers are doing without in the trenches . . .*

Knights of the Sky

When the war broke out, the world's military minds gave no serious thought to the airplane as a weapon. Winning battles, they insisted, required massed troops, artillery, and cavalry—there was no place for those "flimsy contraptions" called airplanes in the scheme of things. So little attention was given to the airplane in training that most ground troops did not recognize the insignia of their own country's aircraft.

The high brass did admit, however, that the plane would be useful for observing troop movements, locating artillery, and landing and picking up spies. These uses made the observer the important man in an air mission: he outranked the pilot and gave all the orders. For a long time pilots remained enlisted men—corporals or sergeants—rather than officers.

BRICKS AND BOMBS

In the early days there were so few flyers among the warring nations that they developed a sort of camaraderie despite the fact they were enemies. They waved at one another as they passed, although later on they began using their hands for throwing things instead. Half bricks were the favorite missiles, but when it proved next to impossible to hit anyone with them, the pilots evolved the "bag of bricks" method. The object was to fly over the enemy's plane and drop a sack full of bricks on the propeller. Records show two German planes were downed this way, but the practice was soon abandoned because the results were not worth the effort.

Bombs were used earlier than most people realize. In August 1914, the very month the war began, a German pilot named Ferdinand von Hiddessen dropped three bombs—if you could call them that—on Paris. The bombs weighed six pounds each, and Hiddessen simply tossed them overboard like so many sausages. They did no damage whatever, but apparently this was the world's first "bombing raid."

WHO FIRED THAT SHOT?

No one knows who fired the first shot from an airplane. The story goes that a German fired a shotgun at a Russian pilot he had been accustomed to waving at. The Russian, incensed at this breach of aerial etiquette, went up next day with a rifle and returned the compliment. Soon all flyers carried rifles and pistols, but there is no record of their shooting anyone down.

When machine guns were first tried, a small problem developed: because there was no way to fire through the propeller, pilots shot themselves down. Mounting a machine gun on brackets for firing over the propeller did not work—aiming the plane was the only way to aim the gun, and the only way to fire the gun was by pulling a cord from the pilot's seat. Also the pilot had to stand up to reload it while holding the "joystick" (control lever) between his legs.

By finding a way to correct these problems, Roland Garros of France became the first air hero of the war. Garros protected the propellers by attaching metal shields to the back of them. The shields were angled so that the bullets were deflected away from the pilot and the plane.

When engine trouble forced Garros down behind enemy lines, the Germans captured him and his plane and learned the secret. They used the method for a short time, then called in Anthony Fokker, a famous Dutch aircraft designer, who found a method of synchronizing the firing of the machine gun with the revolutions of the propeller. Soon all the belligerents learned the system.

For a while, though, the Fokker-designed planes ruled the air. Late in the war the Fokker D-VII emerged as probably the best fighter plane in the world. The wings could be folded back for easy transportation and reassembled in fifteen minutes.

THE "RED BARON"

"Ace" was a term applied to anyone who did something outstanding, but when newspapers began speaking of "that ace among pilots, Roland Garros," the word took on new meaning. After Garros downed his fifth German plane, any flyer who could do the same became an ace.

There were many aces in the war, but the greatest was the German flyer Baron Manfred von Richthofen, who shot down eighty Allied planes. Snoopy in the "Peanuts" comic strip has made him famous as the "Red Baron," but he was not known by that name—he was the "Red Knight."

Richthofen joined the German Army as a cavalryman, but quickly grew bored as there was little for a cavalry officer to do in a war fought almost entirely in the trenches. He transferred to the Air Force and quickly established himself as a skilled fighter. He organized the "Flying Circus," a small fighter group that painted its planes red. While the other planes in the group had markings in other colors, Richthofen's was blood red all over—he wanted every enemy to know their adversary was the Red Knight. In the beginning he flew the heavy German fighter called an Albatros, but became famous piloting his red Fokker airplane.

Richthofen had a silver loving cup made for each of his kills, engraved with the type of plane each was and what nation it belonged to. After two kills the day before had brought his total to eighty, the baron himself was knocked out of the sky and killed. Captain A. Roy Brown of the Royal Air Force—who did not know whom he was fighting—got credit for it, but most scholars today believe the Red Knight's plane was brought down by "Archie," this war's nickname for anti-aircraft fire. (The name came from a popular English song, "Archibald! Certainly not!")

The German ace fell behind Australian lines, where Brown found him and saw that the baron had made a perfect landing. "His face," Brown wrote, "was particularly peaceful, had an expression of gentleness and goodness, of refinement. Suddenly I felt miserable, desperately unhappy, as if I had committed an injustice."

The Australian Flying Corps buried the Red Knight with full military honors. A fourteen-man squad fired three volleys. Wreaths were placed on the grave, including one that read: "To our gallant and worthy foe." The next day a British plane flew over Richthofen's aerodrome and dropped a photograph of the ceremony and the message:

To the German Flying Corps

Rittmeister Baron von Richthofen was killed in aerial combat on
April 21, 1918. He has been buried with all due military honors.

From the British Royal Air Force

THE LAFAYETTE ESCADRILLE

The first American aces flew for the Lafayette Escadrille, volunteering their services to France before the U.S. entered the war. Norman Prince son of a wealthy American family living in France, conceived the idea early in the war, but the proposal got bogged down in red tape and the squadron was not formed until March 14, 1916. At first it was called the *Escadrille Américaine* (American Squadron) N. 124. The "N" stood for Nieuport, the pursuit plane they would fly.

The name was changed when the Germans complained about volunteers from a neutral country fighting against them. Washington was cool at the outset because the U.S., officially, was trying hard to maintain its neutrality. The new name, of course, honored the Marquis de Lafayette, who had served so gallantly with the Continental Army in the American Revolution.[4]

As its insignia, the squadron adopted the head of an American Indian wearing red, white, and blue feathers. Later it adopted a lion cub named Whiskey as its mascot. Whiskey eventually got a girlfriend, Soda, but both lions were given to the Paris zoo when they were grown.

The Lafayette Escadrille's leading ace—who eventually shot down seventeen German planes—was its only non-American member. Raoul Lufbery was born to French parents who had moved to Connecticut when he was small; then he ran away from home to see the world. After serving in the French Foreign Legion he asked for a transfer to the Flying Service.

When America entered the war in 1917, the Lafayette Escadrille became part of the newly organized U.S. Air Service. One day Lufbery was annoyed that a German reconnaissance plane had buzzed the American aerodrome and was going to get away unchallenged. Hopping in his Nieuport, he sped into the air after this smarty-pants "Kraut." As he attacked the German his gun jammed, and horrified spectators on the ground watched his plane burst into flames; the German had made a lucky hit on the gas tank, which was next to the pilot's seat.

Those below knew this ace's greatest fear was of being caught in a burning plane, and they saw him crawl out onto the wing—then jump. They found his body in the lovely garden of a small French home, impaled on a picket fence.

A parachute would have saved Lufbery's life, as well as many other lives, but the American high command refused to let their pilots wear them. All the German flyers did, and many an Allied pilot was happy to see his victim parachute to safety—most of them were only interested in sending down machines, not men.

During World War I the American military never succeeded in making a parachute small enough to fit in a cockpit. The high brass didn't want them anyway. "Pilots would jump out when they did not have to," they said. "We would lose too many planes that way."

RICKENBACKER—"ACE OF ACES"

Like Billy the Kid, Eddie Rickenbacker shot down a man for every year of his life—twenty-six. True, many aces of other countries shot down more planes, but they didn't do it in only seven months—and Rickenbacker was in the hospital with an ear infection part of that time.

Eddie was a well-known racing-car driver who came to France as General Pershing's chauffeur. But the future ace wanted to be a pilot, and after some trouble over his age (twenty-six was thought to be too old to learn to fly) and his seventh-grade education, he wangled a job as an engineer at a new base just opening. One job of an engineer was testing planes after they were repaired, so the Army was forced to teach him to fly. He earned his wings in only seventeen days.

Then came a new setback: the high command thought he was too valuable as an engineer to go out on combat missions. Rickenbacker took care of that problem by pretending to be sick for a few days, forcing the brass to see that his assistant could do the engineering job just as well.

Eventually Rickenbacker became commander of the 94th Aero Pursuit Squadron, which he made the best in the Air Service in one week. It was famous as the "Hat-in-the-Ring" squadron, from its insignia showing Uncle Sam's star-spangled hat inside a ring.

Rickenbacker was replaced temporarily as ace of aces when Frank Luke, the "Arizona Balloon Buster," shot down ten balloons and four planes in an eight-day period—a feat never equaled by anyone, not even Richthofen. On his next mission Luke was killed and Rickenbacker regained his title.

The family name was spelled Rickenba*c*her. Eddie's parents were Swiss-Americans, his mother of French ancestry and his father of German stock. But when he began making headlines he changed the spelling. The newspapers trumpeted: "Eddie Rickenbacker has taken the Hun out of his name!"

Chapter 17

The Roaring Twenties

Prohibition: The Noble Experiment

WORLD WAR I changed America forever. When the nation's young men returned from the battlefields of France, they found it difficult if not impossible to settle again into the sedate ways of living they had accepted as the nature of things before they went off to war. It was hard to taper off from the emotional stimulation the war had provided; they craved excitement and a faster pace to life. And from their contact with continental Europeans they had learned of social standards quite different from the ones they had known in the United States.

So it was not by accident that shortly after the soldiers returned there began a revolution in manners and morals. Young people—"flaming youth"—totally rejected the reigning social mores. Old rituals and old taboos fell by the wayside and were replaced by a philosophy of "eat, drink, and be merry, for tomorrow you die."

Isn't it odd, then, that the decade of the 1920s began with one of the most reactionary measures ever passed by Congress—the Eighteenth Amendment?

The Eighteenth Amendment, which prohibited the manufacture, sale, or transportation of alcoholic beverages in America, was the result of long years of determined lobbying by the Anti-Saloon League. Yet it was strange how the country went on the wagon almost absent-mindedly. The amendment whizzed through the Senate with only thirteen hours of debate, and the House of Representatives considered the matter for only one day. The Volstead Act for enforcement of the amendment passed both houses with even greater ease.

This most ambitious attempt ever to legislate morality was doomed to failure. Lesser attempts to restrict the use of liquor had already shown that people would drink no matter what obstacles were put in their path. Consequently, the Eighteenth Amendment ushered in a period of lawlessness the likes of which the country had never seen. And the problems of enforcement were soon to be seen as insurmountable.

HOME COOKIN'

With the enactment of Prohibition, shops sprang up all over the country selling the necessary paraphernalia for making home brew: malt, hops, yeast, crown caps, rubber hoses, and alcohol gauges. An anonymous New York city rhymester wrote:

> *Mother's in the kitchen*
> *Washing out the jugs;*
> *Sister's in the pantry*
> *Bottling the suds;*
> *Father's in the cellar*
> *Mixing up the hops;*
> *Johnny's on the front porch*
> *Watching for the cops.*

Besides the independent shops, big food chains such as Kroger and Piggly-Wiggly displayed great pyramids of malt syrup cans. The trade in malt syrup was so large, in fact, that it gave birth to two associations of wholesalers. One of them, the National Association of Malt Syrup Manufacturers, published a monthly magazine entitled *Sips*.

Far simpler than brewing beer was distilling alcohol. For only about five dollars, the home distiller could buy a quite serviceable one-gallon copper still. That was not essential, however: steam cookers, coffee percolators, and wash boilers were good enough. Alcohol could be distilled from a number of things, including grain, sugar beets, raisins, and potato peelings. Once the distiller had a batch of alcohol, he could easily simulate the taste of any kind of liquor with additives.

Easiest of all to make was gin. All it took to make a large quantity was alcohol, water, glycerine, juniper oil, and a bathtub. Because it was cheap and simple to make, "bathtub gin" became the most popular drink in the early years of Prohibition.

BY SEA AND AIR

One could not make, sell, or transport liquor, but there was no law against buying it. "Rum runners" plied the coasts, entering U. S. ports in disguise or hovering off the twelve-mile limit while transferring their cargoes to speedy motor launches that would slip into thousands of isolated coves.

Other motor boats sped across the Great Lakes bearing good Canadian whiskey. In Detroit, agents found an underwater cable along which liquor cargoes from Canada were towed on a sledge while customs boats patrolled overhead.

When the Feds began to do a better job of patroling highways and waterways leading out of Canada, many bootleggers turned to aerial rum-running. Farm lots and pastures served as improvised runways, while the headlights of cars illuminated night landings. Some smugglers, taking their cue from the Army's recent mid-air refueling experiments, transferred liquor from Canadian planes to American planes in the same manner. Two planes, both with extra gas tanks filled with hooch, would rendezvous over the border and transfer the stuff by means of hoses.

CAPITAL REPLENISHMENT

One could buy a drink almost anywhere. Liquor was sold by cab drivers, shoeshine boys, bell boys—almost anyone who fraternized with other people. "Speakeasies" sprang up anywhere there was a spare room or two, and as soon as they were shut down they popped up somewhere else.

Bootleggers roamed the Senate and House office buildings, doing business almost openly. In the Capitol itself was a small room furnished with a few chairs, a desk, and row upon row of books. Legislators called the room the "Library," but its books concealed bottles of booze.

President Warren G. Harding was fond of whiskey and poker. A couple of times a week his cronies from back home, later known as the "Ohio Gang," met at the White House for drinks and cards. What bootlegger would have the audacity to bring illegal liquor to the White House? None other than the treasurer of the Republican National Committee.

The Ohio Gang also had booze delivered to its headquarters, a little green house on H Street. The Prohibition Commissioner himself saw to the deliveries, which were made in Wells Fargo trucks guarded by Prohibition agents.

The most unusual cache ever discovered by Prohibition agents was in one of California's giant redwood trees. The tree, twenty-four feet in diameter, had been hollowed out at the base and a still had been installed. The entrance was covered with a piece of canvas painted to look like bark, and the tall flue was concealed in the tree's upper branches. The agents padlocked the tree just as if it were an ordinary speakeasy.

ENFORCEMENT WOES

The authors of the Eighteenth Amendment had not foreseen the tremendous problems enforcing it would bring. How could the government patrol a coastline and two borders amounting to more than 18,000 miles? How could it control the sale of alcohol by druggists, who were allowed to dispense it for medicinal purposes? Near-beer was legal, but the only way to make it was to brew real beer and then remove some of the alcohol; who would know how much was removed? And how could the watchful eyes of the government prevent industrial alcohol from ending up in someone's stomach as rot-gut whiskey?

The answer to all these questions: it couldn't be done.

The Feds kept plugging away anyhow, with the often unenthusiastic help of local law officials. The federal force was woefully small: 1,500 agents in 1920 and still only 2,836 by 1930. An agents salary in 1920 was $1,200 to $2,000, and ten years later $2,000 to $3,000. It was hard to get good men at such wages.

Result: many of the Prohibition agents were a sorry lot. Wrote one newspaper editor: "The dry agent, not alone by the intrinsically unpopular nature of his calling, but by his duplicity, his bad manners, his cheapness and occasional brutality, made himself a symbol of all that is wrong with the law." Some agents were charged with bribery, embezzlement, extortion, perjury, contempt of court, intoxication, theft, conspiracy, and many other crimes.

PROHIBITION PERSPECTIVES

Efforts to end the illegal traffic sometimes ended in tragedy. In Illinois, less than a month after twenty people in Peoria died from drinking poisonous gin, *Time* reported this:

> *Boyd Fairchild, dry snooper, reported to the Illinois State's Attorney a purchase of liquor at the home of one Joseph De King . . . Last week Deputy Sheriff Roy Smith . . . went to the De King home with a warrant. De King refused to let him in. Smith returned with three more deputies. They surrounded the house, threw mustard bombs, rushed the door. De King was clubbed into unconsciousness. Lillian De King, his wife, was at the telephone, screaming "Help! Help!" to their lawyer. Smith fired a shotgun loaded with slugs point-blank into her abdomen. She wilted to the floor, dead. Gerald De King, 12-year-old son, flipped up a revolver, sent a bullet plowing into the fleshy leg of Deputy Sheriff Smith. Later a gallon of weak wine was found.*

There were not only tragic consequences, but tragi-comic ones as well, as this report in *Time* for January 14, 1929, indicates:

> *In a Lansing, Mich., courtroom last week Judge Charles B. Collingwood was sentencing Mrs. Etta Mae Miller. It had taken a jury only 13 minutes to find her guilty. She was charged with having sold two pints of liquor and also with being a "habitual criminal" inasmuch as this was her fourth such offense. So to her said Judge Collingwood. "It is the sentence of this court that from and after this day you shall be confined in the Detroit House of Correction for the remainder of your life."*
>
> *Mrs. Miller has ten children. Her husband is serving his first liquor-conviction sentence. Lest any feel that Mrs. Miller had been too severely punished, Dr. Clarence True Wilson, General Secretary of the Board of Temperance, Prohibition and Public Morals, spoke up . . .: "Our only regret is that the woman was not sentenced to life imprisonment before her ten children were born. When one has violated the Constitution four times, he or she should be segregated from society to prevent the production of subnormal offsprings."*

To further illustrate this lack of perspective, consider this:

In 1929 the penalty on a first offense for manufacturing or selling liquor was a $1,000 fine or up to six months imprisonment. For shanghaiing sailors, the penalty was $1,000 or a year in prison.

A proposal in Congress would make a subsequent offense for selling or making liquor punishable by a $10,000 fine or imprisonment up to five years or both. The punishment for hovering off the coast with slaves for sale was $10,000 or not more than four years in jail.

IF AT FIRST YOU DON'T SUCCEED . . .

By the late '20s, "wets" seemed to be making headway in their opposition to Prohibition. It wasn't prohibiting, they said, and the crime wave that came with it was the worst the country had ever seen. Prohibition agents, frustrated in their efforts to stop the illicit traffic by polite means, were now shooting to kill. When the government began putting wood alcohol and other poisons into industrial alcohol to prevent its diversion, wets charged the government with murder.

As soon as he entered the White House in 1929, Herbert Hoover kept a campaign promise and appointed a special commission to look into the problems of enforcement. In January 1931, nineteen months after its appointment, the commission laid its bulky report on the President's desk. It was one of the strangest documents on record.

First, the report revealed that enforcement agencies were not able to do much enforcing. That revelation came as a surprise to no one.

Second, all eleven commissioners submitted a personal report giving their own views of the problem, and only five of them recommended the experiment be continued without change. Four favored modification of the amendment, and two were for outright repeal.

Third, the commission *as a whole* recommended further trial under the existing laws. A humor columnist for the *New York World* summed up the commission's findings this way:

> *Prohibition is an awful flop.*
>   *We like it.*
> *It can't stop what it's meant to stop.*
>   *We like it.*
> *It's left a trail of graft and slime,*
> *It's filled our land with vice and crime,*
> *It don't prohibit worth a dime,*
>   *Nevertheless we're for it.*

The Adventures of Izzy and Moe

Isadore "Izzy" Einstein and Moe Smith looked as unlike Prohibition agents as any two men could. And that was the main reason for their astounding success.

Both were short, fat, almost bald, and middle-aged. Both were poorly educated, even by the standard of the times, although Izzy, having been brought up on New York's Lower East Side, could get along in several languages. Before they volunteered to catch hooch-crooks, Izzy was a postal clerk and Moe a cigar salesman.

Izzy, who was in the business for a while before Moe joined him, made his first pinch in a fashion that would become his trademark during the next few years. He simply walked up to a speakeasy and knocked on the door. A peephole opened and a voice asked who he was.

"Izzy Einstein," he said. "I want a drink."

"Oh yeah?" said the voice. "Who sent you?"

"My boss sent me. I'm a Prohibition agent."

The door swung open and the owner of the voice slapped Izzy on the back, laughing. "Come on in, bud. That's the best joke I've heard in a long time."

In this first arrest Izzy also learned a lesson: be sure to get some evidence first. He took the drink the man gave him, then suddenly realized he had made a mistake. When the man had found out Izzy really was a cop, he had made off with the bottle.

From then on, Izzy carried a funnel in his vest pocket, connected by a rubber tube to a flat bottle sewed into the lining of his coat. He called it his "evidence collector." When he was sold a drink he would take a sip then pour the rest down the tube.

HOW DRY THEY WERE

By the time Moe joined him, Izzy's name and reputation were so well known among bootleggers many of them kept his picture on a wall behind the bar. Did that slow Izzy down? No, siree. In fact, he once made use of the picture to make an arrest.

When a bartender wouldn't serve him because he didn't know him, Izzy said, "That's me up there on the wall—Izzy Epstein, the famous Prohibition detective."

The bartender laughed scornfully. "It's Einstein. The bum's name is Einstein."

Izzy continued to argue until the barkeep grew furious and made a bet with him: whoever was wrong would buy drinks for the house. Izzy agreed and the bartender called over all nine customers. When they all said the name was Einstein, Izzy admitted defeat and ordered the drinks. The bartender served them—then went straight to jail without passing Go.

Soon Izzy came up with a brilliant idea: he would always carry something with him that made him fit in with the clientele of a bar. In poorer sections of the Bronx, he went to bars in shirt-sleeves carrying a pitcher of milk. In saloons frequented by lawyers and judges, he showed up with a frock coat and a big law book. In places where musicians hung out, he bought a trombone—and when asked to play it he could. He played "How Dry I Am."

SIN ON SUNDAY

When Moe joined Izzy, the two thought up all sorts of imaginative ways to work as a team. For example, they once went to a speakeasy where several other agents had tried to buy a drink. The bartender positively would not sell to anyone he did not know.

The pair picked a cold winter night, and Izzy stood in front of the place in his shirt-sleeves until he was blue and numb with the cold. Then Moe staggered into the place, holding him up and shouting, "Give this man a drink! He's just been bitten by a frost!" When the kind-hearted bartender obliged, Moe grabbed the bottle and placed him under arrest.

Some of New York's best reporters were assigned to cover their exploits, and the pudgy pair always came up with a stunt that was good for a headline. Like Teddy Roosevelt, they had learned that a minor exploit on Sunday was good enough for a big headline on Monday.

One Sunday, the pair, followed by a pack of reporters, set a record by making seventy-one raids in twelve hours.

Another Sunday, the two helped out a preacher by timing their raid on a cafe next to his church to coincide with the dismissal of services. As Izzy and Moe busted beer barrels right and left, the preacher's flock could see the wages of sin right before their very eyes.

MASQUERADE BALLS

The trail Izzy and Moe followed led them to some strange places. At Cornell University they dressed as a couple of overgrown preppies and siss-boom-bahed all over the campus until they located where the illegal booze was coming from. Then they issued their "diplomas"—summonses.

Another time Izzy dressed as an African American, his face blackened with burnt cork, and spoke with a Southern accent as thick as gravy rolling off his tongue. This was to arrest a grocery store owner who was selling whiskey in cans marked "beans" and gin disguised in cans of "tomatoes."

Dressed as a longshoreman, Izzy captured an Italian restauranteur who kept tiny bottles of whiskey in his cash register. Dressed as a bum, he snooped around in pawn shops until he discovered $10,000 worth of liquor wrapped up in old clothes.

Posing as tipsy poultry salesmen, Izzy and Moe got into a club on Eighth Avenue and found a sizeable amount of booze inside a stuffed grizzly bear.

To investigate a snooty delicatessen on Madison Avenue, they got themselves up as Park Avenue dudes, gold-headed canes and all, and found bottles tucked away in baskets of fruit. Next morning, when they returned with a warrant, a young man in a truck yelled, "Hey, mister, I gotta deliver some stuff here and they told me to be careful. Take a look inside and see if everything looks okay."

Izzy took a look and reported that everything seemed all right, then arrested the young man and confiscated the fifty cases of liquor in his truck.

THE ADVENTURE ENDS

In 1925 Izzy and Moe were, more or less, fired. Their names and adventures had appeared in the newspapers so often, other agents—and especially their superiors—were jealous. Izzy was called in by his immediate superior, who frankly told him that he did not like it when Izzy got publicity and he didn't. Higher-ranking officers were the important people in government service, he complained, and they should be the ones to get the credit.

The Prohibition Agency announced the two famous detectives were being laid off "for the good of the service." Izzy and Moe belonged on a vaudeville stage, they said, adding that "the service must be dignified."

Some newspapers thought the whole Prohibition business belonged on the vaudeville stage.

An Era Ends

The Prohibition Era did not end until 1933, but it reached a climax of sorts on St. Valentine's Day, 1929.

At ten o'clock that morning a car pulled up in front of a garage on North Clark Street in Chicago. Three uniformed policemen and two plainsclothesmen got out and went into the garage.

Inside were seven members of the Bugs Moran gang, waiting for the arrival of a shipment of booze from Canada. The five new arrivals frisked the seven, then lined them up against the wall and mowed them down with sub-machine guns and sawed-off shotguns. The five returned to their car, the plainclothesmen walking ahead of the other three with their hands in the air, and sped off. Some of Chicago's finest, thought the handful of bystanders, making another arrest.

The "cops" were gangsters (presumably Al Capone's, but this was never proved) "rubbing out" rivals in the bitter contest for control of bootlegging and other rackets in a city that in the '20s gained an international reputation for unmitigated violence and gore. At the end of the decade, Chicago had been the bloody scene of over 500 gangland slayings, and during one stretch had averaged three killings and two bombings a week. This incredible record inspired some newspaper poet to rewrite part of "The Star-Spangled Banner":

> *And the pistol's red glare,*
> *The bombs bursting in air,*
> *Give proof through the night*
> *That Chicago's still there.*

Chicago was not typical, but law officers in every large city in America realized they had been given the herculean task of enforcing a law that was essentially unenforceable. And it was a law that would never stop what it was supposed to stop. Washington, D.C., officials discovered that in the first four years of Prohibition, arrests for drunkenness in the nation's capital had almost tripled.

The day the Eighteenth Amendment went into effect, the famous evangelist Billy Sunday exulted: "The reign of tears is over. The slums will soon be a memory. We will turn our prisons into factories and our jails into storehouses and corncribs. Men will walk upright now, women will smile, and children will laugh. Hell will be forever for rent."

But John Barleycorn was not dead; he was only in hiding. And in hiding he was infinitely more formidable than when he plied his trade openly.

The Harding Scandals

Warren G. Harding said he did not want to be the best president this country had ever had, just the best-loved one. For a time it appeared he would get his wish—then the sky fell on him.

Harding was the kind of man who never should have been president in the first place. He was a small-town man with a small-town mind. The office was too big a job for him. The presidency took this mediocre man and broke him.

Harding won the nomination of the Republican Party through the behind-the-scenes maneuvering of his mentor, a two-bit Ohio political boss named Harry Daugherty. He won the election of 1920 because he was genial and handsome—the very picture of robust American manhood—and because even Tom Sawyer could have won a majority that year from a public reacting to World War I and the one-worldism of Woodrow Wilson.

Veterans' Benefits

Harding's chief problem, other than being dull-witted, was an inability to judge character. He appointed to high office those he considered good and true friends. Some of these men were merely inept, others were outright crooks.

For director of the Veterans' Bureau, the new President picked Charles R. Forbes, for no reason except that Harding had met him on a senatorial junket to Hawaii and enjoyed some good times with him. Already a deserter from the Army, Forbes turned out to be a thief.

In less than two years in the office, Forbes deprived the country of about $200 million in graft and waste. Examples:

- He gave contracts for new veterans' hospitals to the highest instead of the lowest bidder, and split with the builder the difference between the bidding price and the actual construction cost.

- He bought $70,000 worth of floor wax and cleaner for the hospitals— enough to last a hundred years, some estimated—and paid 98¢ a gallon for it when it was worth less than 4¢ a gallon.

- He sold "surplus" sheets for about 26¢ apiece; they actually were new ones that had cost the government $1.37 each. At one time he was buying sheets at one end of a warehouse while selling them cheap at the other end.

- He sold towels that had cost 19¢ each for $3 each.

Forbes pocketed most of the money from these fraudulent sales. In 1926 he went to the federal penitentiary in Leavenworth, Kansas.

Department of Easy Virtue

Harding made his benefactor, Harry Daugherty, Attorney General of the United States. Daugherty brought to Washington with him, although he had no official office, a country boy from back home in Ohio named Jess Smith. Before long it was common news in Washington's inner circles that all sorts of favors could be won through the discreet use of Jess Smith's "Department of Easy Virtue" within the Justice Department.

Gaston B. Means, a Justice Department agent of unsavory reputation himself, testified that at one time he had reserved two rooms in a New York hotel where bootleggers who expected special favors from the government came to make their payoffs. They put their money, Means said, in a goldfish bowl, and at the end of the day he would count the proceeds and check off each bootlegger's name. He testified that he took in a total of $7 million in this manner, and turned it over to Jess Smith.

Smith kept much of this money buried in a friend's backyard protected by a high wire fence and several signal devices. He also walked around with a money belt filled with $1,000 bills.

Jess Smith, officially at least, committed suicide in 1923. It had become known that he kept a record of all his crooked transactions and was thinking of turning state's evidence against the ringleaders. Means claimed the grafters forced Smith to buy a revolver shortly before his death, although it was well known that the head of the Department of Easy Virtue was afraid of guns.

CHANGING THE NATION'S OIL

The worst scandal of all issued from the Interior Department, where good buddy Albert Fall reigned. Fall convinced the Secretary of the Navy to transfer the Navy's oil reserves at Elk Hills, California, and Teapot Dome, Wyoming, to his department. Then, for certain monetary considerations, Fall leased them to oil magnates Harry F. Sinclair and Edward F. Doheny.

At his hearing Fall claimed he was never paid any money by the oil men.

"But what about the hundred thousand dollars that suddenly showed up in your bank account?" the court wanted to know.

"Oh, that was just a little loan," said Fall, who was an aging and easy-going Westerner.

"A loan carried by a messenger in a black bag? Isn't that a strange way to do business?"

Doheny, on the witness stand, said no, he transacted business with friends that way all the time.

When a witness testified he had heard Sinclair's confidential secretary, G. D. Wahlberg, say he had transferred $68,000 to the manager of Fall's New Mexico ranch, the secretary claimed he hadn't said "sixty-eight thous," but "six or eight cows."

Nevertheless, Fall joined Forbes in prison. Sinclair and Doheny were exonerated, although Sinclair later served a brief stint in prison for contempt of the Senate and for offering a juror "a car as long as a block" if he voted right.

HARDING'S SUDDEN DEATH

When President Harding set out on a tour of Alaska and the Pacific Coast early in 1923, he must have known what was coming. A foul odor was beginning to rise from his administration. "I can take care of my enemies," he said. "It's my friends who are giving me trouble."

When his train reached San Francisco, the public was told the President was ill. He had stomach trouble . . . he had pneumonia . . . he was getting better . . . he had a stroke . . . the President was dead.

Harding had taken no liquor with him, in itself an unusual circumstance. He had not taken his cronies, the men he drank and played poker with, but men who had his trust and the nation's. He was nervous and upset and wanted to kill the time by playing bridge fourteen hours at a stretch. Before leaving Washington he had told his lawyer to draw up a will.

His death is still something of a mystery; the details of it have never been made public. When the President became ill, two highly reputable doctors from the San Francisco area were called in, but apparently they were never allowed to treat him. He was attended only by his personal physician, good old "Doc" Sawyer from back home in Ohio. Sawyer had spent two terms in a medical school.

Mrs. Harding was alone in the room with her husband when he died. She would not allow an autopsy.

Is there more to Harding's death than meets the eye? It is a question that probably will never be answered.

"Silent Cal" Coolidge

Calvin Coolidge believed the best government was the one that governed least. Therefore, he said, he was going to be the least presidential president this country had ever had. He was.

Coolidge became a national figure when as governor of Massachusetts he put an end to the Boston police strike. His pronouncement that no one had the "right to strike against the public safety anytime, anywhere" caught the nation's fancy. The same backroom cabal that had nominated Warren Harding for president had slipped Coolidge in as the vice-presidential candidate.

In keeping with his theory that government should govern little, Coolidge snoozed away part of every afternoon at the White House, his feet propped up on the presidential desk. Someone figured out he averaged about four hours of work a day. When he was not snoozing away problems, he was ignoring them. When told by Treasury Department officials that if something wasn't done to check the nation's wild love affair with the stock market the country was going to go bust, Coolidge went down to the White House basement to count the apples in a barrel an old friend had sent him.

At any other time in American history, perhaps, Calvin Coolidge would have been condemned as a do-nothing President. However, Coolidge was fortunate enough to be counting sheep in the Oval Office at a time of unparalleled national prosperity. Business was booming, and the people quickly put the Harding scandals out of mind and got on with the pursuit of wealth as never before. Coolidge was loved simply because he happened to be in the right place at the right time.

A CREATURE OF HABIT

The droll, parsimonious little man the country remembers today was in part a creation of bored newspapermen on the White House beat. With seldom any important news to report, they recounted instead tales of Coolidge's domestic adventures calculated to tickle the public's fancy. Though related to the reading public as amusing capers, most of the President's antics were more in the nature of practical jokes and whoever was the butt of his jokes didn't always find them amusing. It seems certain his wife did not laugh when she found her husband walking up the train of her evening gown, nor the servants when he rang for them and disappeared before they got there.

The President's parsimony, the reporters appeared to indicate, was a virtue rather than a fault: he was merely trying to save the country money. But the White House's chief cook did not think much of this virtue when his boss inspected his kitchens and storerooms every day; he quit in disgust. Neither were other members of the staff impressed when the President checked their accounts all the time. There is no record of what Grace Coolidge, a truly charming lady, thought when her husband checked her accounts.

"HOW CAN THEY TELL?"

Was the man known to millions as "Silent Cal" really so silent? From inside accounts Coolidge was apparently more garrulous than we have been led to believe, but only in private. In public he was generally disposed to say as little as possible. Everyone remembers his famous retort when asked if he intended to be a candidate for reelection in 1928: "I do not choose to run."

At social gatherings he was also reticent. When he was Vice-President, a woman sitting next to him at a dinner party confided, "Mr. Vice-President, I have a bet with friends that I can get you to say at least three words tonight."

"You lose," snapped Cal.

When Coolidge died five years after leaving office, someone asked the noted writer and wit Dorothy Parker if she had heard the former President was dead. "How can they tell?" asked Miss Parker.

Chapter 18

The Great Depression

How Bad Was It?

"**I** KNEW IT WAS BAD," joked Groucho Marx, "when the pigeons in Central Park began feeding the people." How bad was the Depression? It was this bad:

In the countryside, children ate roots, violet tops, dandelions, and forget-me-nots.

In the coal-mining regions of Kentucky and West Virginia, little babies, famished for food, chewed their hands.

City mothers fought homeless dogs for possession of spoiled produce discarded on the docks or for leftovers thrown into the alley behind a cafe. "I take off my glasses," said a little old widow, "so I won't see the maggots."

A woman shot and killed her husband for spending in a gin-mill $1.85 she had saved for Christmas presents for the children.

A father suffocated his three small daughters rather than have to watch them starve to death.

When a man who had pounded the pavement for two years searching for a job, finally landed one, he promptly had a heart attack and died.

A BIG RELIEF

One could not go six blocks in any large city without coming across a long line of destitute men, their hats pulled low over their heads in embarrassment, waiting for a government handout of bread, beans, and coffee; or bread, soup, and coffee; or bread, oatmeal, and coffee. Some went from one line to another all day, finally managing to get full after four or five meals.

Some people were too proud to go on relief, even when starving. A black farmer in Georgia, who was blind and had no horse, refused offers of relief and hitched himself to his plow. When a Pittsburgh man who had refused to go on the public dole was caught stealing a loaf of bread, he was so ashamed he hanged himself. Rather than accept charity, a New York dentist and his wife killed themselves with gas; the little money they had was left to his brother with instructions that the city was not to touch their bodies, for they had a great horror of charity burials.

An old man who finally accepted $15 a week for his large family went out every day and swept the streets of his small town. "I want to do something in return for what I get," he explained.

The typical Depression story of former millionaires selling apples on the street corner is an exaggeration: only one was ever found. There were, however, thousands of ordinary citizens selling apples, although the practice lasted less than two years.

The street-corner peddling was an idea of the International Apple-Shippers' Association in 1930. Unemployed men lined up at dawn every day at the association's big city warehouses and bought a crate of apples for $1.75. If they sold all their apples at the standard price of 5¢ each, they would make a net profit of $1.85 a day. Sometimes they did, but as often as not many apples were spoiled or bruised, and they lost money.

"HOOVEROCRACY"

President Herbert Hoover couldn't stand to see the people suffering. When his limousine passed a relief station he turned his head. He thought of economizing in the White House, but changed his mind because he thought it would be bad for the country's morale.

He continued to have seven-course dinners and wore a black tie to the table. The butler and footmen—all of whom had to be the same height—stood at attention, silent. Marines in dress blues stood in the doorways. Buglers announced his arrival and departure, even when he and his wife dined alone.

Meanwhile, on the outskirts of the capital sprang up the tent cities and tarpaper-shack villages that became known as "Hoovervilles." They were growing up around every large city in the country as homes for many of the nation's destitute, who were tired of bumming rides on the highway and "riding the rails" from one place to another in search of work that was never there. Some of these settlements grew quite extensive. Many came from far away to live in Washington's several Hoovervilles, partly as a protest against a government that seemed powerless to do anything to solve the country's economic woes.

"Hooverocracy" was in full flower. People everywhere were calling sacks of belongings "Hoover bags," sawed-off flivvers with mules attached to the front "Hoover carts," old newspapers to sleep in "Hoover blankets," empty pockets turned inside out "Hoover flags," and jackrabbits caught for food "Hoover hogs."

A popular joke about "Hoover hogs" had one man saying "The Depression is over. I seen a jackrabbit and they wasn't nobody after him." The second man replied, "That ain't the reason. Can't afford to kill jackrabbits no more. Catch 'em and milk 'em and turn 'em loose. One you seen prob'ly gone dry."

The unfortunate President took his lumps from everyone. On stage a comic said, "What, you say business is better? You mean Hoover died?" His partner followed with a story that Hoover asked Secretary of the Treasury Andrew Mellon for a nickel to phone a friend. Mellon gave him a dime and said, "Phone both of them." Mellon himself was the butt of much criticism. Even children were singing:

Mellon pulled the whistle,
Hoover rang the bell.
Wall Street gave the signal,
And the country went to hell.

SUFFER THE LITTLE CHILDREN (AND THEIR TEACHERS)

Schools suffered more than many institutions because they were victims of local government's inadequate tax base. Some closed for several months of the year. Some had to put desks in the halls. Some used textbooks until they fell apart. Teachers "boarded round," meaning they stayed with, or at least took meals with, their students one at a time.

New York found that twenty percent of the city's schoolchildren were suffering from malnutrition. In the mining regions of Kentucky, Ohio, West Virginia, and Illinois, the rate was sometimes as high as ninety percent. One teacher told a little girl to go home and get something to eat. "I can't," the girl said. "It's my sister's turn today."

Teaching was—at least at first—considered a "safe" job; there would always be a need for teachers. But every job opening brought a flock of applicants. Eventually school boards started inventing reasons for not hiring those applicants who did not make it. A New York City board told a grossly overweight woman she was not being hired because the board feared she would present a fire hazard in the halls!

Teaching was not a good Depression occupation for long. When the money began to run out, many courageous teachers went on working anyway, sometimes feeding children out of their own meager pocketbooks.

The story of the Chicago schools is almost epic. Teachers taught on despite "payless paydays" or payment in scrip that bankers would not redeem. Many lost their homes to loan sharks who charged as much as forty-two percent interest.

Having a college degree did not guarantee work. In Oskaloosa, Iowa, an unemployed teacher and her two children spent two winters living in a tented hole in the ground. A Brooklyn bum hauled into court for spending forty-six days in a vacant lot turned out to be an alumnus of the University of Colorado who had worked as an engineer in South America and China.

College graduates who found work might be office boys or elevator operators. Unemployed architects turned out jigsaw puzzles. An unemployed draftsman named Alfred Butts, with no work on his desk, began fiddling around with word puzzles and later patented one of them. He called it Scrabble.

Students in colleges knew they would come out into a world that had no place for them, and they sang:

> *I sing in praise of college,*
> *Of M.A.s and Ph.D.s.*
> *But in pursuit of knowledge*
> *We are starving by degrees.*

THE PLOWMAN'S PLIGHT

The American farmer, long proud of his self-reliance, suffered as much as anyone else—and in many cases more. He had the food for sale, but no one to buy it. At the same time, there was no comparable decline in the things he needed to buy, and fixed charges such as interest rates and taxes remained high.

Farm produce brought such low prices, dairy farmers poured milk into the streets to make it scarce and up its price. Others fed mutton to buzzards and burned corn in stoves. When Hoover proposed federal loans to farmers for feeding livestock, outraged citizens taunted him for thinking it all right to feed animals but not men, women, and children.

In some states there were riots when bankers threatened to foreclose on farms. Pitchfork-bearing farmers blocked the roads to Sioux City, Iowa. Wisconsin dairy farmers dumped 34,000 pounds of milk and poured gas in the vats. Bitter over a system that paid them 2¢ for a quart of milk that a distributor would sell for 8¢, they railed against the money-changers of the marketplace. Some sang:

> *Let's call a farmers' holiday,*
> *A holiday let's hold.*
> *We'll eat our wheat and ham and eggs*
> *And let them eat their gold.*

GONE WITH THE WIND

As if the farmers didn't have enough trouble, the drought and dust storms of the early '30s magnified them tenfold. The 1920s had been a period of high moisture in the grasslands of the West, but in 1930 the rains stopped abruptly, as they did in other arid parts of the world.

It was the worst in Oklahoma, Kansas, and Texas—the "Dust Bowl." Small lakes dried up, streams disappeared. Field mice crept into country schools to drink from ink wells.

When the dust storms came they buried cars and telephone poles. Street lights burned at noon. People wore handkerchiefs and goggles, and tried to seal cracks in their house with gummed paper, but the dust seeped in nevertheless. Sleepers put wet towels over their cracked lips, but the grit got in their teeth anyway.

Cattle rustling increased, and police arrested anyone who used water illegally. The earth was so hard after the topsoil blew away a farmer had to use two or three mules where he used to need only one.

The effects of drought and dust were felt in twenty-two states of the Great Plains and Midwest, but even the eastern seaboard was not immune. Dust storms that started in the Plains deposited grit not only in the eastern states but as far as 200 miles out to sea.

In one day 50 million tons of topsoil blew away, and in May 1934, when 300 million tons of dust blew over the East, congressmen who had previously opposed such measures gritted their teeth (literally) and voted $5 million for controlling soil erosion.

Despite it all, people still told jokes like these three:

> A raindrop hit a fellow over in the next county yesterday and they had to throw three buckets of dirt on him to bring him to.

> A rancher hauled a load of gravel to his house and threw it on the roof so his children would know what rainfall sounded like.

> A man went to the bank for a loan on his farm, but the banker glanced out the window and saw the farm blowing past.

SOME FOR THE ROAD

Thousands left the Dust Bowl and headed for greener climes, especially California. The largest outpouring, at first, was from Oklahoma, but before long all Dust Bowl emigrants were called "Okies" no matter where they came from. In *The Grapes of Wrath* John Steinbeck brilliantly recorded their odyssey in prose, while Woody Guthrie captured the essence of the movement in song.

> *"Almost everybody is a Okie now days," said Guthrie. "That means you ain't got no home, or don't know how long you're gonna have the one you're in. Sort of means, too, that you're out of a job. Or owe more than you can rake or scrape. Okies has come to include all of the folks the rich folks has et up."*

Many states had to adopt stringent methods of dealing with Okies. At first California put them in forced labor camps, but eventually posted guards on the border to keep them out.

"Riding the rods"—riding on a train without a ticket—became a national practice. City officials in Kansas City, one of the nation's railroad hubs, estimated that 700 train-hoppers a day passed through their yards.

In 1932, the worst year of the Depression, the city of Chicago estimated that on a given night 200 women could be found sleeping in Grant Park.

In Pittsburgh, unemployed steel workers slept in the steel pipes their former employers could no longer sell, or in the coke ovens they once stoked.

In New York's Central Park, a man made his home in a large baby buggy.

In Oakland, California, former city sanitation workers slept in sewer pipes.

In Los Angeles, a street railway company donated fifty ancient trolley cars for living quarters.

All over the country, desperate citizens burrowed out rooms in large abandoned sandpiles, their smokestacks sticking out the top.

HOME, SWEET HOME

Those who had homes fought desperately to keep them. On any given day a judge's case load was nine-tenths eviction cases or vagrancy charges. During the first three weeks of 1932 one judge handled—or tried to handle—425 eviction cases a day. But if a landlord dumped a tenant's furniture in the street, the installment company had better pick it up right away. If not, it would disappear in a hurry, piece by piece. Some of the thieves burned the furniture to keep warm.

Some city employees saw their homes auctioned off for failure to pay, say, $35 in back taxes, while the city owed them several hundred dollars in back pay.

One woman came home to find her house padlocked, with her three children, including an infant, inside. Afraid to touch the lock, she climbed in a window, nursed the baby, then climbed out and went to the police to appeal to them to let her children out.

Some tenants with no money concocted elaborate deceptions to avoid paying the rent. A favorite technique was to knock holes in the walls, then demand they be repaired before paying up.

Some Harlem blacks found a way to get rent money and have fun at the same time: the house-rent party. They would charge a small admission price in addition to selling pigs' feet and chitterlings. They might send invitations like this one in rhyme:

> *There'll be plenty of pigs' feet*
> *And lots of gin.*

Just ring the bell
And come on in.

Parties were usually held on Thursday or Saturday nights—the days off for most domestic servants—and could go on all night. Next day the landlord got his rent money. The idea spread to other large cities, and some whites picked it up as well.

HOME ECONOMICS

With little or no money to spare, Americans economized in ways that might seem pathetic today. These are some eocnomies used in the home:

1. Reweaving socks.

2. Resoling shoes with rubber from old ties.

3. Relining coats with old blankets.

4. Splitting sheets up the middle, flipping them, then resewing them to equalize wear.

5. Steaming off postage stamps to be used again (if the Post Office's marking machine had missed the stamp, as it often does).

6. Sharpening old razor blades.

7. Using only 25-watt bulbs.

8. Rolling one's own cigarettes.

Some families opened a "parlor grocery" in their homes; some converted their lawns into miniature golf courses; and some textile workers set up looms in their living rooms. The poor saved on heat by warming up only their kitchens and by cooking only once a week—if they had anything to cook. Down at the office, the boss had pulled all clocks from the wall to save electricity.

FDR and the New Deal

It is hard to say when a depression begins and ends, but it is safe to say this one started soon after the cataclysmic stock market crash in 1929 and didn't completely stop until the United States entered World War II. It was the sudden wartime boom that put the finishing touches on that unhappy era, but before that, President Franklin D. Roosevelt had done his best to bring it to an end—and in large measure had succeeded.

At the beginning of his administration, during the famous Hundred Days in which opponents agreed to a moratorium on criticism, Roosevelt inaugurated more federal programs than had all three presidents before him. And it is a tribute to his success that many of these programs outlasted his time and some are still in use today: the Social Security System, Federal Depositors Insurance Corporation (FDIC), Tennessee Valley Authority (TVA), and Federal Housing Authority (FHA), for example.

The people of this ravaged land knew there was a determined spirit in the White House when their new president did not go to his own inaugural ball (he sent his wife Eleanor, though), but stayed in his office to start work on Depression remedies. He took down Hoover's elegant trappings and replaced them with plain, traditional ones. There were no more footmen or buglers. Gone also were the seven-course meals; guests, in fact, sometimes complained of the monotonous fare at the White House table. The president ordered that anyone phoning the White House in distress should not be put off; some member of the staff must be found to listen to him.

"No president in so short a time has inspired so much hope," the *New York Times* editorialized. One congressman compared FDR to Jesus Christ. In a poll of New York schoolchildren, God ran a poor second to Franklin D. Roosevelt.

THE RED DEAL?

Although Roosevelt seemed like the Almighty to schoolchildren and was considered a savior by many adults, he certainly was not without his critics. Some critics said he went too far with his Depression remedies, others not far enough. The President's most encompassing program was the National Recovery Act (NRA), which sought the cooperation of business and industry in complying with government codes on prices and competition. Before the Supreme Court struck down the NRA as unconstitutional, critics had a field day with it. Some laughed that the initials stood for "National Run Around" or "No Recovery Allowed." They said Roosevelt was "Franklinstein" and the NRA his monster.

Critics from the far right called NRA—and the whole New Deal—a gigantic communist conspiracy. They enjoyed with bit of verse written in the editorial rooms of the *New York American*:

> *A Red Deal with a Soviet seal*
> *Endorsed by a Moscow hand.*
> *The strange result of an alien cult*
> *In a liberty-loving land.*
> *The truth is out and there is no doubt*
> *Of the trend of the New Deal heads.*
> *Their plans are made and their courses laid*
> *With the blessings of the Reds . . .*

Of many other criticisms in verse, prose, song, and oratory, this parody called the "23rd Spasm" seems to have been the most popular:

> *Roosevelt is my shepherd, I am in want.*
> *He maketh me to lie down on park benches.*
> *He leadeth me beside the still factories.*

He disturbeth my soul.
He leadeth me in the paths of destruction
    For his party's sake.
Yea, though I walk through the valley of recession,
I anticipate no recovery.
    For he is with me.
His promises and pipe dreams they no longer fool me.
He preparest a reduction of my salary
    In the presence of my creditors.
He anointeth my small income with taxes.
Surely unemployment and poverty shall follow me
    All the days of the New Deal,
And I will dwell in a mortgaged house forever.

WE PIDDLE AROUND

Of all New Deal programs, the WPA took the worst beating from critics. Instead of Works Progress Administration, the opposition said WPA stood for "We Piddle Around."

Criticism of the new agency brought the word "boondoggle" into our language. A WPA handicrafts teacher told reporters he was teaching cowboys how to "boondoggle"—to make saddle trappings and belts out of odd bits of leather. It was a legitimate activity and its products useful items, but critics seized upon the word and used it as a derisive term for a deliberate waste of the government's money. Some felt the term an apt one when one of its first uses was to describe a WPA project reporters had turned up in New York City: several unemployed research assistants had been hired to make a study of ancient safety pins.

But the WPA put thousands to work, and not just building roads, public housing, and football stadiums. It also gave employment to writers, actors, and artists. Although many congressmen did not like giving money to people who "push a pen," the agency's projects saved the talents—and perhaps even the sanity—of many writers who were put to work on government books and pamphlets.

Although some applicants had little connection with the world of art, they were kept busy painting posters, designing stage sets, embroidering seat covers, and ransacking old houses for antiques worthy of preservation.

The Federal Theater Project brought theater to people who had never seen a play—or a real live actor before. Such professionals as Burt Lancaster, Orson Welles, and Joseph Cotton took part.

Still the opposition never missed a chance to get in a dig at the agency. They applauded when a Massachusetts woman put her foot in the way of a WPA wall being built and refused to move it. And they whooped with delight when the agency had to halt construction of a fish hatchery in Florida because a cow ate the blueprints.

Some favorite WPA jokes:

> A farmer asked the druggist for "some of that WPA poison. I hear it won't kill squirrels, but it will make them so lazy I can stomp them to death."

> A WPA worker sued the government for damages suffered when the shovel on which he was leaning broke.

> There is a new cure for cancer, but nobody can get any of it: it's sweat from a WPA worker.

> Don't shoot our still life. It may be a WPA man at work.

FDR's Critics

EVERY MAN A KING

Who, specifically, were FDR's critics, and what did they propose in place of New Deal measures? One vociferous one, the outspoken and powerful Senator Theodore Bilbo of Mississippi, thought we should send all 12 million American blacks to Africa to ease the unemployment problem. H. L. Mencken, the writer known for his caustic wit, thought Roosevelt was on the verge of establishing a monarchy. He proposed we go ahead and make FDR king; then we could dispose of him in the traditional manner—by beheading him.

Bernarr Macfadden, a well-known physical culturist, said why not put all the unemployed in cold storage and revive them when prosperity returns. Walter P. Chrylser, president of the Chrysler Corporation, thought the Depression would end if everyone bought an automobile; that would put more money in circulation and provide innumerable jobs. (Does this sound familiar?)

Serious challengers to Roosevelt's leadership included Senator Huey P. Long from Louisiana; Father Charles E. Coughlin, a radio priest; and Frances E. Townsend, an unemployed doctor. FDR called Huey Long the most dangerous man in America. Long, while still governor of Louisiana, had gotten himself elected senator from that state. Afterwards he consolidated his power and became the virtual dictator of Louisiana, controlling its politics from Washington. At first the "Kingfish" (a name he adopted from the enormously popular radio show "Amos 'n' Andy") supported Roosevelt, but then became angry at the entire New Deal when his tax returns were questioned, and when federal patronage was withheld and WPA projects were suspended in his state because of irregularities in local administration.

Long had been elected on the slogan "Every Man a King, But No Man Wears a Crown." (The rule did not apply to Huey, however.) His program to lift the country out of the Depression, called the "Share-Our-Wealth Plan" would give every family a house and a lot worth $6,000, an annual income of about $2,500, a radio, an automobile, and a washing machine. Every youth would have a free college education, every veteran a bonus, and every aged person a pension. The government would get the money for this largesse by soaking the rich: no one would be allowed an annual income of more than $1 million. Needless to say, Long had widespread support among the poorer classes.

Long was considered a serious threat to FDR when he announced his intention to run for president in 1936, but before he could do so he was shot to death on the steps of the Louisiana state capitol.

FATHER COUGHLIN'S GOSPEL

Father Charles E. Coughlin was a spectacularly successful radio salesman of the gospel, but it was the gospel according to Father Coughlin. His rich, musical voice attracted millions of listeners to his regular broadcasts over a Detroit radio station and later over a national network. After a few months on the air, he was receiving more mail than anybody in the United States, including the President. His success soon went to his head, and he began interlacing his sermons with heavy doses of his peculiar brand of politics.

Like Huey Long, Coughlin was at first a firm supporter of FDR, telling his faithful flock that "the New Deal is Christ's Deal." Later disillusionment set in; he did not think Roosevelt was going far enough. He began lambasting the President in almost every broadcast, once recommending FDR's leadership be terminated with a bullet.

The good Father accused Roosevelt of catering too much to big business and high finance. He thought the government should nationalize banks and abolish the Federal Reserve System. His Fascist leanings showed themselves when he advocated forming the entire nation into a corporate state, as Hitler and Mussolini had done.

As time went on, Father Coughlin became increasingly bitter and virulent, finally mounting an open campaign of anti-Semitism. His influence then began to wane.

ONWARD TOWNSEND SOLDIERS

One day early in the Depression, Dr. Francis E. Townsend glanced out the window of his modest home in Long Beach, California, and saw three old women clawing through garbage cans in search of food. Gripped in a cold fury, he decided then to do something about the national dilemma. Townsend himself had just been laid off from his job as assistant city health officer.

The doctor's prescription for national recovery was for everyone over sixty to retire on a monthly pension of $200. They would thereby be removed from the labor market, but they must spend all of the pension money each month in order to keep plenty of cash in circulation. Money for the pensions was to come from a 2¢ tax on every business transaction; this levied in addition to the existing local, state, and federal taxes.

It seemed a simple enough remedy for the nation's ills, and tens of thousands of elderly people joined Townsend Clubs across the country. Some of them sank all their savings into the movement. They also bought Townsend stickers, Townsend buttons, Townsend tire covers, and Townsend auto plates. And they sang their marching song:

Onward pension soldiers,
Marching as to war,
With the plan of Townsend
Going on before.
This great pension leader
Bids depression go;
Join him in the battle,
Help to fight the foe.

Townsend's influence over the post-sixty generation brought him a considerable amount of political weight for a time. In 1936 he joined with Father Coughlin in an ill-fated attempt to form a third party; after which he followed the priest into decline.

TO THE POORHOUSE IN A CAR

Historian Caroline Bird says the Great Depression has not been given its proper due in the chronicles of America. It did more, she claims, to shape American life than any other event in this century.

But the Depression has also been misunderstood. It was not a period of great scarcity, but a period of unparalleled glut. There was too much of everything: too many factories turning out too many cars, radios, washing machines, and refrigerators; too much money around and too much of it going into the hands of a few wealthy people, who reinvested it in more factories and other means of production; and too many people getting too much easy credit, which caused a further overstimulation of production.

The country's ability to produce had outstripped its ability to pay—and the nation paid for the mistake. As Will Rogers said, "America will be the only country that ever went to the poorhouse in an automobile."

 Chapter 19

World War II

The Soldier at Home and Abroad

T HE NATION'S FIRST PEACETIME DRAFT began in 1940, before America entered the war. The draft began with eighteen-year-olds, but a boy could enlist at seventeen if his parents signed the papers. One high school lad, who wanted to be a fighter pilot, ate so many carrots to sharpen his vision he became temporarily orange.

Sixteen million men were drafted or enlisted, while 5 million others were rejected. Three million were turned away on account of emotional instability; other causes were hernia, flat feet, and bad eyes or teeth. Another cause of rejection was illiteracy, but later the Army inducted most of those cases and sent them to school until they reached fourth-grade level. By 1943, the draft had also lowered its physical standards to rock bottom: anyone five feet tall and weighing 105 pounds would be accepted.

The clown prince of draft evasion was a young man from Valley Station, Kentucky, who kept appearing at his draft board in various disguises to report on his rapidly deteriorating health. He came as his sister, a half-brother, a crippled old uncle, and finally, dressed in a wig and floppy hat, as his mother. The "mother" reported that her son had died, but the "deceased" boy was drafted anyway.

Almost 43,000 American men were officially classified as "conscientious objectors," those who refuse to bear arms for moral, religious, or philosophical reasons. Over half of these eventually agreed to serve in duties not requiring them to bear arms, while many others worked in Civilian Public Service Camps, which were similar to the Civilian Conservation Corps of the Depression. Six thousand, however, went to federal prisons.

WHIRLWIND ROMANCES

For a year or so after Pearl Harbor about a thousand servicemen a day got married. All too many of them were hurry-up romances, while some were between partners who had just met the night before. Private Mickey Rooney, the film star, met a seventeen-year-old girl and proposed to her on their first date; they were married after a whirlwind courtship of seven days. "I married Betty Jane because I was determined to marry some-one," he later wrote. "I'd had some drinks, was hurt and lonely, reached and grabbed."

Like Mickey Rooney and Betty Jane, the serviceman and his girl were looking for some sort of emotional anchor amid the uncertainties of the day. On the other hand, there were "Allotment Annies," women who married a uniform just to receive the $50 a month allotted a serviceman's wife and to become the beneficiary of his $10,000 life insurance policy.

Some "Annies" specialized in combat pilots because of their high mortality rate. One preyed on sailors shipping out from Norfolk Naval Base in Virginia and was married to several at the same time. Two soldiers, sipping beer in an English pub, got to comparing pictures of their wives and discovered they were married to the same one. Military police broke up the fight.

This Is the Army, Mr. Jones

The recruit soon learned the Army had a reason for everything it did, but to him the reason often made no sense. To determine his shoe size he had to hold two buckets of sand weighing a total of fifty pounds, the weight of his marching pack. When his feet spread under the weight, that was his "correct" shoe size. A man who wore a size nine shoe would be issued a size ten. Sometimes his clothes did not fit much better, especially if he was unusually large or small.

Everything the soldier received was marked "G.I." meaning "Government Issue," and from that came the nickname. The new G.I. soon learned the meaning of other terms: "mess hall" for dining room; "chow" for food; "on the double" for hurry up; "SNAFU" for "situation normal—all fouled up"; and "SOS" for chipped cream beef on toast, a culinary abomination fed him for breakfast. The initials stood for "something on a shingle" although soldiers usually used another word for the first "S."

Life in the barracks was a revelation to young men who had never been exposed to that kind of group living. The language was of the foulest sort imaginable, and some of the recruits were personally as foul as their language. When one of these had gone without a bath for as long as his comrades could stand it, they threw him in the shower. Many sergeants were abusive, and in one camp the commanding officer used a sergeant who was a former boxer to handle complaints from enlisted men by roughing them up.

Training in the field was rigorous and sometimes perilous, as recruits learned to dodge bullets and to hug the ground as artillery shells roared overhead. One G.I. wrote home: "I know what President Roosevelt meant when he said that we had nothing to fear but fear itself."

JIM CROW GOES TO WAR

African-American servicemen, to their dismay, found they generally faced more discrimination after donning a uniform than they did as civilians. In the beginning, the Navy accepted them only as mess attendants, the Marines not at all. In the Army, camp life was strictly segregated, and in no unit could an African-American officer outrank a white officer. Even blood plasma was segregated. (Ironically, Dr. Charles R. Drew, who perfected the method of preserving blood plasma, was himself an African-American.)

Many generals, even high-ranking ones, considered blacks inferior intellectually. They pointed to the African-American soldiers' poor performance on the Army General Classification Test as proof. Later psychologists would determine such tests biased in favor of middle-class whites.

Overseas, African-American soldiers were often treated better by the local populace than by white soldiers. In England their fraternization with local girls sparked a number of clashes between them and white G.I.s. British bystanders sometimes joined in on the side of the blacks.

Here at home many training camps were in the South, which brought African-American soldiers into conflict with local segregation laws. In one of the periodic outbreaks of violence—an hour-long gun battle with military police—two African-Americans were shot to death, becoming the first American casualties of World War II.

Shortly after the war began, the civil rights leader, A. Philip Randolph, threatened to lead a march on Washington if the government did not end discrimination in defense plants. Eleanor Roosevelt, the African-American's best friend in Washington, tried to dissuade Randolph with the argument that there would be no place for the demonstrators to stay or eat—Washington was a thoroughly segregated city. When it appeared the demonstration would be huge, President Roosevelt issued an executive order forbidding discrimination in defense industries and set up a commission to enforce it.

Though the order did not come close to ending discrimination, it was a big step forward. At least now there would be no more factories with separate production lines, restrooms, and drinking fountains for blacks. One factory even had a bomb shelter labeled "For Colored Only."

A year before the war ended the Army ordered all of its training facilities desegregated, but compliance was slow. A shortage of infantry replacements in the Battle of the Bulge prompted the Army to take a tentative step toward battlefield integration by attaching platoons of African-Americans to white platoons.

Yet it was not until 1948—three years after the war—that President Harry Truman signed an order officially ending segregation in America's armed services.

THE G.I. AS PACK ANIMAL

Soldiers at the front were not like the slicked-up actors who play them on the screen. Often they did not have the time—and were too tired to have the inclination—to shave, cut their hair, or take a bath. And they were likely to lose many of the other arts of civilization, such as a preference for going to the bathroom privately.

Life at the front could be degrading and dehumanizing. The G.I. became a beast of burden, carrying an average daily load of eighty-four pounds. In addition to his essential equipment—helmet, rifle, bayonet, knife, canteen—he had a belt with cartridges and hand grenades, an entrenching tool (collapsible shovel), and first-aid pouch. On his back was a pack containing a poncho, mess kit, C-rations, and gas mask. Besides this personal equipment, he might be required to carry part of his unit's heavy weapons—mortars, machine guns, Browning automatic rifles.

What the G.I. needed most was socks—clean and dry. Without a frequent change of socks, mud accumulated inside his shoes and he soon had trenchfoot. The pain was excruciating, and sometimes his feet swelled so much that his boots had to be cut off.

ROTTING IN THE JUNGLE

Fighting in Europe was of the conventional sort and against a conventional enemy. But in the Pacific the opponent was unconventional and had an entirely different sort of national background. The Japanese soldier looked like a World War I American doughboy—small, round helmet and leg wrappings—but his appearance was deceptive. He was tough, disciplined, and fanatically devoted to the pursuit of victory. Since childhood he had been taught that to die for his homeland was the greatest honor possible and that to surrender was a fate worse than death. He also thought that it was disgraceful for an enemy to give up and sometimes executed those who did.

Yet the worst enemy in the South Pacific was geography. Americans knew virtually nothing about the geography of that part of the world when the war began. The U.S. Navy started out using eighteenth-century maps and General Douglas MacArthur's men had to find out where they were from captured Japanese maps.

Americans at home tended to think of the "South Seas" as an island paradise where the weather was always perfect and all the women were as gorgeous as Dorothy Lamour, an actress who made a number of movies about those locales.

The islands could be more menacing than the Japanese Navy. Sea battles were broken off because neither commander knew where the bottom was. A triple typhoon halted the battle of Leyte Gulf in the Philippines, and a month later a storm sank three U.S. destroyers. Volcanic steam hissed through the rocks of Iwo Jima. At Cape Gloucester twenty-five Marines were killed by falling trees. Sharks sometimes ate shipwrecked sailors and those who made it to shore might be eaten by headhunters.

As much as sixteen inches of rain might fall in a single day, and when rain stopped, suffocating waves of steam rose from the marshes. Trails could be covered with waist-deep slop. Crocodiles and pythons lurked in the bayous and at night the G.I. might have to tear leeches from his rectum and genitals.

Not much light appeared through the thick vines overhead, vines that crawled with fleas, chiggers, biting ants, poisonous spiders, and unidentifiable blood-sucking insects. When scratched, bug bites turned into festering sores. Waving away swarms of flies and mosquitoes was called the "New Guinea salute," named for one of the larger islands.

G.I.s in the South Pacific called themselves "jungle bunnies." Hardly any escaped "jungle rot," hideous ulcers that formed on feet, arms, bellies, chests, and armpits. Many had dengue fever, beriberi, malaria, hookworm, dysentery, yaws, blackwater fever, and ringworm. Many ran a fever much of the time, but it was a rule of thumb in the high command that no one went to the hospital unless his temperature was over a hundred.

The Home Front

World War I was a singing war. Though World War II had its share of popular tunes, none ever became *the* song as "Over There" did in the first war. "I'll Be Seeing You" and "The White Cliffs of Dover" came close.

Songwriters worked hard, but in trying to find *the* song they often came up with such duds as:

> *You're a sap, Mr. Jap,*
> *To make a Yankee cranky.*
> *You're a sap, Mr. Jap,*
> *Uncle Sam is gonna spanky.*

Other notable flops were "The Japs Don't Have a Chinaman's Chance" and "We're Gonna Find a Feller Who Is Yeller and Beat Him Red, White and Blue."

For a time there seemed to be a concerted effort to make "Praise the Lord and Pass the Ammunition" *the* song. Disc jockeys (a term just becoming popular) played it so often, federal officials asked them to slow down lest the public tire of the song too quickly.

Most of the popular songs, unlike those in World War I, were overly sentimental. They spoke of separation and heartbreak. The best in that genre was probably "I'll Be Seeing You." Of those that referred directly to the war, the most popular were "The White Cliffs of Dover" and "When the Lights Go On Again All Over the World."

There were songs addressed to women left without romance while most of the able-bodied men marched off to fight. Such songs as "They're Either Too Young Or Too Old" lamented the fact that although a woman could once get any man she liked, she now had to like any man she could get. The sad maiden in that song found that the only males available were ones who had to be "held off or held up," and concluded her lament with a reply to another popular song, "I *can't* sit under the apple tree with anyone else but me."

Perhaps *the* song of World War II was "Lili Marlene," a German song popular on both sides. Among patriotic songs, "God Bless America" virtually replaced the difficult-to-sing "Star-Spangled Banner." Irving Berlin had written it in 1918, but put it aside until offering it to Kate Smith in 1938.

THE BIRTH OF "BLUE EYES"

The war brought with it a new phenomenon: a separate entity, almost a subculture, called the "teenager." The word had never been used for young people before, but caught on quickly after "teener" failed and the die-hard grammarians gave up.

Along with "teenager" came "bobbysoxer." The bobbysoxer's uniform was long socks and saddle shoes, rolled up blue jeans, and a boy's white dress shirt with the mandatory shirttail flapping. Mismatched shoes and socks were also the rage, as were "slumber parties" and that noble new product the "yo-yo."

On December 30, 1942, New York bobbysoxers birthed a legend when a frail young man stepped onto the stage at the Paramount Theater and began to sing in a quavering voice. Down front a girl who had skipped lunch fainted. Her companion jumped up and screamed and within a minute every girl in the audience was on her feet shrieking.

That was how it started, but from then on pandemonium broke loose everywhere the young crooner went. He received about 5,000 fan letters a week; autograph hounds, not all of whom were teenagers, ripped off his clothes. At the Waldorf-Astoria a middle-aged woman tore open her blouse and insisted he autograph her brassiere.

The young man (he was twenty-five, but looked nineteen) went on to build a pink house in Hollywood that had all the latest gadgets, including an automatic drape-opener. He did not go to war because he could not pass the physical examination.

His name was Francis Albert Sinatra; some liked to call him "Ol' Blue Eyes."

MOBILIZING SCHOOLS

The kids got a chance to do their bit for the war effort by taking part in parades, scrap drives, and bond sales. Large numbers joined the high school Victory Corps, which taught them close-order drill and the manual of arms with a wooden gun. The uniform, for both boys and girls, was a white shirt, dark trousers or skirt, and a white paper cap with a large "V" on it. Schools gave academic credit for belonging.

From 1942 on, the American school took on an entirely different complexion. There were regular air-raid drills, and the curriculum was strong in vocational-technical subjects and physical education. Practical courses—cooking, sewing, health—abounded.

Many schools offered auto mechanics, map reading, aeronautics, navigation, and even preflight training. Spelling lessons were sprinkled with military terms, English classes learned propaganda analysis, and arithmetic lessons used airplanes instead of apples.

The military also took over much of college education. Classroom studies included the chemistry of explosives, camouflage techniques, map reading, military law, and German and Japanese. Outside the classroom, students learned marksmanship and the art of the bayonet. Open campus areas became rifle ranges and obstacle courses.

Colleges began granting three-year B.A.s, while medical and law schools also lopped a year off their requirements. In some cases, the senior year of high school was lumped in with the freshman college year.

"SCRAP THE JAP"

Virtually every American, it seemed, pitched in to help the government with its scrap drives. The steel scrap drive of 1942 was inaugurated with such slogans as "Slap a Jap With Scrap!" and "Hit Hitler With Junk!" Bing Crosby recorded the song "Junk Will Win the War."

The scrap turned in included parts of the *Maine* dredged up from Havana harbor and a pair of horseshoes from Robert E. Lee's horse, "Traveller." Citizens were asked to drop old keys in "Key Kans" strategically placed everywhere. San Francisco courts would take a traffic violator's bumper in lieu of a cash fine.

The government asked for 4 million tons of scrap metal in the first two months of 1942—and got 5 million tons in three weeks. Peetz, Colorado, claimed the championship of the 1942 drive when its 207 citizens rounded up 225 tons, more than a ton per person.

Metal was not the only thing saved for the war effort. With the world's chief rubber-producing lands in the hands of the Japanese, rubber was also in short supply. Sally Rand, the famous striptease artist, donated fifty of the balloons she used in her act.

President Roosevelt turned in the floor mats from all White House cars, while at gas stations Boy Scouts begged motorists for theirs. The Senate and the House of Representatives gave up the mats under their spittoons.

When citizens were asked to turn in old newspapers and magazines, the paper piles in some cities became so big they had to be burned to chase off the rats. When the government called for phonograph records to recover their precious shellac, they piled up by the millions.

PLAYING HARD TO GET

The biggest sacrifice made by most people on the home front was giving up so many things they wanted and needed, items they had always taken for granted. Some twenty items, from gasoline to tomato ketchup, were rationed; some others, such as nylon stockings, were hard to find whether rationed or not.

Nylon was needed to make parachutes. Canned foods were rationed because tin was needed for armaments and the containers for the soldiers' C-rations. Coffee was rationed not only because it was the soldier's standard drink, but because the ships that used to bring the beans from South America had been drafted for military purposes. Sugar, the first item to be rationed, was hard to get for similar reasons.

Rationing was a cumbersome business. Each month some 3 billion stamps, each smaller than a postage stamp, changed hands. There were red stamps for meat, butter, and fat (fats were used to make explosives) and blue ones for canned goods. Everything worked on a point system: meat was so many points, butter so many, and so forth. The points were marked on the stamps and on the goods to be sold, but the consumer could not always rely on the system. The number of points needed to buy something fluctuated with that product's availability, especially in the case of meat.

Rationing of gasoline was even more elaborate. Motorists received a windshield sticker indicating their priority as gasoline users. Pleasure drivers received an "A" sticker, the lowest priority; they could have from three to five gallons a week, depending on the supply and the region of the country. At the other end of the scale was the "E" sticker, for emergency use only; it was reserved for police and firemen.

Rationing, and ceiling prices too, were managed by the OPA (Office of Price Administration). Over 5,000 local OPA boards operated much the same as local draft boards. The agency, as one might expect, became everyone's favorite wartime scapegoat. The whole nation guffawed when the Philadelphia office forgot to ration enough heating fuel for its own use, and had to shut down for the rest of the month.

Among the items shoppers simply could not find, rationed or not, were lawnmowers, alarm clocks, beer mugs, boxed candy, brushes made of hair or bristle, and glass eyes. (Most of the glass eyes were imported from Germany.) The demand for alarm clocks was so great, however, that the government finally authorized production of a "victory model" that contained very little metal.

Many Americans doubtless agreed with the rhymester who wrote:

> *And when I die, please bury me*
> *'Neath a ton of sugar, by a rubber tree.*
> *Lay me to rest in an auto machine*
> *And water my grave with gasoline.*

The Issei and Nisei

GENERATIONS OF VIPERS?

There were some courageous home-front soldiers not in uniform; they were, in fact, behind barbed wire. They were the Issei, first-generation Japanese Americans, and their children, the Nisei—and their treatment during the war was a national disgrace.

Their troubles did not begin after Pearl Harbor, as one might expect, but after a long string of Japanese victories in 1942. Americans wanted the vengeance they could not achieve on the battlefield.

The majority of Japanese-Americans lived in California, and everyone assumed that state would also be the first to suffer in the event of a Japanese attack. So that is where the trouble began for the Issei and Nisei. Suddenly they found insurance companies had cancelled their policies; milkmen would not deliver milk to them; grocery stores would not sell them groceries; banks would not cash their checks; gas stations refused them service; and they were not allowed to use the public toilets.

Signs appeared in barber shops: "JAPS SHAVED—NOT RESPONSIBLE FOR ACCIDENT"; and in restaurant windows: "THE MANAGEMENT POISONS RATS AND JAPS."

When a New Jersey farmer hired five Nisei workers, vigilantes burned his barn and threatened to kill his child.

Then came the thunderbolt: an executive order from the White House told all people of Japanese descent they had forty-eight hours to dispose of land, homes, and businesses before moving to "relocation centers" in various parts of the country. They could take with them only what they could carry in hand luggage.

Then the government found it had a problem—state governors did not want to turn over any of their facilities to house these pariahs. That meant the centers had to be built on land owned by the federal government—and those areas were invariably far out in the boondocks.

In the meantime, the Issei and Nisei were taken by truck convoy to fifteen assembly areas, including the Rose Bowl and the racetracks at Santa Anita, where many lived temporarily in horse stalls. Liquor and razors were confiscated and the right of appeal denied.

After moving to the "relocation centers" (actually concentration camps with barbed wire, watchtowers, and floodlights), Japanese-Americans found themselves living in 20' x 25' "apartments" without heat or running water. The only toilet facilities were latrines, the only bathing facilities open shower stalls where women had to bathe in full view of sentries.

Hollywood was busy meanwhile helping the government prepare the American public to accept this outrageous situation. The film *Little Tokyo, U.S.* showed Los Angeles's "Little Tokyo" district to be a hotbed of espionage, while *Air Force* tried to prove Hawaii's Japanese-Americans were double-dealers also. In *Betrayal from the East*, a popular Nisei cheerleader at Stanford turned out to be a spy.

PROVING PATRIOTISM

Despite everything, the Issei and Nisei proved themselves to be unfailing patriots. In the camps they raised the American flag every morning and saluted it while their own Boy Scout drum and bugle corps played the national anthem. In the evenings they sang "America, the Beautiful."

They planted trees, experimented with artificial rubber, and painted recruiting posters.

In 1943, when young Nisei men were allowed to enlist, they joined up in droves, taking the oath while still behind barbed wire. The Army formed them into two units, the 100th Infantry and the 442nd Infantry; both served with distinction in Italy, and neither ever had a desertion.

Nisei soldiers, of course, had a point to prove, and the 442nd in particular more than proved it. The unit emerged from the war as the most decorated regiment in the history of the United States Army. It won 3,000 Purple Hearts (some soldiers had a whole pocketful of them), 810 Bronze Stars, 342 Silver Stars, 47 Distinguished Service Crosses, and 17 Legion of Merits. Hardly a man was not decorated, and many were decorated numerous times. The regiment had become a legend.

Nisei soldiers had proved their loyalty and their fighting mettle, but they also hoped this would help their families reclaim lost property in California. Alas, that did not happen, and when the Issei and Nisei returned, they still were not treated well for some time. Public opinion changed only gradually.

America Under Attack?

"JAPS DROP BOMBS ON WEST COAST" "SABOTEURS LAND ON LONG ISLAND AND FLORIDA COAST!" No, these headlines never made the papers, but they could have if the government hadn't suppressed the information until the war was over.

The headlines would have been misleading, however. The bombing of the West Coast was done by a single plane carrying two incendiary bombs. The plane, a fighter known as a Zero, had been brought to the coast in a special watertight compartment aboard a submarine and was launched from the deck with a catapult. Its mission was to drop the bombs in an Oregon forest and start a firestorm that would sweep down the coast. It failed because the fire the bombs set off refused to spread and sputtered out.

The plane returned to the launching site and landed on pontoons. Three weeks later it tried again, with the same results.

Shortly before these "raids," German submarines had launched two sets of saboteurs, four each in Florida and on Long Island. All had lived in the United States before the war and spoke fluent English. Those who landed in Florida split into two groups, one going to New York, the other to Chicago.

The four who landed on Long Island were caught with their pants down: an unarmed Coast Guardsman saw them while they were changing into civilian clothes on the beach. He reported them to the FBI, which discovered their cache of arms and explosives. Meanwhile, the spies had gone into New York, bought clothes on Fifth Avenue, and dined at Dinty Moore's restaurant. Two of them, both naturalized Americans, became disillusioned with their project in pretty short order and blabbed to the FBI. All four were arrested, along with the two later arrivals from Florida and the two in Chicago.

All of them were sentenced to death, but President Roosevelt commuted the sentences of the two defectors to thirty years in prison, of which they served five. The other six were electrocuted.

There was one air raid, if you could call it that, that was successful to some degree. Late in the war, the Japanese sent in our direction thousands of large paper balloons, each carrying several thirty-pound bombs timed to explode three to five days after launching. The balloons were released in Japan to ride the high-velocity stratospheric air currents across the Pacific. They were ingeniously designed to dip toward the ground, drop one bomb, then soar upward again to distribute the rest of the load in the same manner.

About 300 bombs reached the U.S. and Canada—some coming as far inland as Iowa and Kansas—and set off several fires. Most of them did not explode, but one that did took six lives. That one landed on Oregon's Mount Gearhart, where it was found by a woman and five children who were on a church camping trip. They were the only victims of Japanese "air raids" in the United States.

Chapter 20

The Black Revolution

No to Jim Crow

THE MONTGOMERY BUS BOYCOTT

THE BLACK REVOLUTION began in Montgomery, Alabama, in 1955 when Mrs. Rosa Parks, a forty-two-year-old seamstress, was arrested for sitting in the "white section" of a city bus. Mrs. Parks said later she was not trying to start anything; she was just tired and her feet hurt.

Civil rights leaders in the South rejoiced over the arrest. The white power structure had erred grievously. The police should have arrested Mrs. Parks for disorderly conduct or disobeying the orders of a bus driver, as they usually did in such cases. Instead they charged her with violating a city ordinance requiring blacks to sit in the back of a bus. Now this Jim Crow law could be tested in court.

The case gave birth to the Montgomery Improvement Association, which the young minister Martin Luther King rather reluctantly agreed to shepherd. The association brought forth a long list of complaints against the city bus service: drivers had called African Americans "black apes"; a pregnant black woman had been made to give her seat to a white woman; a driver had shut the door on a blind man's leg and sped off; and in one case a black man had been forced from the bus at gunpoint because he did not have the correct change. There was also the ridiculous procedure of having blacks pay in front, then go out and reenter through the rear door, even in a pouring rain. During rush hours, the driver sometimes roared off and left customers standing there.

While the world watched, Montgomery blacks boycotted city buses for a year, a move later adjudged to have been ninety-five percent effective. Blacks walked to work or carpooled. Some whites paid cab fare for their domestics or picked them up themselves.

So many churches in the North and East sent station wagons that every black church in Montgomery had one of its own. No company, though, was willing to insure the station wagons. In desperation, civil rights leaders appealed to Lloyd's of London, the international firm that boasts it will insure anything. Without knowing even the makes or motor numbers, Lloyd's provided a binder on "nineteen station wagons, nineteen Christian churches, Montgomery, Alabama."

Montgomery police arrested carpool drivers for operating a franchise without a license, but while the cases were before the judge, the U.S. Supreme Court ended the matter by declaring discrimination in public transportation unconstitutional. The ruling came in early December, and as a white man entered a bus next day he said, "I can see this isn't going to be a white Christmas." The black man sitting next to him smiled and nodded.

A LITTLE TROUBLE IN LITTLE ROCK

The trouble in Little Rock in the fall of 1957 had political rather than racial roots. Orval Faubus intended to run for a third term as governor of Arkansas; only one Arkansas governor had ever won a third term, and that had been more than seventy years before. The two-term tradition, Faubus knew, would be hard to beat.

Hence the governor created a problem that, regardless of the outcome, would make him a hero to countless numbers of segregationists—and win him enough votes to stay in the governor's mansion for another two years.

The city of Little Rock had developed a model seven-year integration plan that was to begin that fall by placing nine black students with 2,000 whites at Central High School. No one expected any trouble, and apparently no one planned any—no one, that is, except Faubus. The governor began creating the kind of climate he needed by warning the U.S. Attorney General's office that there might be violence on the first day of school. He then asked the State Supreme Court to set aside the school district's integration plan because of impending trouble. The court obliged, but a U.S. District Court quickly overturned the ruling. Little Rock's mayor was astonished by this tempest in what appeared to be an empty teapot, saying, "We had no reason to believe there would be violence. There was no indication whatever." Five hundred FBI agents sent to the city found no evidence of unrest.

On statewide television Faubus announced that because the city was on the brink of riot he was stationing National Guard troops around Central High with orders to prevent the nine blacks from entering. The red now rose in a lot of necks, and on the opening day of school a crowd of some 1,000 gathered in front of the school. Some were merely curious bystanders, but others had mayhem on their minds. A band of toughs began attacking reporters who didn't have Southern accents, and while they were doing so, the nine blacks slipped into the school unnoticed. Because of the explosive situation, however, the mayor ordered the school closed for the day.

The same sort of crowd, except larger, gathered every day until President Dwight D. Eisenhower took matters into his own hands. First he federalized the National Guard, taking authority over them away from Faubus; then he sent in a crack battle group of the 101st Airborne Division. Part of the paratroopers forced the mob back with bayonets, while others ushered the blacks into the school. The troops remained on the campus, setting up tents behind the tennis courts, until November, when things seemed under control. Some soldiers were stationed in the halls, where Faubus accused them of paying overdue attention to the female students.

Faubus got his third term, and another three after that—twelve years altogether.

The Push Toward Freedom

SIT-INS DOWN SOUTH

The "sit-in" movement began in 1960 when four black students from North Carolina A&T College in Greensboro decided to sit down at the lunch counter in a Woolworth's store and remain there until served or arrested. Nothing happened; the management didn't know what to do. Next day, twenty other students helped occupy most of the seats all day. On the fourth day, white students from the University of North Carolina Women's College joined them.

The movement spread throughout the city to shopping centers, drive-ins and drugstores. Before long there were so many volunteers they had to operate in shifts, with hundreds more on the waiting list. When the management pulled up the seats, the students continued to occupy the space standing up. When the movement spread to other cities, CORE (Congress of Racial Equality) and SNCC (Student Non-violent Coordinating Committee, pronounced "Snick") began training courses for sit-in volunteers.

Sometimes more happened to a sitter than simply being refused service or arrested. John Lewis, a student organizer in Nashville, Tennessee, tells of being locked in at a hamburger stand in Nashville while the manager fumigated the place. He and his sitters got out only after the Nashville Fire Department arrived and broke out the windows. Lewis, who became a leader in the sit-in movement, also tells what happened when his group tried to desegregate the lunch counter of a Trailways bus station in Nashville:

> *[They] just closed down the counter and closed the restaurant. And we got very sleepy and we would put our heads down, and this waitress would walk around with this big knife, hatchetlike, and she said, "This is not a hotel. There will be no sleeping here." And little things came out of that whole effort. Somebody said, "We can't serve you. We don't serve niggers," and somebody said, "Well, we don't eat them."*

GETTING RICH'S

Students at the all-black University of Atlanta mounted a propaganda campaign against that citadel of the white elite in Atlanta, Rich's Department Store. They began by asking the store's black customers to "close your account with segregation" by mailing in to them their charge cards, which the students kept in a safety-deposit box.

When it came time for sit-ins in the store's restaurant, the students called on their most distinguished alumnus, Martin Luther King, to lead them. At first King demurred: he was on probation after being arrested in De Kalb County for not transferring his driver's license back to Georgia after returning from Montgomery. His advisers told him that sitting-in at that time was risky. Knowing he could not let his followers down, King later agreed, and led seventy-five students, all singing "We Shall Overcome," to the store's Magnolia Room.

Dick Rich, the owner, wept when he saw King sit down, but he had all seventy-six arrested. When the judge remembered King was on probation, he had him remanded, in chains, to the De Kalb County Court. For violating his probation on a simple first-offense traffic charge, the civil rights leader was sentenced to four months at hard labor in the state penitentiary at Reidsville, where blacks were sometimes beaten and even shot. He was locked up in solitary confinement.

It was only a week before the 1960 presidential election. Richard Nixon missed a chance to endear himself to black voters by protesting such treatment; he was more concerned with maintaining his slim lead in the polls in three Southern states.

Not so with the Kennedy brothers. John F. Kennedy called King's wife Coretta and expressed his concern. Robert Kennedy, JFK's campaign manager, went a step further by telephoning the judge and asking him to allow King out on bail. The call aroused national attention and the judge agreed to the request. Reverend Martin Luther King, Sr., told a cheering crowd, "If I had a suitcase full of votes, I'd take them all and place them at Senator Kennedy's feet."

The following Sunday thousands of black preachers around the country praised the Kennedys from their pulpits. On election day seven out of ten black voters cast their ballots for John F. Kennedy, providing the margin of victory for the young senator in several states, and quite possibly giving him the election.

FREEDOM RIDING

As early as 1946 the U.S. Supreme Court had outlawed segregation in interstate travel, but the South had widely ignored the decision. In May 1961, CORE wrote the President, the Justice Department, and the Greyhound and Trailways bus companies that they intended to do something about that by riding across the South in the front of the bus—and for good measure would desegregate restrooms, lunch counters, and water fountains.

Through Virginia and North Carolina two busloads were not bothered, and through South Carolina and Georgia only a little. It was when they hit Alabama and Mississippi that the Freedom Riders knew they would become Rough Riders.

The rough part began at Anniston, Alabama, where a mob tossed a firebomb inside the Greyhound bus and held the doors so the Riders could not get out—until the mob ran away for fear the bus would explode.

The Trailways bus escaped the mob in Anniston and made it safely to Birmingham, but there the Freedom Riders' good fortune ended abruptly when a group of whites armed with baseball bats and chains beat them unmercifully for close to half an hour. The attack came on Mother's Day, and when Birmingham Public Safety Commissioner Eugene "Bull" Connor was asked where his police were he replied, "Visiting their mothers." A Ku Klux Klansman, who had been a paid informer for the FBI at the time of the attack, told a Senate committee in 1975 that Connor had promised Klan leaders he would not let his men interfere for at least fifteen minutes after the bus arrived.[1]

The Riders spent the night in jail, and next day police took them in patrol cars to the Tennessee-Alabama state line, dumped them, and told them to find a way home. They returned, however, and vowed to continue their ride through the South. When they sat down in the white waiting room at the Jackson, Mississippi, bus station, the Riders were immediately arrested and taken to jail. Meanwhile, more than 300 other Freedom Riders poured into Jackson and filled all the jails.

They were not physically mistreated in the Jackson jails, but there were not-so-subtle forms of psychological brutality. The food was made so unpalatable, mostly by dumping salt in it, that the prisoners could scarcely eat it. Those who smoked were tormented by guards walking by and blowing smoke into their faces. They were all told to strip and were issued undershorts to wear—nothing else. The larger men got little shorts, the smaller men big ones, and the Riders were mixed up in the cells in such a way that there could be no switching. The larger men tried to keep theirs shut, while the smaller ones fought to keep theirs up.

The Riders had planned to stay in jail until the city of Jackson went broke supporting them, but after finding out forty days was the maximum one could stay in jail and still file an appeal, CORE bailed them all out on the fortieth day—and almost went broke themselves.

THE "BATTLE OF OLE MISS"

In the fall of 1962, James Meredith became the first black student to register at the University of Mississippi in Oxford, but not without two deaths and a bloody battle between white segregationists on one hand and United States marshals and Army troops on the other.

The courts had ordered that Meredith, a nine-year veteran of the Air Force, be admitted to "Ole Miss," but when he first tried to register he was greeted by mobs of white students singing "Glory, glory, segregation." He was then officially turned away by the segregationist governor, Ross Barnett, who read a grandiloquent proclamation denying him admittance—and then presented the embossed document to Meredith as a souvenir.

In his capacity as U.S. Attorney General, Robert Kennedy telephoned Barnett and talked to him about the problem.

"It would be best for him not to go to Ole Miss," insisted Barnett.

"But he *likes* Ole Miss," Kennedy said.

After Meredith was turned away a second time, this time by Lieutenant Governor Paul Johnson, Kennedy entered into some ridiculous bargaining designed to allow Barnett to save face with his segregationist followers and at the same time avoid violence. Kennedy suggested a scenario that would have thirty marshals escort Meredith to the campus and when one of them pulled an unloaded gun Barnett would step aside. No, Barnett said, that wouldn't be good enough—all thirty marshals had to draw.

"How about if the other marshals just slap their holsters?" Kennedy wanted to know.

No, that wasn't good enough either, said Barnett. Kennedy reluctantly agreed to the deal, but at the last minute Barnett backed out. He called Kennedy to say that the crowd was too angry; he didn't think he could control it. Realizing he was the only one who knew of the deal, the governor was also afraid he might be the only one to step aside.

After a circuit court found Barnett in contempt of court and ordered him to pay $1,000 a day until the new student was registered, Barnett asked for another deal. This time he would divert the crowd at Oxford while marshals registered Meredith in Jackson. Kennedy agreed, but the night before the registration was to take place Barnett again reneged.

Finally the governor arranged for a quiet registration on the campus at 5:00 P.M. on a Sunday, when few students would be around. Assistant Attorney General Nicholas Katzenbach flew down to take charge of 400 marshals, all white Southerners. The locals found out, however, and a crowd of some 3,000 gathered and shouted, "Two, four, one, three, we hate "Kennedy!" Unaccountably, a contingent of state troopers was ordered by radio (by whom no one knows) to leave the campus.

When the snarling mob began throwing rocks and bottles and then sniping at them, the marshals took refuge in the school's administration building. Kennedy had ordered them not to use their weapons unless Meredith's life was in danger, and since Meredith was secreted away in another part of the campus, the marshals could fire only gas grenades. Troops from Memphis, who had promised to be there within two hours of being called, took five hours to arrive. They had to fight their way in.

It was a long, bloody night, and when it was over there were two dead and forty soldiers and 166 marshals injured. Ironically, the two deaths were those of an Oxford bystander and a French journalist, who was executed with a bullet in the back of the head. James Meredith got his quiet registration at eight o'clock the next morning. As he left, a white student shouted, "Was it worth two lives, nigger?"

BIRMINGHAM BATTLEGROUND

In 1963, leaders of the Black Revolution zeroed in on Birmingham, Alabama, which many said was the most segregated city in America. There was even a city ordinance forbidding blacks and whites to play checkers together. Dr. King and the staff of his Southern Christian Leadership Conference (SCLC) came in and organized workshops for those volunteering to take part in peaceful protests. "Birmingham is the testing ground," King told them. "If we fail here we fail everywhere. . . . We've got to break the back of segregation here . . . Some are going to die, but this is the cost. It'll be another down payment on freedom."

The protests began with picketing and sit-ins. At the airport restaurant five blacks rushed the door before the management could lock them out, and they demanded to be served. They each had a ham sandwich and a glass of tea. Cost for each: $10.25. One of them didn't eat his sandwich; he took it home and put it in the refrigerator, and later in federal court introduced it as evidence. When the restaurant manager took the stand, the judge asked him if all customers paid that much for a sandwich.

"Well, no sir, judge," the manager admitted.

"Then why did you have to charge these persons $10.25 for a sandwich?"

"They were special guests."

"What made them so special—because they were black?"

When the street marches began, Bull Connor sought to stop them by siccing police dogs on the marchers and by dousing them with water from fire hoses. The tremendous pressure of the hoses knocked many off their feet. At the height of the marches upwards of 3,000 demonstrators were in jail, while hundreds more sat on the curb hoping to get in. Connor filled the Birmingham jails, the county jails, and then the jails of surrounding towns.

White racists retaliated with various acts of destruction, especially bombings. So many explosions took place in one black residential neighborhood, it became known as "Dynamite Hill." The city itself was sometimes called "Bombingham."

After the church of Fred Shuttlesworth, a civil rights activist, was bombed, the congregation rebuilt it with a sentry box in front, and someone guarded it every night. Still the church was blown up one more time.

The worst instance of bombing was at the Sixteenth Street Baptist Church, where an explosion killed four small black girls in a Bible class. When Birmingham blacks heard the news, thousands rushed into the streets. During the ensuing riots police, who claimed they "fired over their heads," killed two black boys.

In 1977, after the state of Alabama had reopened the case, Robert "Dynamite Bob" Chambliss, a well-known Birmingham Klansman, was sent to prison for life for the church bombings.

WALLACE'S LAST STAND

When George Wallace was sworn in as governor of Alabama, his inauguration address ended with the words, "Segregation now, segregation tomorrow, segregation forever!" Shortly after taking office he outfitted his state troopers with helmets and license tags decorated with Confederate flags. He threatened to send the troopers to take over in his name any school that bowed to a federal court's order to integrate, and promised that he himself would "stand in the schoolhouse door" if necessary.

In the spring of 1963 when two black students announced their intention to enroll at the University of Alabama at Tuscaloosa, Wallace had a chance to make good on his promise. He also saw a chance to become the apotheosis of the will of segregationists everywhere by striking this note of personal defiance. If he could manage to get Alabama "occupied" by federal troops, all the better.

About 3,000 federal troops did arrive in the state, and at a bivouac site near Tuscaloosa the commanding general trained a special squad to whisk Wallace away—to literally pick him up by the arms and carry him off—if he attempted to block the door of the school's administration building. The commander of the federalized Alabama National Guard, however, talked the general out of such a foolhardy scheme.

On June 11, Wallace sent his staff ahead to choose a good spot for him to make his stand, one providing the best camera angle. The staff even marked the place with white chalk. When the head of the state police announced press coverage of the event would be severely restricted, the governor quickly countermanded the order.

When Nicholas Katzenbach led federal marshals up the steps of the administration building, Wallace struck a grave pose and thrust out his hand to stop them. After the two exchanged a few words, Katzenbach left. Four hours later, when his own National Guard general arrived with state troops, Wallace stepped aside and allowed the students to register. The famous last stand ended in an inglorious fizzle.

"FREEDOM SUMMER"

In 1964, civil rights workers from across the nation descended on Mississippi, one of segregation's strongest bastions, to organize the state's blacks as a voting bloc. It was known as "Freedom Summer."

When blacks tried to register, they found certain "literacy tests" had been designed for them that were virtually impossible to pass. They were asked such questions as how many words are in the Constitution and what side of the earth the moon is on. When SNCC workers began training prospective voters to pass these tests, officials made up an entire book of such tests, and no registrant knew which one he or she would get.

Some who went to register never got there. They were intimidated by cars full of angry whites who followed them toward the courthouse. The whites might not do anything, but the blacks grew afraid and returned home. One busload going down to register was stopped by the law, and the driver was fined $100 for driving a bus with too much yellow in it!

Others gave up trying when they received letters implying their welfare checks would cease coming if they persisted in trying to vote. Some went ahead anyway and were supplied with food from outside the state, much of it paid for by the black comedian and civil rights activist Dick Gregory.

It was during that summer that the most publicized civil rights murders took place. Three SNCC workers—Michael Schwerner, 24, of New York; Andrew Goodman, 21, of New York; and James Chaney, 21, of Mississippi—were arrested in Philadelphia, Mississippi, by a sheriff's deputy for speeding. They were fined $20 and released, but none of the three was ever seen alive again.

When he heard of the disappearance of the youths, Dick Gregory hopped the next flight out of Washington and took part in the search. He quickly established himself as a hero among local blacks by his audacious badmouthing of white law officers.

> *I did something else, too [Gregory said]. I would wear a big white cowboy hat . . . because I felt that the mentality that I was dealing with was a cowboy mentality, and the big white cowboy hat could make me the good guy, and it would scare 'em. As a consequence, I never went to jail in Mississippi . . . My cowboy hat and talkin' to 'em in the way I talked to 'em, they became the boy and I became the man. They became the nigger and I became the white man.*

Gregory borrowed $25,000 and put it up as a reward for finding the missing youths. The FBI responded by putting up $30,000, and as a result, informants brought the information to both the comedian and the FBI. Still the federal agents did not act (most blacks believed they entered the case only because two of the youth were white) until Gregory held a press conference and said, "If the bodies ain't up in eighteen hours, I will lead the press down there."

The FBI men found the bodies later that same day, buried under an earthen dam on a farm. Goodman and Schwerner had both been shot in the head. Chaney, the black, had been brutally beaten to death.

The deputy sheriff, Cecil Price, and twenty other white Mississippians were tried in federal court on charges of conspiring to deny the three dead youths "life or liberty without due process." No one was charged with murder since that is not a federal offense, and state authorities had refused to prosecute the case.

The charges were dropped, but in 1967, on the basis of new charges and in a changed racial atmosphere, Price was convicted on the federal conspiracy charge and spent forty-four months in prison. The bodies of the three young men were not the only bodies found in Mississippi that summer. In searching for the victims, federal agents found several unidentified corpses, one of them a fourteen-year-old boy wearing a CORE T-shirt.

THE GREAT SELMA MARCH

The march from Selma to Montgomery in March 1965, was the grand culmination of all civil rights marches, a triumph from beginning to end. A first attempt, however, failed when the posse of Sheriff Jim Clark stopped the would-be marchers at a bridge over the Alabama River on "Bloody Sunday." Swinging billy clubs and wet bullwhips and firing tear gas, the lawmen scattered the demonstrators and badly beat many of them. The Reverend James Reeb of Boston was clubbed to death after leaving a black restaurant.

Martin Luther King flew in on Tuesday to lead the marchers, now numbering over 3,000, on the fifty-four-mile trek to the state capital on Route 50, the Jefferson Davis Highway. Governor Wallace, who had forbidden the march, appealed to President Lyndon Johnson for help. He got more than he bargained for: almost 2,000 National Guardsmen, a battalion of military police, 250 federal marshals, several FBI men, helicopters overhead, and a team of demolition experts to search roads and bridges for hidden explosives. In addition, the government provided the hikers with huge tents for overnight sleeping, a 600-gallon water truck, latrine trucks, garbage trucks, ambulances, and scout cars.

By this time, the civil rights movement knew how to organize a march for maximum effect, with a cross-section of American life always prominent. In the lead were King, Ralph Bunche, a rabbi, a priest, a nun, a pretty coed, a sharecropper in overalls, and a one-legged man on crutches. Racists strung out along the highway made obscene gestures at the nun, while others counted cadence for the one-legged man: "Left, left, left."

By the time the procession arrived in Montgomery, five days after starting, it had swelled to 25,000. By this time a second death, that of an Episcopal seminary student, had occurred. Afterwards Mrs. Viola Liuzzo, a Detroit housewife who had taken part in the march, was shot to death while driving her car back to Selma.

Fire in the Streets

THE WATTS RIOT

"Burn, baby, burn!" was the slogan of a disc jockey popular with Los Angeles blacks; ironically it was also the slogan for clean-up week of the Student Committee for the Improvement of Watts, a black section of Los Angeles. When a young black shouted the words at the beginning of the Watts riot, it was picked up by others and later became a familiar cry in other riots around the nation.

Watts was the first of hundreds of racial outbreaks, large and small, during the summers of 1965–1968. The rioting there began after a lone policeman arrested a black youth on suspicion of drunk driving. When an angry crowd gathered, the cop called for reinforcements. It was the fourth day of a brutal heat wave and tempers were short. The crowd began throwing things at the police, and by nightfall some 2,000 blacks roamed the streets, overturning cars, setting fires, and breaking into pawn shops, supermarkets, furniture stores, and liquor stores. They even broke into the Post Office—twice. That night Dick Gregory toured the area calling for order over a bullhorn; he got a bullet in the leg for his trouble.

On the third day—and for the rest of the six-day duration—rioting continued into the daylight hours as well, and the National Guard was called in. A hundred fire companies could not put out the blazes; as soon as they had one under control, two more broke out. Constantly harassed by sniper fire, the firemen took to wearing bullet-proof vests.

When it was over, thirty-four were dead, 898 injured, and 4,000 arrested. About $45 million in damages had been done.

BAD NEWS IN NEWARK

In some respects the rioting in Newark, New Jersey, was worse than anywhere else. Newark was a crowded, slummy city with the nation's highest rate of crime, venereal disease, and condemned housing. It was second only to Washington, D.C., in its percentage of blacks. Newark was a powder keg, and riot-watchers knew it would take only a minor police incident to set it off. The incident came on the night of July 12, 1966, when police arrested a black cabby for a traffic violation and a fistfight broke out. Rumors that he had been beaten to death spread quickly, and soon the plundering, arson, and sniping were on.

As in most other street riots, the blacks at first attacked only white-owned businesses, especially those exploiting them by selling second-hand merchandise at top-quality prices, by using weighted scales, or by signing them to trick installment contracts. "This is owed me!" was a familiar cry as rioters carried off TV sets or household appliances. It gave them the feeling they were justified in breaking the law. Later the blacks attacked black-owned businesses as well, although the owners tried to stave off that prospect by painting "Soul Brother" in large letters on the window.

Sometimes even middle-class blacks took part in rioting. Some waited until the rioting reached fancier parts of town where they could steal expensive items such as furs. One black executive said he stopped to throw bricks on his way to a suburban cocktail party.

Newark's 1,400-man police force could not handle the situation. Their basic tactic was to speed through ghetto streets—too quickly to be struck by bricks—merely as a show of force, but the sights and sounds of police simply spurred the looters on.

When the five days of violence were over, twenty-six lay dead and 1,200 had been injured.

DESTRUCTION IN DETROIT

A week after the Newark riots ended, Detroit blew—and it was the worst of all. As usual, it began with a police arrest distorted by wild rumors. A crowd gathered when police raided a liquor store selling after hours, and the main rumor was that a handcuffed black youth had been kicked down a flight of stairs.

During the next eleven days there were 1,600 fire alarms. Eighteen blocks of 12th Street and three miles of Grand River Avenue were burned to the ground. Aerial photos showed the city to look like Berlin in 1945. Henry Ford II called the riot the "greatest internal violence since the Civil War." Thanks to the booming auto business, Detroit had a large, prosperous black middle class, and the mayor had been elected with black support. Nevertheless, widespread destruction was visited upon black homes and black businesses by black rioters.

Detroit was the culmination of the 159 riots across the nation in 1967, the worst year for what the President's riot commission called "civil disorders." There were forty-three dead and more than 7,000 were arrested. Almost 5,000 paratroopers and 800 National Guardsmen had been called in.

QUICK CHANGE—THANKS TO TV

In a fierce decade of civil rights activity, and mostly by nonviolent confrontation, blacks won most of the rights they had been denied for a hundred years. Not only were the militant days of the civil rights movement over in an incredibly short time, the changes they ushered in came quickly and—to the surprise of many—were accepted without much fuss. It all started with the first Greensboro sit-in of 1960. By the mid-1970s Greensboro's city fathers, who had staunchly resisted change at the time, were bragging that their town was where it all began and were putting up signs to that effect. Atlanta elected a black mayor, Governor Jimmy Carter hung a picture of Martin Luther King in the Georgia state capitol, and over at Tuscaloosa, George Wallace, all smiles, crowned a young black woman homecoming queen at the University of Alabama. The times they had changed.

More than anything else, the civil rights movement proved the phenomenal power of television as an instrument for mobilizing public opinion. Time after time, TV viewers watched as passively resisting demonstrators were cursed, spat upon, hit with rocks, fists, and clubs, and finally hauled off to jail. Around the world went scenes of blacks being set upon by German shepherds and washed down the streets with fire hoses. Although it was sometimes a toss-up as to whether the television cameras came to cover a newsworthy event or whether the demonstrators turned it into a newsworthy event because the cameras were there, there is no doubt such brutal scenes changed many minds and did more than anything else to alter the mood of the country. It is difficult to know whether the movement would have succeeded without television.

Chapter 21

The Korean War

Undeclared, But Bloody as Any

WHAT PRESIDENT HARRY S TRUMAN called a "police action" in Korea lasted thirty-seven bitter months and left 8 million dead, eighty percent of them civilians. And when it was all over, the divided country returned to the *status quo ante bellum*, with nothing essentially changed.

Most of the American casualties came in the early months of the war and were the result of unpreparedness and a lack of flexibility. No U.S. troops were equipped, trained, or mentally ready for the type of war they found in the cold hills and rice paddies of Korea. American armies were used to linear strategies where battlefronts and objectives were clearly defined, and neither the North Koreans nor the Red Chinese fought that way.

Enemy troops were hard-muscled and uncomplaining. They could live for days and cover incredible distances—on a pocketful of rice. They came on in waves and when they met an obstacle they simply dissolved into guerrilla bands, flowing through the rice paddies and hiding in the hills.

Although United Nations forces had a near monopoly in air power, it made no difference. They relied heavily on wheels, and wheels were of little use where there were no roads to fight on, march on, and retreat on. When American planes shot up an enemy supply train, the enemy simply disappeared, each soldier carrying part of the equipment by hand.

There was no shade in the hills, only scrub growth. When U.S. soldiers pursued the enemy into the hills, they dropped like flies. Their legs couldn't stand the pull. Although winters were bitterly cold, the summers were scorching. G.I.s sweated under the sweltering sun until their shirts rotted. Salt tablets were at a premium and were often air-dropped with the ammunition.

On the other hand, they often had to fight in twenty-below-zero cold, especially after the push into North Korea early in the war. Medical officers often reported as many casualties from the cold as from enemy fire. Some froze to death, and only quick work by litter teams prevented more from doing so.

"Breach of the Peace"

On June 25, 1950, the North Korean People's Army (NKPA) suddenly invaded the Republic of South Korea. It was superbly equipped with the latest in weapons and tanks—all made in Russia. It was, at the time, probably the best army in the Far East. It should have come as no surprise. The NKPA had been practicing by making small raids across the border for months, and the Central Intelligence Agency (CIA) had alerted Washington to the fact that an immense buildup of Northern troops along the border couldn't mean anything else. The CIA had even predicted the NKPA would attack in June 1950.

Republic of Korea (ROK) troops, only 65,000 of them, were no match for the Northern invaders. They were armed with ancient Mauser rifles, short-range artillery only, obsolete bazookas, and they had no tanks or warplanes. A U.S. advisory group had been training ROK troops as military police only, and Congress had cut out the $60 million President Truman had earmarked for Korea in his 1950–51 budget.

The United Nations declared the invasion a "breach of the peace" and quickly approved Truman's decision to provide ROK troops with air and naval support, but it was not soon enough. ROK defenses crumbled, and in less than a week half of the ROK army had been killed, wounded, or captured.

Truman ordered General MacArthur, based in Japan, to fly in and take a look at the situation. MacArthur said U.N. troops must be thrown into the breach at once, and on the seventh day of the crisis the United States was at war again—without even consulting Congress.

But U.S. forces crumbled just like the ROK troops. They were unprepared, out of condition, and outnumbered twenty to one. Many were cut off and surrendered almost immediately, including Major General William F. Dean, commander of the 24th Infantry. Many of these were green troops who were quickly afflicted with "bug-out fever," but giving up so soon came to a screeching halt when the G.I.s learned the North Koreans often executed prisoners.

Surprise at Inchon

MacArthur allowed his defenders to withdraw slowly to the port city of Pusan in the southeastern part of the country. There he set up a perimeter defense, and there his U.S. and ROK survivors were joined by troops from twenty-one other U.N. countries.

Then MacArthur thought up a brilliant stratagem. "The history of war," the general said, "proves that nine times out of ten an army has been destroyed because its supply lines have been cut off." His plan was to leave half his force at Pusan and secretly land the other half 150 miles behind enemy lines at Inchon. The North Koreans knew a landing was coming, but like the Germans on D-Day, they thought it would come elsewhere. The Inchon landing, spearheaded by the First Marine Division, which had secretly departed San Francisco, was a complete tactical surprise.

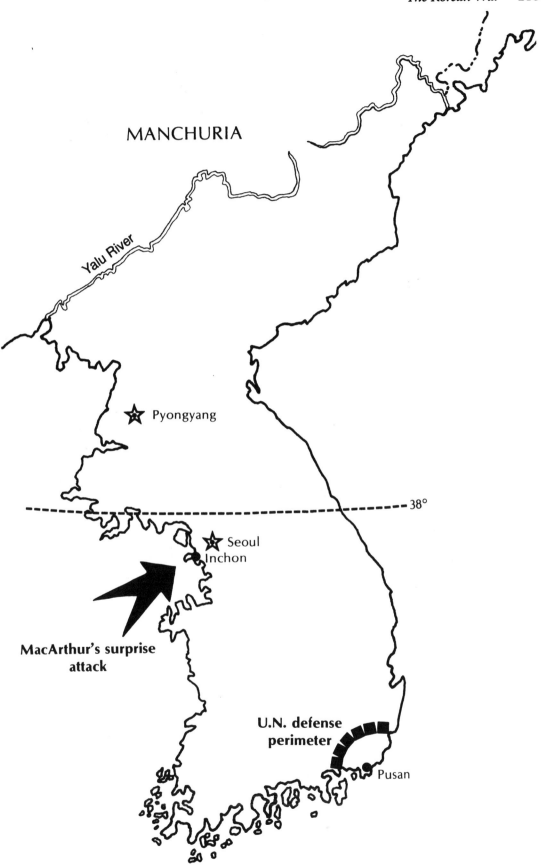

MANCHURIA

Yalu River

☆ Pyongyang

38°

☆ Seoul
Inchon

**MacArthur's surprise
attack**

**U.N. defense
perimeter**

Pusan

At the same time, U.N. troops broke out of Pusan and raced to tie up with the troops from Inchon. In an incredibly short time the North Korean army was broken and pushed back across the 38th parallel into its own country.

After waiting for U.N. approval, MacArthur sent seven splendid U.S. divisions and six seasoned ROK divisions flying into North Korea. The Northern capital, Pyongyang, fell quickly, and the general talked of having "his boys" home for Christmas. He did not know that 250,000 North Korean peasants were hiding in the bleak hills where aerial observation could not spot them. He *did* know that large numbers of Red Chinese troops were massed along the Manchurian border, but he thought that was only a protest move, a show of force in case the U.N. had any thoughts of invading China.

"RETREAT, HELL!"

MacArthur found out he was wrong when, on the day after Thanksgiving, 1950, thirty-three Red Chinese Divisions—300,000 men!—began to pour across the Yalu River. What followed was a total rout; *Time* called it the "worst defeat ever suffered by a U.S. army." The ROK divisions in the center of the U.N. line caved in, and men of all nations began fleeing south.

But not all. Red Chinese attacking a ridge were shocked to come across a brigade of fierce Turks who charged into them with bayonets fixed. After forty-eight hours of continuous action, the Turks were short of food and ammunition, but were still fighting with knives, fists, and stones. U.S. tank units that went forward to rescue the trapped unit found them preparing to attack. Ordered to pull back from positions where they were surrounded by swarming Chinese, the Turks said, "Withdraw? What for? We are killing lots of them." A U.S. doctor said it seemed a Turk waited until he had at least three wounds before asking for medical attention.

Their courage became legendary, but most of the Turks were wiped out.

Meanwhile, the First Marine Division had been cut off and surrounded. When a war correspondent asked the commander if he intended to leave the field, the general replied, "Retreat, hell! We are just attacking from a different direction." A regimental commander told his men, "The enemy is in front of us, behind us, to the left of us and to the right of us. They won't escape *this* time!"

With help from parts of two other U.S. divisions and one ROK division, the Marines hacked their way through the Chinese for fourteen days, climbing icy trails in sub-zero temperatures. Casualties were heavy: one column buried 117 Marines in one grave, while another unit carried its 2,651 dead and wounded every step of the way for four days. When one unit seemed stopped by an impassable gorge, pilots of the Combat Cargo Command dropped them a suspension bridge.

This was the most heroic tale of the Korean War.

MacArthur and Truman

SACKING THE QUARTERBACK

After U.N. forces were pushed back below the 38th parallel, the war bogged down—and it would remain a dreary stalemate until 1953.

Douglas MacArthur was the first American general to be handcuffed by a limited war for limited goals, and he could not—or would not—accept that: "There is no substitute for victory," he said. MacArthur, who since the beginning of World War II had been criticized for playing God, never forgot for a moment that he was the major figure on the historical stage of the period. He wanted authority to expand the war into Communist China, and even to drop atom bombs if necessary. When he did not get it, his messages home became increasingly petulant and ill-tempered. Trying to get around the President, he appealed to Congress and the Pentagon, asking for a full-scale assault on the administration.

When Truman sent the text of a cease-fire agreement to the general for his comment, MacArthur announced to the press that he was prepared to deal with the enemy himself. It was the last straw for Truman, who thereupon fired his field commander. "MacArthur left me no choice," Truman later wrote. "I could no longer tolerate his insubordination."

The President sent the message to Secretary of the Army Frank Pace who was in Korea, and told him to deliver it personally. But Pace's plane was grounded by a hailstorm, and MacArthur first heard he had been sacked on the radio.

THE EMPEROR RETURNS

Back home, meanwhile, the announcement was greeted by a hailstorm of protest. How dare this former National Guard captain fire a five-star general who had so brilliantly distinguished himself in three American wars, was the attitude of many Americans. Cries of "Impeach the President" went up; state legislatures censured him; mobs burned him in effigy; flags were flown upside down. Bars served "Truman beer," which was just like any other beer except it didn't have a head. A favorite joke: "This wouldn't have happened if Truman were alive."

MacArthur accepted an invitation to speak at a joint session of Congress and came home for the first time in fourteen years. Everywhere he received a tumultuous welcome, first in San Francisco, then Washington, then New York.

In Washington he received a seventeen-gun salute and a silver tea service from the Joint Chiefs of Staff, who had just helped fire him. He ended his speech to Congress by quoting the refrain from an old barrack-room ballad popular during his West Point years: "Old soldiers never die, they just fade away." Within days Tin Pan Alley had five versions of the song on the market.

In New York a ticker-tape parade in MacArthur's honor was bigger than the one for Charles A. Lindbergh when he returned from his Atlantic flight, and bigger than Dwight D. Eisenhower's after he returned from his "Crusade in Europe." MacArthur checked into a $130-a-day suite at the Waldorf-Astoria and was treated like an emperor, which he apparently thought he was. The hotel switchboard got 3,000 calls a day from citizens wanting to speak to the emperor.

Truman predicted the fuss over MacArthur would die down in six weeks, and he was correct to the letter. Many of his admirers thought the firing of MacArthur was the most courageous act of Truman's career—a career that also included the decision to drop the atom bomb, remember. "Courage didn't have anything to do with it," snapped the peppery President. "General MacArthur was insubordinate and I fired him. That was all there was to it."

Chapter 22

Assassination!

Malcolm X

THE 1960s IN AMERICA was a decade of assorted violence, including the assassinations of John F. Kennedy, Malcolm X, Dr. Martin Luther King, Jr., and Robert F. Kennedy. Never had so many well-known citizens been gunned down in such a brief interlude.

Malcolm X (birth name: Malcolm Little) was shot to death, apparently by other Black Muslims, in New York on February 21, 1965, as he walked on the stage to make a speech. Why? Probably because he had lately backed off from his hard-line ideas on black supremacy and strict segregation from whites. A year earlier he had broken off completely with the Black Muslims and formed his own religious sect, the Muslim Mosque.

As Malcolm X prepared to make his speech, a disturbance broke out somewhere in the hall. A member of the audience shouted, "Get your hands off my pockets! Don't be messin' with my pockets!" This was followed quickly by a small fire in the back of the hall, which, according to the police, was caused by someone setting ablaze a sock filled with something flammable. During the confusion a man stepped on the stage and fired a shotgun blast through the plywood lectern and into Malcolm X's chest. Two other men fired into his prone body.

It had not been long since Malcolm X had declared, "I have never had a bodyguard. Your best bodyguard is your own alertness." Yet on this occasion he had six bodyguards. One of them chased a suspected assassin to the door of a ladies' restroom, but declined to follow him inside; the man was never seen again. Another fired into the crowd, hitting one assassin but also wounding two innocent spectators; this bodyguard disappeared and the two bystanders were never called to testify at the trial.

Three Black Muslims (though one denied being a member of the order) were convicted of the crime, but there was enough conflicting testimony to cast doubts about who was really involved. One of the defendants had gone to the doctor earlier on the day of the crime and had a bandaged leg; there was some evidence suggesting he was not even at the hall. Testimony varied on which man wielded the shotgun, and some witnesses seemed to be unaware that a shotgun had been used at all.

There are still many unanswered questions concerning Malcolm X's assassination, and there has yet to be a complete investigation of the case.

Martin Luther King, Jr.

Martin Luther King, Jr. seemed to prophesy his own death when he said in a speech, "We've got some difficult days ahead, but it really doesn't matter with me now because I've been to the mountaintop . . . Like anybody else I would like to live a long life . . . but I'm not concerned about that now."

A few hours later—on April 4, 1968—he was struck down by an assassin's bullet in Memphis, where he had gone to help out in a strike by sanitation workers. He was thirty-nine years old.

The assassin was James Earl Ray, a small-time crook who had been involved in a number of burglaries, smuggling operations, and armed robberies. A year before the assassination he escaped from a Missouri prison, but law enforcement authorities thought so little of him they offered only fifty dollars for his return.

Martin Luther King, Jr. was standing on the balcony of the Lorraine Motel when a single bullet struck him in the neck and severed his spinal cord. Ray had fired from the bathroom window of a rooming house across the way and quickly made off in a white Ford Mustang, not the kind of car for a man on the run to use.

The search spread from Memphis to Canada to London, where Ray was arrested at Heathrow Airport after he accidentally showed authorities two different passports. The court sentenced him to ninety-nine years in prison.

Throughout his days in prison Ray maintained his innocence. He claimed that someone he knew only as "Raoul" gave him money and instructions; he took the money and followed the instructions, Ray said, but someone else actually shot Dr. King. Ray's father agreed, telling the media that his son "couldn't have planned it alone—he isn't smart enough."

Some thought the FBI was involved. A retired agent told the media there were not a lot of kind feelings toward King in the Bureau, and that there were some who actually jumped for joy upon hearing news of the assassination. He also accused the FBI of deliberately sidetracking any conspiracy investigations. A Memphis police detective claimed he was jerked off the case immediately after he suggested the department take better precautions against assassination than the ones they had planned.

It was well known in government circles that FBI director J. Edgar Hoover detested Dr. King, calling him "burrhead" and "the most notorious liar in the country." He ordered King's home wiretapped, had him shadowed, publicly criticized his selection as winner of the Nobel Peace Prize for 1964, and sent anonymous letters to Coretta Scott

King implying that her husband was seeing other women. Another letter suggested King commit suicide as "the only thing left for you to do."

Robert F. Kennedy

"An assassin never changed the course of history," remarked Robert Kennedy after his older brother John was shot to death. He was wrong, for on June 5, 1968—two months and a day after the King assassination—he himself was shot and killed in a Los Angeles hotel.

Kennedy was struck down as he and an enthusiastic crowd of supporters celebrated winning the Democratic primary in California, an essential victory in his bid to be the Democratic nominee for president in 1968. The assassin was twenty-six-year-old Sirhan Sirhan, who had come to America from Jordan when he was thirteen.

Sirhan used a .22-caliber pistol holding eight bullets. Three bullets struck Kennedy and five wounded people in the crowd. However, two bullets were recovered from a counter and one from a door frame, making ten altogether. This of course led many to believe in a conspiracy, with Sirhan being only the executioner.

The coroner said the fatal bullet struck Kennedy behind the right ear and in his professional opinion was fired from only three or four inches away; Sirhan probably was never closer than three feet. Several criminologists concluded that two guns were fired from two different positions. A security guard behind Kennedy pulled his gun when Sirhan's first shot rang out and he later admitted that it "might have discharged," possibly accounting for the two extra bullets.

There were reports of a woman at Sirhan's side just before the shooting. She seems to have disappeared just before Kennedy came into the room, but a witness claimed to see her and two other persons stampeding past her. The woman—hard to miss in a polka-dot dress—shouted "We shot him! We shot Kennedy!"

The police brought in someone they thought might be the mystery woman, but the witness was unable to identify her. Shortly after Sirhan was convicted, the woman was found dead in a motel room.

According to his mother, Sirhan began acting strangely a few months before the assassination. Some experts thought he was mentally disturbed. Others suspected he had been programmed to do his dastardly deed, which seems a distinct possibility since Sirhan was never able to recall pulling a gun and shooting Robert F. Kennedy.

John F. Kennedy

Crime: Murder of John F. Kennedy, 35th president of the United States.
Place: Dallas, Texas, while riding in a parade.
Date: November 22, 1963
The Assassin: Lee Harvey Oswald, who two days later was himself murdered.

These are the essential facts in the crime of the twentieth century—everything else is in dispute. Inquiring Americans want to know the answers to these questions: How many shots were fired and from what directions? Did the bullet that probably killed Kennedy come from the back or the front? Did Oswald act alone or as part of a conspiracy? Why was Oswald killed so quickly? Was there a government cover-up of the facts?

Oswald fit the classic profile of an assassin—a loner and misfit who deeply resented the fact that the world had not noticed his existence. When he was a boy a social worker noted that he seemed to be "emotionally frozen" and was "just floating along in the world." Perhaps the most telling argument in favor of the belief that Oswald acted alone is: What self-respecting conspirator would have entrusted a job like that to a man like Oswald?

According to the polls, a considerable majority of Americans suspect a conspiracy. And who wouldn't with such an implausible storyline as this:

At the height of the Cold War a nineteen-year-old former Marine defects to the Soviet Union. After the KGB (the secret police) denies him political asylum, he tries to commit suicide. After two and a half years he returns to the U.S with a pretty Russian wife.

Just days before Kennedy comes to Dallas he gets a job filling orders on the sixth floor of the Texas School Book Depository, directly overlooking the president's motorcade route. With the high-powered rifle he smuggled in that morning he fires three quick shots—hard to do with a bolt-action weapon—that kill the president and wound Texas Governor John Connally. What's more, the public is asked to believe the bullet (called the "Magic Bullet" by assassination buffs) that wounded Connally has already passed through JFK's body.

Despite the tight security, Oswald leaves the Book Depository and escapes—on foot. (He does not know how to drive.) After stupidly killing a policeman, he is arrested and jailed. Two days later, while being transferred from one jail to another, he is shot to death in front of a live TV audience while surrounded by more than seventy officers of the law. His killer, Jack Ruby, was a nightclub owner with ties to the mob.

Who would believe such a fanciful tale? It sounds like the plot of a grade-F movie. For many Americans it seems inconceivable that such an enormous crime could be committed by such a puny criminal. They want to add something more to Oswald's part of the story, giving the matter more balance and investing the president's death with more meaning.

Ironically, John F. Kennedy probably was in the best health of his adult life when he was killed. Not until 1993—the thirtieth anniversary of his assassination—was it made public that Kennedy had suffered from Addison's disease, an affliction of the adrenal glands that could be fatal. For it he took cortisone through injections, pills, and pellets implanted in his thighs. For emergencies his father had cortisone stashed away in safety deposit boxes all over the world.

Kennedy had a bad back that gave him great pain from time to time, sometimes obliging him to walk with the aid of a cane or crutches and to use a rocking chair for sitting. He also had persistent venereal disease, stomach problems, difficulty hearing in his right ear, and allergies so bad they sometimes prevented him from doing much of anything.

Kennedy's image as a man of strength and vigor was a carefully cultivated illusion. In fact he retired early, slept late, and took a nap in the afternoon. The doctors gave him novacaine injections that provided him with temporary relief from his back pain; he also downed amphetamines, with or without the doctors' knowledge.

DOES HISTORY REPEAT ITSELF?

There are some spooky coincidences between the assassinations of John F. Kennedy and Abraham Lincoln:

- Lincoln was elected in 1860, Kennedy in 1960.

- Both were slain on Friday, sitting beside their wives.

- Lincoln was shot in Ford's Theater; Kennedy was shot in a Lincoln automobile, made by the Ford Motor Company.

- Both of their successors were Southerners and Democrats (though Lincoln was a Republican). Both were senators and both were named Johnson.

- Andrew Johnson, who succeeded Lincoln, was born in 1808; Lyndon Johnson, who succeeded Kennedy, was born in 1908.

- John Wilkes Booth shot Lincoln in a theater and was cornered in a warehouse; Lee Harvey Oswald shot Kennedy from a warehouse and was captured in a theater.

- Booth was born in 1839, Oswald in 1939.

- Both assassins were slain before a trial could be held.

Another oddity in presidential history is the "zero factor." All four assassinated presidents were elected in years ending in a zero. In fact, since 1840 every president elected in a year ending in zero (they come every twenty years) died in office:

- William Henry Harrison, elected in 1840 and died of pneumonia a month later.

- Abraham Lincoln, first elected in 1860 and killed just after being inaugurated for a second term.

- James A. Garfield, elected in 1880 and assassinated six months after taking office.

- William McKinley, elected in 1900 and assassinated six months after taking office.

- Warren G. Harding, elected in 1920 and died under mysterious circumstances three years later.

- Franklin Roosevelt, elected in 1940 (for the third time, but for the only time in a year ending in zero) and died shortly after his fourth inauguration.

- John F. Kennedy, elected in 1960 and assassinated three years later.

The only presidents escaping the twenty-year curse were Thomas Jefferson in 1800 and James Monroe in 1820. (Had the curse not begun yet?) Apparently Ronald Reagan ended the curse in 1980, though it almost got him when he barely escaped an assassination attempt a month after he was sworn in.

Chapter 23

The Vietnam Experience

Looking for Charlie

WHAT HAPPENED TO THE UNITED STATES in Vietnam was at the same time less than a war and more than a war. It was an experience no American who lived through it would be eager to repeat. On the battlefront it was a limited engagement, without front lines or specific objectives; at home supporters of the war ("hawks") duked it out with opponents ("doves"), often violently and sometimes with tragic results.

The only objective of the American soldier was to "find, fix, and finish" Charlie. "Charlie" was the GI's nickname for the Vietcong, the communist guerrillas trying to overthrow the government of South Vietnam. Finding Charlie was not easy to do, for Charlie was found only when he wanted to be found. Mostly he attacked at night in black pajamas, and often stayed close to U.S. troops to avoid being bombed by U.S. warplanes. The Vietcong was not an army in the usual sense of the word. Charlie could be the innocent villager who shined your shoes in the daytime and attacked you at night; the lady who ironed your pants in the day and helped mortar your camp after dark; or the little beggar boy with sad eyes who suddenly blew you up with a hand grenade—and perhaps himself as well.

For this was a war of endless barbarities on both sides. The dead were mutilated, hospitals attacked, whole villages wiped out on a suspicion that some of the inhabitants were Vietcong. My Lai ["Me Ly"], one such village, became notorious in the United States; not because it was a worse incident of barbarity than others, but just because it caught the attention of the media. The American military tried to keep these incidents quiet. One officer said of My Lai: "It didn't happen, and besides the Vietnamese deserved it."

If innocent villagers were killed—women and children included—they might be added to the "body count." In a war where there was no territory to capture, adding up corpses seemed to be the only way to measure how well the troops were doing. Sometimes, especially in mercenary units, an ear was proof of a kill.

"Grunts," as foot soldiers were called in this war, were not "in country" long before they became resolutely opposed to dying and as a result developed all sorts of superstitions. A grunt who had narrowly escaped death more than once was believed to lead a charmed life, finding himself surrounded by new friends who wanted to be near him in the next firefight. Good luck charms included not only the usual crosses and St. Christopher medals, but locks of hair, a girl friend's underwear, and in one case an oatmeal cookie that a soldier carried throughout his tour of duty, lovingly wrapped in foil and three pairs of socks.

Grunts on search-and-destroy missions might develop search-and-avoid tactics. They lingered in the jungle for a while—eating, sleeping, and smoking (some even smoked cigarettes)—and then returned to camp, "mission accomplished."

Drugs were plentiful and easy to come by. The army estimated eighty percent of soldiers smoked the cheap local marijuana and about five percent were addicted to heroin. The heroin was good quality, flown in from Laos while customs officials were paid to look the other way. Fights among soldiers increased when heroin was scarce.

Fights might be race-related. Some African-American soldiers saw the war in a new light after realizing that Vietnamese were also nonwhite, and they began to wonder if they were fighting the "honkey's" war for him. News of Martin Luther King, Jr.'s killing sparked a rash of fights and shooting incidents.

G.I.s in Vietnam were the youngest in any American war, the average age just over nineteen. There was no cross-section of American youth, as in other wars: about half were African-American or Hispanic, the others from the lower or lower-middle class. Many middle-class and upper-class youths avoided the draft through deferments, exemptions, and legal maneuvering.

The U.S. Air Force had a role in this war it was not accustomed to. Without many of the usual targets—factories, railroads, bridges, and such—it tried to bomb people. It used, not very effectively, fragmentation bombs that sent bits of shrapnel flying everywhere. The point was not to kill the enemy, but to cause so many deep wounds it would create impossible medical problems for the Vietcong. Fire bombs—napalm and white phosphorus—were also used.

The Air Force also carried out what military strategists call "resource denial," meaning the systematic destruction of crops and foliage. Without crops the Vietcong had little to eat; without foliage there were few places to hide. Defoliation, done with toxic chemicals including the notorious agent orange, ruined thousands of acres and damaged large numbers of people, some of them Americans.

A special task force carried out defoliation. It was called the "Ranch Hands" and its motto was: "Only we can prevent forests."

PROTESTS AND PEACE

The war dragged on, not changing much. As a critic said near the end: "We have not been in Vietnam for nine years, but one year nine times." Some saw the South Vietnamese government, considered corrupt through and through, as more of a problem than the Vietcong. One dissenter suggested that the best way to end the war was to load all the South Vietnamese onto ships and take them out to sea. Then bomb the country flat. Then sink the ships.

In a man-on-the-street TV interview, one fellow said what the United States ought to do about the war was "go over there and bomb that *island* off the face of the earth." This man was a typical American—he did not know what Vietnam was, could not locate it on a map, did not understand why we were there, and didn't care anyway. Like others, he just wanted the war to end.

Americans, like other Westerners, did not understand the Oriental mind. Douglas MacArthur did, and on his deathbed he warned the president, Lyndon B. Johnson, that Asians had infinite patience and that the United States would never win a war in that part of the world unless thy were willing to fight for twenty or thirty years.

Ho Chi Minh, the North Vietnamese leader, predicted the war "will be won on the homefront, not the battlefield. We will discourage their population. They will not support their combat troops and eventually they will leave."

It was exactly what happened. For the Vietnam War divided this nation like no other war, perhaps like no other event. Most Americans seemed to support the conflict to begin with—when it was believed the U.S. was protecting its national interests—but not after the war effort grew larger and larger and the casualty lists grew longer and longer. "Hawks" fell in behind Senator Barry Goldwater and John Wayne (a movie action hero who never served in the military), and "doves" rallied to Senator George McGovern and actress Jane Fonda. Between the two extremes was a large body of citizens who did not know what to think.

Young people—especially college students—were in the vanguard of the protest movement. After President Johnson stepped up draft calls, they took to the streets chanting, "Hey, hey, LBJ, how many kids did you kill today!" There were draft-card burnings, campus demonstrations, "lie-ins" at the local draft board, and "bleed-ins" where students collected blood not for American soldiers but for the North Vietnamese civilians U.S. planes bombed. For college protestors the new Great American Tradition was, "Work hard, study hard, get ahead, kill!"

As the protest movement grew, there were riots on college campuses as students faced off with administrators, police, or the National Guard. Dozens of colleges shut down temporarily after nervous National Guardsmen fired into a crowd and killed four students at Kent State University.

Older Americans demonstrated en masse. At a rally of 250,000 people in Washington, D.C., the police arrested some 12,000 without having the space to hold them. Those not jailed were football-stadiumed.

President Johnson was surprised—and angered—by the uproar his escalations of the war brought. As the conflict dragged on, it dragged him with it. He seemed to look upon Vietnam as a personal commitment: it was *his* war, *his* troops, *his* bombers. In the end it was *his* defeat, for the war weighed so heavily on him he declined to run for reelection in 1968.

His successor, Richard Nixon, inherited the war but did not seem to know what to do with it either. Declare victory and get out quickly, said some advisers; but Nixon was not willing to do that. Instead he announced a policy of "Vietnamization"—turning over the war to the South Vietnamese army while gradually withdrawing American forces. According to critics, this plan did little more than "change the color of the corpses."

The killing continued and the protesting went on until American participation in the war ended on January 23, 1973. On-again, off-again peace talks had been going on in Paris since 1968, but the delegates had been unable to agree on much of anything, beginning with the shape of the conference table.

As agreed, the United States removed its troops from South Vietnam within sixty days after the armistice. So abrupt was the departure they left behind a huge amount of supplies and equipment. Fighting between North and South Vietnam continued until Saigon, the South Vietnamese capital, fell on April 30, 1975.

The evacuation of Saigon was chaotic as thousands of refugees swarmed into the city. When the last American diplomats and Marine guards took flight in helicopters, they took aboard as many refugees as they could with still more dangling from the landing gear until the choppers reached the waiting U.S. ships. Some pregnant South Vietnamese women gave birth in the helicopters or soon afterward on the ships.

The Vietnam War was over, but the Vietnam Experience lingered on. For ten years there seemed to be a tacit agreement among Americans that they would not discuss the war, then in the 1980s it emerged as an important piece of unfinished business. Veterans of the war—Vietvets—were angry because they had not been recognized as other veterans had been—no parades, no cheering crowds, no claps on the back. Instead some returnees had been greeted with jeers or shouts of "How many babies did you kill?" Some were spat upon.

Some Vietvets suffered from "post-traumatic stress disorder," known in World War II as "combat fatigue" and in World War I as "shell shock." Its victims were plagued by depression, anxiety, and violent behavior. Some relived their experiences in nightmares or flashbacks while awake. The suicide rate among Vietnam vets was thirty-three percent higher than among the general population. Some did not leave their homes for months or even years; said one of them, "All the feeling I have seems to be in my trigger finger—it makes my folks real uptight.

It was more than ten years before Americans could begin to examine the Vietnam Experience dispassionately. As articles, books, and movies began to sweep the country a national catharsis took hold. More important, a memorial went up at last—a somber black granite one in Washington, D.C.

By the 1990s it appeared that America finally had recovered from its own post-traumatic stress disorder. It had passed through the usual stages: grief, anger, depression, and finally acceptance.

Chapter 24

The Moon Walk

Live from the Moon

IT WAS THE GREATEST SHOW off Earth—the landing of two American astronauts on the surface of the moon on August 20, 1969. It was watched by countless millions around the world. It was a triumph of American ingenuity, both in landing a spacecraft on the moon and in being able to show it on live television everywhere.

The three Apollo Il astronauts—mission commander Neil Armstrong, Edwin "Buzz" Aldrin, and Michael Collins—were surprised when they awoke on the morning of the big day. Mission Control in Houston suggested they keep an eye out for a lovely Chinese girl named Chango, an inhabitant of the moon for the past four thousand years. And watch too for her only companion, a big rabbit standing on its hind feet under a cinnamon tree.

Mission Control was beginning this momentous day with a little humor, hoping to loosen up the astronauts. The legend of Chango and her four-legged accomplice had appeared in a Chinese newspaper the previous day.

Later that day Armstrong and Aldrin broke out the landing craft, nicknamed the *Eagle*, and descended to the moon's surface. After the *Eagle* sat down near a depression called the Sea of Tranquility, viewers around the world heard the first intelligible words from the moon when Armstrong said calmly, "Tranquillity Base here. The *Eagle* has landed."

Armstrong and Aldrin were supposed to spend the next eight hours in the *Eagle*, sleeping most of the time. But they were too excited to sleep, and Houston gave them permission to begin their exploration without further ado.

Still it took the pair six hours to get ready. They had to depressurize the *Eagle* and prepare their multilayered pressurized suits and life-support backpacks. The equipment allowed them to breathe for up to seven hours and protected them from temperatures of up to 250 degrees and down to 200 degrees below zero. They called the suits "moon cocoons."

While working, the two gaped out the window at an alien landscape. "The sky is black, you know," said Armstrong later. "But it still seemed more like daylight than darkness . . . It's a peculiar thing, but the surface looked warm and inviting, as if it would be a nice place to take a sunbath."

Before venturing onto the lunar wastes, Armstrong and Aldrin had their last meal in the *Eagle*. Aldrin gave himself communion with a wafer, tiny chalice, and thimble of wine. He made no mention of this, wanting to avoid a public controversy like the one stirred up by the noted atheist Madalyn Murray O'Hair when the Apollo 8 astronauts read from Genesis.

ONE GIANT LEAP

What followed soon was perhaps the most riveting drama in human history, and a television camera attached to the *Eagle* recorded it. The world watched by satellite as Neil Armstrong cautiously backed down the *Eagle*'s ladder and gingerly touched a toe to the moon's surface. At that moment he said those immortal words, "That's one small step for man, one giant leap for mankind."

Actually he blew the immortal line. Though he had rehearsed the words over and over, he still blew the line. What he meant to say was, "That's one small step for *a* man, one giant leap for mankind."

Does it make any difference? Quite a bit. Without the *a* the line is redundant because "man" and "mankind" mean the same thing.

Never mind. Nobody thought much about it at the time, and nobody has complained since.

Buzz Aldrin followed Armstrong to the ground, a bit miffed because he was not first to touch the moon. It wasn't long though before he had to use the collection device built into his spacesuit, thereby becoming the first person to relieve his bladder on the moon. "It was a unique feeling," he later said. "The world was watching, but I was the only one who knew what they were really witnessing."

The pair found the surface of the moon like fine powder, no trouble to walk in. The one-sixth gravity was comfortable enough, though they had to move about in what they called a "kangaroo hop." Aldrin said he felt balanced and comfortably upright when leaning forward slightly.

The smallness of the moon altered perceptions, they discovered. The horizon seemed to curve downward and away from them, instead of flat as it did on earth. This could be disorienting.

The astronauts erected a plaque reading "Here Man from the planet Earth first set foot on the Moon, July, 1969 A.D. We came in peace for all mankind." It was signed by the three astronauts and President Richard Nixon.

Planting an American flag was not easy, light gravity making it difficult to keep the pole erect. The piece that was supposed to keep the flag stretched out refused to work. It was left as it was, drooping and crooked.

Armstrong and Aldrin spent two and a half hours on the moon. They set up a solar wind detector, a seismic detector, and a laser reflector. They checked the *Eagle* for damage. And they gathered up forty-seven pounds of rocks, the moon's chief products.

Why a bag of worthless rocks? Scientists can learn a lot by studying rocks and those from the moon were, as one NASA scientist said, "worth more than all the gold in Fort Knox." The rocks were astonishingly old, more ancient than any ever found on earth.

The astronauts took time out for a long distance—*very* long distance—telephone call from President Nixon. "This certainly has to be the most historic telephone call ever made," Nixon said to them while the world eavesdropped. "I just can't tell you how proud we all are of what you have done. For every American this has to be the proudest day of our lives. And for people all over the world I am sure that they too join with Americans in recognizing what an immense feat this is."

As our intrepid men in the moon cocoons bounded around the lunar landscape, obviously having the time of their lives, those at home enjoyed the most splendid television show of all time. Some viewers were disquieted, however. Having grown up with tales of intergalactic horror, they halfway expected weird creatures with antennae to suddenly pounce on our unsuspecting heroes and tear them apart.

Nothing of the sort happened, of course. Scientists had known for a long time that there was no life on the moon. There were no monsters, no Chinese lady, no rabbit under a cinnamon tree. Not even a cinnamon tree. Not even a tree.

If someone from outer space ever visits our moon, the visitor will know that earthlings have been there. A lot of trash was left behind: over 5,000 pounds of cameras, backpacks, and tools.

Thanks to the Apollo ll mission, we now know much more about the moon—age, composition, landforms. We have made some headway in understanding where the moon came from, the best theory being that it was the result of a collision between the earth and a giant asteroid or comet about 4.5 billion years ago.

It changed things on earth as well. The knowledge necessary to put a person on the moon brought on the high-tech explosion that both thrills and threatens us today: computers, microelectronics, and thousands of spin-off technologies.

"It's the beginning of a new era," said Neil Armstrong upon his return to earth. He did not know how right he was.

Chapter 25

Watergate and Its Legacy

Watergate

WHEN POLICE ARRESTED five burglars in Democratic Party campaign headquarters at the Watergate Building in Washington, D.C., no one dreamed the incident would one day pull down the president of the United States. It was 1972, an election year, and the burglars were looking for something they could use to incriminate the Democratic Party. It was a terribly bungled attempt, but the cover-up of it—and the cover-up of the cover-up—brought Richard Nixon's presidency low.

The burglars were hired by the "Plumbers," a group of the president's men charged with "fixing leaks" in the administration. Their funds came from the Committee to Re-Elect the President, known as CREEP. John Mitchell, a former attorney general, headed the committee.

In telephone conversations with Mitchell, Nixon instructed him to tell the burglars to "stonewall it . . . Plead the Fifth Amendment, cover up or anything else." He also ordered chief of staff H. R. Haldeman to get the CIA to obstruct the FBI's investigation of the case. These phone calls, secretly taped in the Oval Office, were the "smoking guns" that later proved Nixon not only knew about the Watergate affair but took part in its cover-up.

When the investigations began and the media started to move in, Nixon decided the best thing to do was throw out a sacrificial lamb—that is, get someone in the administration to accept responsibility for the break-in and then resign. That ought to settle the matter.

Not surprisingly, no one wanted to be the sacrificial animal. So Nixon, hoping to save his own skin, cleaned house by firing a number of top aides. Some of them later went to jail where they served short sentences and wrote long books about their misadventures in politics.

The misadventures were not public knowledge until Nixon's private tapes were subpoenaed. The courts, to their dismay, discovered that some tapes were missing and that on one, eighteen minutes of a critical conversation had been erased.

The tapes revealed the president as something of a paranoid egomaniac. And he used a lot of words parents would not want their children to hear, words that appeared in the press as "expletive deleted." Billy Graham, Nixon's close friend, called reading transcripts of the tapes "a profoundly disturbing experience."

The tapes damned Nixon beyond redemption, for they showed him to be, in the words of one newspaper, "devious, immoral, vacillating, profane, unprincipled." Nixon, it appears, had no idea how much the public would be shocked by such revelations.

The tapes revealed that the Nixon administration had given preferred treatment to certain business concerns, circumvented the Fair Campaign Practices Act, and used the FBI, CIA, and Internal Revenue Service to harass those he considered political enemies. Some White House staffers even drew up an "enemies list" that included private citizens such as the outspoken Hollywood liberals Barbra Streisand, Paul Newman, and Jane Fonda. No one knows why Joe Namath's name was included unless it was because of his reputation as a carouser and womanizer. Also on the list was the president of the Otis Elevator Company, apparently because the Otis elevator in Nixon's San Clemente, California, home did not work properly.

Adding to Nixon's problems, Vice-President Spiro Agnew was accused of tax fraud and taking kickback from contractors, both as governor of Maryland and as vice-president. Agnew angrily denied the charges, but later pleaded no-contest to charges of income-tax evasion and resigned.

Nixon blamed his troubles on the media, which he claimed were out to get him. Before he could be impeached, he too resigned and retired to his San Clemente home. He was the first president in American history to resign, setting a precedent; Agnew had already set a vice-precedent.

Nixon had no sooner left office than rumors began to fly that the new president, Gerald Ford, planned to pardon him. (Nixon had appointed Ford to the vice-presidency after Agnew resigned, making him the only person in American history to be both president and vice-president without being elected to either office.) When the news media asked him about the rumors Ford said, "I don't think the people of the United States would stand for it." Shortly afterwards he issued a "full, free, and unconditional pardon for all offenses against the United States." There was a firestorm of protest, but like all storms it passed.

The Watergate Legacy

Gerald Ford said he had pardoned Nixon because it was time to "fully close and seal" the book on Watergate. By this time "Watergate" had come to mean not just a bungled burglary that eventually brought down a president, but a whole series of inter-related crimes, misdemeanors, and sordid political tricks carried out by Nixon and the White House underground. It included:

- Bugging newsmen.

- Surveillance of political figures.

- An aborted plan to bomb the Brookings Institute, an ultra-liberal research organization.

- An attempted break-in at the headquarters of George McGovern, Nixon's presidential opponent in 1972.

- Forging a document that attempted to implicate John F. Kennedy in the assassination of South Vietnam's president, thus discrediting the Democratic Party.

- Sending out phony press releases, stealing documents, and trying to sabotage fund-raising dinners of their opponents.

- Spying on an enemy's family to dig up dirt.

- Publishing phony letters accusing opposing candidates of sexual misconduct.

- Calling up television stations and, pretending to be the opposing candidate's media adviser, cancelling his appearance.

When Congress passed the Fair Campaign Practices Act, requiring all campaign contributions over $100 to be made public, Nixon wanted to veto the bill but did not dare to. But he delayed signing it to give his people time to round up as many campaign contributions as possible. By the time the law went into effect the Republican Party had raised $58 million for the 1972 campaign, the largest sum ever. The Democrats scared up only $14 million.

It was alleged that Nixon's reelection campaign accepted a $100,000 cash contribution from billionaire industrialist Howard Hughes, who was trying to get government approval of some planned mergers of his. The campaign claimed the money was left in a safety-deposit box for three years and then returned to Hughes; others believed Nixon converted the money to his personal use.

Certainly Nixon could have used the money—he needed huge sums to keep up his two private residences. The San Clemente home, a twenty-eight-acre estate overlooking the Pacific Ocean, had a guest cottage, a $100,000 swimming pool, and a private golf course with a presidential seal on each tee. The General Services Administration, which oversees government expenditures, admitted that the president had spent $700,000 of the people's money on the San Clemente home and $1 million on another residence in Florida.

At the presidential retreat in Camp David, Maryland, Nixon added a pool, bowling alley, and archery range, sending its yearly upkeep from $147,000 to $640,000. He also maintained, at public expense, sixteen jet airplanes and sixteen helicopters.

In April 1974, when citizens all over the nation were filling out their income tax returns, the government announced that their president owed the treasury almost half a million dollars in back taxes. Nixon blamed everything on his tax accountants.

The government had also found that Nixon took advantage of a large tax break by donating his vice-presidential papers to the National Archives. In 1969, the year Nixon took the office of president, Congress had made such donations ineligible as tax write-offs. But Nixon, or someone, had back-dated his gift.

Nixon himself was soon back-dated, afterwards retiring to the San Clemente estate where he started on his memoirs and nursed his phlebitis, a painful inflammation of veins in the legs. Before he got an advance on his book and lined up a series of TV interviews, the estate took on such a seedy look, his extremely wealthy neighbors complained. A Nixon friend persuaded a Boy Scout troop to spend some Saturdays cleaning up around the place.

Nixon, who loved the trappings of power, could not have been more embarrassed.

Chapter 26

Middle East Muddles

OPEC Cripples the U.S.

IN THE 1970s Arab states of the Middle East began to flex their muscles, creating continuing problems for the United States. The muscles were well-oiled, petroleum being the principal product of those countries.

OPEC (the Organization of Petroleum Exporting Countries) created an energy crisis in the United States when it slapped an oil embargo on Western nations. There was not only a lack of gas and oil, but the ban affected the manufacture of plastics, fertilizer, paint, ink, and many other products using petroleum.

In America there was sudden chaos. At gas stations there were long lines of cars filled with very angry citizens; occasional fistfights erupted and there were even a few murders. The government suggested several energy-saving measures: Sunday closings of gas stations; lower speed limits; a rationing system based on license plate numbers, with those having even-numbered plates buying gas one day and those with odd-numbered plates the next day. A newspaper columnist rewrote some favorite Christmas carols to reflect the time:

> *You better watch out, you better not shout,*
> *You better not pout, I'm telling you why,*
> *Ra-tion-ing is coming to town.*

> *Deck the halls with boughs of holly,*
> *Fa la la la la, la la la la.*
> *To plan a trip would be sheer folly,*
> *Fa la la la la, la la la la.*

When it became apparent to OPEC members—mainly Saudi Arabia, Kuwait, Iraq, and Iran—that the embargo brought them great power, they raised oil prices from three dollars a barrel to twelve dollars a barrel. Though American industry as a whole suffered because of the embargo, American oil companies seized on the opportunity to raise their own prices. What resulted was a few years of inflation and stagnant economy dubbed "stagflation."

The crisis seemed beyond the control of the country's leadership. It began in Richard Nixon's last days. His successor, Gerald Ford, hoped to "WIN"—"Whip Inflation Now"—but had no success. Under Jimmy Carter the country began a slow and agonizing climb back to normal while trying to end the nation's dependence on foreign oil. The auto industry chipped in by working on more fuel-efficient cars.

The Hostage Crisis

The nightmare began on November 4, 1979, when an Iranian mob stormed the American embassy in Teheran. For over fifty American hostages the ordeal would not end for 444 days.

Ten months earlier a revolution had ousted the American-backed Shah of Iran and replaced him with an Islamic fundamentalist leader, the Ayatollah Khomeini. But Khomeini's revolution was faltering and when the mob took over the embassy he seized upon the incident as a means of winning a propaganda victory over the "Great Satan," as he called the United States. He vowed to hold the Americans in the embassy until the hated Shah and his wealth were returned to Iran.

When television showed blindfolded American hostages being paraded in the streets of Teheran, a cold fury gripped the nation. Americans marched in the streets in protest. Workers refused to unload Iranian ships or refuel Iranian airplanes. President Carter ordered all Iranians in the United States to report to the Immigration and Naturalization Service, and several hundred were deported.

Khomeini used the crisis to whip Iranians into a fever pitch. In a radio broadcast he warned his countrymen not to eat canned beans from America because the CIA had booby-trapped them. He ordered the release of eight black soldiers and five women in an apparent attempt to win over America's minorities. The other fifty-six hostages were not released, Khomeini claimed, because they were spies. The televised press conferences announcing the releases were propaganda circuses.

The captives were treated harshly from time to time. Some stayed in a room where the light burned all night; some slept on a hard floor; some were bound at the wrists and ankles for long periods to time. In the beginning they were forbidden to speak to, or even look at, one another. Those trying to escape were beaten with rubber hoses.

At least three of the hostages were CIA agents. Two of them spent most of the 444 days in solitary confinement, with one of them being badly beaten for trying several times to escape.

Some hostages were taken to the basement of a warehouse and stuck in small cubicles with no windows and only dim light. "It was like living in a tomb," said one. They called their quarters the "Mushroom Inn."

At the Mushroom Inn the rules were on the wall: four cigarettes a day; a shower every five days; laundry once a week; talking only with permission; and no trips to the bathroom without a guard. One hostage drew on the wall a picture of Khomeini standing in front of a church belfry full of bats; the Iranians did not understand what the picture meant.

Prisoners killed time by playing Monopoly, before their captors decided the game was "too capitalistic" and took it away; reading the Bible over and over; jogging in place; or throwing paperwads at a wastebasket in what they called "hostage basketball."

FREE AT LAST

A small group of U.S. commandos tried to rescue the hostages. The plan was to fly them by helicopter to a rendezvous with six transport planes in the Great Salt Desert of Iran, after which they would slip into Teheran and free the hostages. Then they would return to the rendezvous, board the helicopters and transport planes, and fly away to live happily ever after.

Unfortunately this was not what happened, the poorly planned strike ending in tragedy instead.

On the way to the rendezvous three of the eight helicopters developed mechanical problems. One headed back for the aircraft carrier they had come from; one was abandoned in the desert; and the third, though still flying, was deemed incapable of carrying out the mission. After conferring with President Carter, the commander aborted the mission.

But an orderly abortion had not been practiced by the team. While preparing to leave the desert base, one of the helicopters crashed into a transport plane and eight men were killed. The mission, critics said later, was too complicated to succeed.

The long hostage ordeal ended when the U.S. and Iran worked out a deal. The United States government pledged not to interfere in Iran's affairs, to unfreeze Iran's assets in the U.S., and to drop all economic sanctions against Iran.

American foreign policy, suspect under Carter anyway, looked feeble indeed after the rescue fiasco. How could the strongest nation in the world be confounded by a street rabble? Why couldn't a nation that put men on the moon keep a few helicopters in working order?

Some foreign affairs experts think the U.S. made a mistake in dealing with a band of terrorists in the first place. A better way, they say, would have been to declare the hostages prisoners of war, appoint a third nation as mediator, bring in the Red Cross to check on the prisoners' health, and then sit back and wait. The hostages' value to their captors would have run dry quickly.

The Iran-Contra Scandal

The hostages were released on the same day Ronald Reagan was sworn in as president. Television showed both events on a split screen and newspapers proclaimed both in double-deck headlines. The Iranian mess had helped Reagan go into office by a landslide vote.

Reagan was conservative to the core, as one might expect from a man who wore custom-made suits with buttons on the fly. To his legions of supporters it did not seem to matter what Reagan said or did or what sort of misadventures his appointees had. All criticism seemed to roll off him, prompting the media to christen him "the man in the Teflon suit."

However, one affair of his presidency refused to go away, even following him into retirement. It was called "Iran-Contra" and the public still does not know its details due to the silence of some involved and the death of the CIA director. In the beginning this scandal also involved hostages, taken captive in chaotic Lebanon presumably by Iranians.

Apparently the Reagan administration worked out a deal to trade American arms to Iran in return for freeing the hostages though both Reagan and George Bush, then vice-president, later claimed no knowledge of the arrangement.

Meanwhile the government was secretly supporting a rebel army known as the Contras that was fighting against the ruling communist regime in Nicaragua. American financial support for the Contras allegedly came from the sale of arms to our old enemy Iran. As these doings came to light, president Reagan issued a stream of denials that were usually contradicted as soon as he made them. The *New York Times* called him "a man confused, distracted, and remote . . . At times the president sounds like the inhabitant of a never-never land of imaginary polices."

Both Congress and a special commission investigated the Iran-Contra matter, finding that a lot of people had engaged in lies, deceptions, and illegal maneuvering. Marine Lt. Col. Oliver North, who seemed to be the chief conspirator, was eventually convicted on a number of charges stemming from the Iran-Contra investigations, though not on any of the more serious charges. Calling him a "fall guy" for more important people, a judge gave him a suspended sentence and ordered that he do community service work.

President Reagan called North "an authentic American hero."

Managing the Gulf War

The War in the Persian Gulf was in large part a war of words and illusions, perhaps more so than in any other war the United States has fought. Media manipulation and censorship climbed to new heights and truth was one of the war's first casualties. Here are some facts few Americans were aware of:

- Saddam Hussein, the Iraqi dictator, invaded Kuwait after Kuwait soldiers continued to make incursions into a neutral zone between the two countries. Kuwait had also been swiping some of Iraq's oil.

- Saudi Arabia encouraged Iraq's threats of war, hoping a good scare would prompt Kuwait to stop charging higher prices for its oil than the other OPEC nations.

- The U.S. ambassador in Iraq may have unintentionally encouraged the invasion by implying that the United States would not interfere.

- The U.S., by accident or on purpose, may have scuttled an attempt by other Arab countries to mediate the growing fraction between Iraq and Kuwait.

- The bases American troops used in Saudi Arabia had been built for just such a purpose using secret Saudi funds.

- The international embargo against selling goods to Iraq was more effective than the U.S. government admitted.

- About seventy percent of American bombs missed their targets.

- More often than not Patriot missiles failed to intercept Iraqi Scud missiles. In many cases what TV viewers thought was the explosion of a Scud in the night sky was in fact caused by the Scud abandoning its fuel tanks.

Hoping to desensitize certain dreadful but inevitable results of war, the U.S. military used a variety of obfuscating terms such as:

Attrition: killing the enemy.
Collateral damage: unfortunate civilian deaths.
Assertive disarmament: defeat of the enemy, also known as *servicing the adversary.*
Discriminate deterrence: precision bombing.
Intelligence assets: spy satellites.
Human remains pouches: a more palatable term than the "body bags" of the Vietnam War.

Saddam Hussein was skillful in the use of euphemisms and symbolisms. His favorite word during the war was "treachery." All those arrayed against him, Westerners and Arabs alike, were treacherous. He would cry, "The treacherous have committed treachery" and ranted against "the cowards who have perfected the acts of treachery and treason."

Several times Saddam accused American bombers of destroying factories producing babies' milk instead of hitting military targets. This may or may not have been true, but frequent use of the word "milk" probably was a calculated stroke of propaganda. In the Arab world milk is a powerful symbol, suggesting fertility and life itself.

The Iraqi dictator often referred to the Gulf War as a *jihad*—a "holy war"—in hopes of gaining sympathy in the Arab world. Crushing defeats of Iraqi troops were reported by Radio Baghdad as "a total rout of the infidel armies." Iraq's allies around the world, claimed Radio Baghdad, were delivering fatal blows to other American forces and President Bush was becoming a prisoner in his own home, the "Black House."

Iraq tried to enlist the sympathy of other third world countries by accusing the U.S. military of rounding up the poor men of Bangladesh and transporting them to the Gulf to fight for them. Other reports said the Americans forced thousands of Egyptian women to go to the front and entertain the troops. Though Iraq made sure the world saw televised images of charred bodies after allied air attacks on Baghdad, Saddam Hussein promised to "cut the legs off" any reporter or cameraperson nosing around Kuwait, where he or she might see the victims of Iraqi torture and execution.

The Kuwaiti government-in-exile had its own propaganda machine, spending about six million dollars in the United States alone. Most of the money went for media advertizing blitzes showing Americans how cruelly their homeland had been treated under the yoke of Saddam Hussein. It also wanted the world to know that not all Kuwaiti refugees left the country in a Mercedes or BMW (though some did) and that not all of them danced or gambled away the nights in whatever country they had taken up a temporary residence, as some news programs reported.

Pooling the News

Remembering the Vietnam experience, the U.S. military kept strict control over what kind of news went out from Saudi Arabia where allied troops were congregated. Good news went out quickly, but bad news was either skirted or allowed to seep out a little at a time so its effect would be lessened. The military managed this by using "pools."

A pool contained a number of reporters and got most of its news from a daily briefing by allied officers. The military loved the idea; every newsman hated it. "We are not allowed to report news," complained Christiane Amanpour of CNN. "If we happened to stumble across news, we couldn't report it because it had to be cleared." Forrest Sawyer of ABC News called the pool system "a strange, distorted form of public relations . . . A great deal of history was lost because of it."

The pool system, in effect, made a reporter an unpaid employee of the Defense Department. Unlike in other American wars, newsmen were not allowed on the battlefield without a military escort, who often told them what questions they could ask and even told soldiers the answers to give. Of course there were newsmen who ignored the rules and went off on their own in search of a good story; in a number of cases these strays were picked up by military police and detained for several hours. "I've covered wars for twenty-five years and this is the first time I've been held prisoner by my own military," complained one reporter.

To question the pool system, as one newsman said, was "like asking whether a smoothly functioning dictatorship was working well." Another reporter, who had been covering wars for twenty years, said the only nation more restrictive than the U.S. was Iraq.

The media were not allowed to take pictures of dead soldiers of either side, and in at least one case a reporter who tried to was clubbed with a rifle. Reporters could not interview bomber pilots, prisoners of war, military doctors, or even chaplains (called "morale officers" in deference to the Saudis, their Muslim hosts). All news copy had to be read and edited at pool headquarters, where it often stayed until it was too stale to use.

The Pentagon orchestrated a stream of public announcements designed to fool the American people as well as the Iraqis. It announced that whole units had left for deployment in the Persian Gulf when in fact only some parts of the units had. It planted false reports of air force landings in Iraq and Kuwait and another about sixty Iraqi tank crews defecting to the allies.

An article about pilots on the aircraft carrier *U.S.S. Kennedy* watching pornographic films before flying missions was suppressed. In other cases profanity used by airmen was deleted.

This unparalleled muzzling of the press did not escape public criticism. The august Walter Cronkite said the military was "trampling on the American people's right to know" and compared the situation to the way Nazis covered up what happened in the concentration camps. "The fact that the military apparently feels there is something it must hide can only lead eventually to a breakdown in homefront confidence," said Cronkite.

P. J. O'Rourke, a columnist for *Rolling Stone*, summed up the management of news by the U.S. government by writing: "If we got our news at home the way we're getting it here, the only time you'd know about a fire would be when the kids playing with matches lit the living-room drapes."

Chapter 27

The Clinton Beginning

A New President

FOR MONTHS AFTER the Gulf War, President Bush rode a high tide in the popularity polls. Not much more than a year before the election of 1992, he looked like a shoo-in for a second term.

But matters changed swiftly. Thanks to an ever-increasing federal deficit and a sinking economy, Bush saw his chances slipping away. Toward the end of the campaign he looked more like "the Wimp" he was accused of being rather than the heroic leader of a successful war. He grew increasingly shrill, in the end calling Bill Clinton and Albert Gore, his Democratic opponents, "those two bozos."

Bill Clinton was born William Jefferson Blythe IV, later adopting the last name of his stepfather. In high school he was a drum major and an all-state saxophone player. He graduated from Georgetown University, Yale Law School, and studied in England as a Rhodes Scholar. He set his sights on becoming president after meeting John F. Kennedy while at Boy's Nation.

Clinton was frank in attributing his victory to three factors, all of them coming under the heading of luck: (1) Because Bush was riding high on the strength of his Gulf War successes, big-name Democrats stayed out of the race; (2) The other Democratic candidates appeared tentative and in the end came off as merely ambitious; and (3) A bad economy continued to worsen.

Clinton the candidate promised he would not have a cabinet of mostly living white males—as his predecessors had—but one that "looks like America." He kept that vow, his cabinet almost exactly mirroring the racial and ethnic makeup of the nation:

- 14 percent African American (actual makeup 12 percent).

- 6 percent Hispanic (actual 9.5).

- 3 percent Asian American (about the same).

- 0.6 percent Native American (about the same).

In addition the cabinet was fifty-four percent men and forty-six percent women, close to an even split. There were more women than in any other president's cabinet, including the first-ever female attorney general.

Yet the new president was notably slow in filling other appointments. (He was operating on "Clinton Standard Time," said those who criticized his inevitable lack of punctuality.) More than a year after taking office he still had not filled many vacancies.

Once in the Oval Office, Clinton discovered that the national debt was much larger than the two Republican administrations before him had let on, making the problem of what do do about it more acute. The debt went down from 290 billion to 255 billion during his first year in office, but few critics seemed to notice.

The critics instead were busily lambasting him for alleged extra-marital affairs, possibly shady financial dealings, and what appeared to them to be a schoolboy approach to running the country. At the same time, being politicians, they must have admired his uncanny ability to wriggle out of tight spots. An Arkansas newspaper, years before, had dubbed him "Slick Willie."

The Hillary Factor

Bill Clinton met Hillary Rodham while both were going to Yale Law School. Later they married. They had a daughter and named her Chelsea after a recording by singer and good friend Judy Collins.

During the years Clinton was governor of Arkansas, Hillary mostly stayed out of the political limelight. But during the presidential campaign she emerged as a strong-willed and ambitious woman, apparently striking fear into the hearts of some voters; the American electorate was not used to a candidate for First Lady of the land being so visible and so outspoken. In some quarters there seemed to be an uneasy feeling that Hillary might become not only First Lady but co-president. "Buy one, get one free," quipped her husband.

Clinton's team advised that Hillary stay more in the background for the rest of the campaign; most of the time she dutifully did, though her presence was still felt. After the election a headline in a German newspaper trumpeted: "HILLARY'S HUSBAND ELECTED."

After becoming First Lady, Hillary immediately proceeded to redefine the job. Not since Eleanor Roosevelt had a First Lady been so active and not since Edith Bolling Wilson, who ran the country while Woodrow Wilson was gravely ill, had a president's wife wielded such power.

Eleanor Roosevelt, an early champion of civil rights and feminist causes, was one of Hillary's idols. Mrs. Roosevelt also suffered at the hands of the public and the press. Anti-Roosevelt critics wore a button reading: "I DON'T WANT ELEANOR, EITHER."

But there were great differences between Eleanor and Hillary. Mrs. Roosevelt was trained, in the tradition of her day, to be a wife and mother; Mrs. Clinton was a lawyer and an advocate of children, the elderly, and the poor.

Hillary Clinton was a unique product of her time, the first presidential wife to arrive in the White House on something approaching equal footing with her husband. The President asked her advice on almost everything. If the Constitution did not forbid it, she probably would have become a cabinet officer.

It seems likely that Hillary Clinton will radically—and perhaps permanently—change the way Americans view a First Lady's role. As a Little Rock newspaper columnist wrote, "Maybe we elected the wrong Clinton."

Footnotes

CHAPTER 1

[1]Apparently the horses of the Plains Indians were descendants of runaways from the herds of Francisco Coronado, even though records of his expedition show only two mares among them. Anthropologists believe this was a reintroduction of the horse into this continent, as fossilized remains have been found dating back before the Ice Age. The original horse, called by scientists *Eohippus*, was about the size of a fox terrier. After its evolution into the modern horse, it emigrated to the Old World by way of the Bering Strait, thereafter becoming extinct in this hemisphere. (See Davies in Notes on Sources, p. 260)

Native Americans were terrified of horses at first and thought they ate people. Some natives, having never seen either before, thought the horse and its white-skinned rider were one animal, at least until trouble erupted and they found out the top of this strange beast would come off.

CHAPTER 3

[1]For the information here that is contrary to general opinion about the Pilgrims, see George F. Willison, *Saints and Strangers*, and especially Francis Dillon, *The Pilgrims*. For the origin of the term "Pilgrims" and the history of Plymouth Rock, see Dillon's notes in the back of his book.

CHAPTER 5

[1]See Daniel Boorstin, *The Americans: The National Experience*, chapter 39.

[2]See Boorstin again, chapter 42.

[3]"Old Glory" was only one of several flag designs used by Americans for over a hundred years after the Revolution. It wasn't until 1912 that President William Howard Taft, by executive order, made today's flag design the official one.

The Betsy Ross story has no foundation in history. It was first told by her grandson in an address to the Pennsylvania Historical Society in 1870. See Boorstin, pp. 373–375, and especially p. 1,242 in *The People's Almanac #2* (Bantam Books, 1978) by David Wallechinsky and Irving Wallace.

CHAPTER 11

[1]It could almost be said, silly as it sounds, that the Civil War was won by a whisker. Most of the good generals—on both sides—wore beards, while most of the poor ones did not.

Those who bearded the lion in his lair were U.S. Grant, Robert E. Lee, William T. Sherman, Stonewall Jackson, Nathan Bedford Forrest, and J.E.B. Stuart. Those with clean-shaven Achilles chins included George B. McClellan, Ambrose Burnside, Joseph Hooker, George G. Meade, and others too numerous to mention.

[2] Grant has gone down in history under false pretenses: his name was Hiram Ulysses Grant, not Ulysses Simpson Grant. The congressman who got him an appointment to the U.S. Military Academy made the mistake and Grant, characteristically, never bothered to correct it.

When upperclassmen saw the name "U.S. Grant" on the roster of incoming cadets, they joked that the initials must stand for "Uncle Sam," and throughout Grant's pre-Civil War military career he was known as "Sam" Grant.

CHAPTER 13

[1]Custer was not a general nor did he command the 7th Cavalry. In wartime an officer may be swiftly moved up to higher rank. The rank is a temporary one called a *brevet*; when the emergency is over, the officer returns to his permanent rank, although he is usually moved up a notch or two in recognition of his services. Custer was a *brevet* major general in the Civil War, but when the conflict ended, he returned to his permanent rank of captain. When he died, he was a lieutenant colonel. As a courtesy, however, it was a military custom to call an officer by the highest rank he had ever attained, whether temporary or permanent.

Custer was second in command of the 7th. Its commander, Colonel Samuel Davis Sturgis, was on detached duty at the time of the Little Big Horn expedition.

CHAPTER 14

[1]In his biography of Thomas Edison (see Notes on Sources, p. 265), Robert Conot claims Zenas Fiske Wilbur, a Patent Office official, allowed Bell to see plans for a smaller but better device filed by the Edison Laboratories. Wilbur, an alcoholic always in need of money, then let Bell file an amendment to his application.

CHAPTER 15

[1]The Army sent its soldiers to Cuba, where the weather is always mild, in heavy winter clothing, including overcoats. Summer uniforms finally caught up with them—in New York, after they had come home from the war.

CHAPTER 16

[1]In the nineteenth century a "doughboy" was a small, round doughnut served to sailors. In the Civil War, the word referred to the large, globular buttons on an infantryman's coat, then to the infantryman himself. The term was not very commonly used until World War I.

[2]Early in the war, the Germans had an enormous sawed-off howitzer that fired a two-ton shell nine miles. One shell penetrated ten feet of concrete, six feet of dirt, and a wooden wall thirty inches thick. Near the end of the war, the Krupp Munitions Works, famous all over the world, invented a gun that shelled Paris from almost eighty miles away. It weighed 150 tons and fired a long, slender projectile weighing 200–230 pounds. The barrel had to be replaced after sixty-five firings. This was the notorious *Pariskanone* (Paris gun), nicknamed "Big Bertha" after the large and fleshy Bertha Krupp, wife of the munitions maker. Today, even in Germany, the earlier howitzer is mistakenly referred to by the nickname.

[3]The Allies used this name for propaganda purposes, implying that the Germans were as barbaric as the hordes of Attila the Hun, some of whom settled in Central Europe. Other uncomplimentary appellations were Krauts, Jerries (the British favorite), Heinies, and Boche.

[4]It was not General Pershing, as generally believed, who said "Lafayette, we are here," but an aide, Captain C. E. Stanton. Later, some doughboys, unhappy that the war did not end sooner after they arrived, said, "Lafayette, we are *still* here."

CHAPTER 20

[1]"Bull" Connor is usually spoken of as the Birmingham chief of police; commissioner of public safety, an administrative position, is superior to the chief of police. He was a small man, acquiring his nickname because of his booming voice.

Notes on Sources

CHAPTER 1

The New World (Duell, Sloan and Pearce, 1946) is old, but still one of the most readable books on the subject. Other general treatments are *Indians of the Americas* (National Geographic Society, 1955) and *The American Heritage Book of Indians* (1961).

CHAPTER 2

For those who might have visited here before Columbus, see *The Quest for America* (Praeger Publishers, 1971) by Geoffery Ashe, *et. al.*; *The Viking Settlements of North America* (Clarkson N. Potter Publisher, 1972) by Frederick J. Pohl; and especially *Voyagers to the New World* (William Morrow, 1979) by Nigel Davies.

For the most comprehensive account of explorers of the coasts and coastal waterways, there is none better than Samuel Eliot Morison's *The European Discovery of America: The Northern Voyages* (Oxford University Press, 1971) and *The European Discovery of America: The Southern Voyages* (Oxford University Press, 1974).

For land explorations, *The Eyes of Discovery* (Lippincott, 1950) by John Bakeless is certainly no conventional treatment, but is one of the most interesting history books ever written. Bakeless concerns himself not with what the explorers did, but what they saw. *They Saw America First* (Lippincott, 1957) is a junior version of the book.

Certain land explorers are covered well in *Explorers of the Mississippi* (Knopf, 1968) by Timothy Severin.

CHAPTER 3

For the Jamestown story, see *Behold Virginia: The Fifth Crown* (Harcourt, Brace and World, 1951) by George F. Willison, and S.E. Morison's *The European Discovery of America: The Northern Voyages, op. cit.* Chapter 1.

For the Pilgrims, Willison's *Saints and Strangers* (Reynal and Hitchcock, 1945) is old, but good. More recent books include *The Mayflower* (Stein and Day, 1974) by Kate Caffrey, and *The Pilgrims* (Doubleday, 1975) by Francis Dillon.

For the colonies in general, read *The American Heritage History of the Thirteen Colonies* (1967) and *Land Where Our Fathers Died* (Doubleday, 1962) by Marion L. Starkey.

For the slave trade, I used *Black Cargoes* (Viking, 1962) by Daniel P. Mannix.

CHAPTER 4

For an understanding of colonial life, one book is essential: *Colonial Living* (World, 1957) by Edwin Tunis. It is an oversize book with a wealth of information and wonderful drawings. Other books are *American Manners and Morals* (American Heritage, 1969) by Mary Cable; *The Americans: The Colonial Experience* (Random House, 1958) by Daniel Boorstin; and *Death in Early America* (Thomas Nelson, 1976) by Margaret M. Coffin (and with a name like that she ought to know).

Then there are the classics in the field: *Everyday Things In American Life, 1607-1776* (Scribner's, 1937) by William Chauncy Langdon; *Colonial Days and Ways* (Frederick Ungar, 1900) by Helen Evertson Smith; and *Customs and Fashions in Old New England* (Macmillan, 1893), *Home Life in Colonial Days* (Macmillan, 1898), *Child Life in Colonial Days* (Macmillan, 1899), and *Stage Coach and Carriage Days* (Macmillan, 1900)—all four by Alice Morse Earle. All of these classics have been reprinted.

CHAPTER 5

Perhaps the most interesting book you could read on the American Revolution is *The Revolutionary War: Being a De-Mythed Account of How the Thirteen Colonies Turned the World Upside Down* (Dial Press, 1954) by the Civil War novelist James Street. There is some on the Revolution in the very entertaining *George Washington: The Image and the Man* (Boni and Liveright, 1926) by W. E. Woodward, although the author wrote in a time when debunking was in style and has been criticized in later years for being too cynical. A good general treatment of the war and its background can be found in *The History of American Wars* (Knopf, 1981) by T. Harry Williams, who died after finishing World War I. Other books are *The American Revolution* (Harper and Brothers, 1954) by John Richard Alden; *The Family Quarrel* (Duell, Sloan and Pearce, 1959) by Elswyth Thane; and *The Birth of the Nation* (Knopf, 1969) by Arthur Schlesinger, Sr.

For military buffs there are *The Crossing* (William Morrow, 1971), Howard Fast's story of the battle of Trenton; *The Way of the Fox* (Greenwood Press, 1975) by Dave Richard Palmer, a study of Washington's strategy; and *The Battle of Cowpens* (Doubleday, 1958) by the historical novelist Kenneth Roberts. Roberts has also written some fine novels about the period, *Oliver Wiswell, Arundel,* and *Rabble in Arms.* (His best novel is *Northwest Passage*, about the French and Indian War.)

Other specialized books are *Inventing America: Jefferson's Declaration of Independence* (Random House, 1978; Vintage paperback, 1979) by Garry Wills; *The Loyalists* (Crown, 1973) by Donald Barr Chidsey; *1776: The Year of Decision* (Norton, 1975) by Thomas Fleming; *Under the Guns: New York, 1775–1776* (Harper and Row, 1972) by Bruce Bliven, Jr.; and *The Peacemakers: The Great Powers and American Independence* (Harper and Row, 1965) by Richard B. Morris.

CHAPTER 6

For Lewis and Clark, I prefer two old books: *Lewis and Clark: Partners in Discovery* (Morrow, 1947) by John Bakeless, or *No Other White Men* (Dutton, 1937) a junior book by Julia Davis. The National Geographic Society has a book called *In the Footsteps of Lewis and Clark* (1970) by Gerald S. Snyder. There is also the classic treatment by Bernard De Voto in *The Course of Empire* (Houghton Mifflin, 1952) and Lewis and Clark's original *Journals*.

For the Louisiana Purchase itself, see *Eminent Domain* (Charterhouse Publishers, 1973) by John Keats, and *So Vast, So Beautiful a Land* (Little, Brown, 1974) by Marshall Sprague.

For frontier life there is none better than the pictures-and-text book by Edwin Tunis, *Frontier Living* (World, 1961). You can make some use of *Frontier America: Its First Three Centuries* (Doubleday, 1949) by Carl W. Drepperd.

CHAPTER 7

There apparently aren't many good books on the War of 1812 except old ones. I think the best—certainly the most entertaining—is the two-volume account by Glenn Tucker, *Poltroons and Patriots* (Bobbs-Merrill, 1954). Some libraries, because it is in two volumes, I suppose, keep it in the reference section. A shorter review of the war is in *The History of American Wars, op. cit.* Chapter 5. For the Chesapeake campaign, see Walter Lord's *The Dawn's Early Light* (Norton, 1972). For the battle of New Orleans, look up *The British at the Gates: The New Orleans Campaign in the War of 1812* (Putnam's, 1974) by Robin Reilly.

CHAPTER 8

For everything in this chapter, I relied heavily on the excellent junior book *The Romance of American Transportation* (Thomas Y. Crowell, 1962) by Franklin M. Reck. For river craft and stagecoaches *Frontier Living, op. cit.* Chapter 6, is good, and for those subjects plus early railroads, helpful books are *Everyday Things in American Life, 1776–1876* (Scribner's, 1941) by William Chauncy Langdon and *The History of Travel in America* (originally published by Bobbs-Merrill, 1915, and reissued by Tudor Publishing Co., 1937) by Seymour Dunbar.

For the transcontinental railroad, my best source was Dee Brown's *Hear That Lonesome Whistle Blow* (Holt, Rinehart and Winston, 1977).

CHAPTER 9

For the Alamo, see *A Time to Stand* (Harper and Brothers, 1961) by Walter Lord; *13 Days to Glory* (McGraw-Hill, 1958) by Lon Tinkle; *Glory, God and Gold* (Doubleday, 1954) by Paul I. Wellman; and for a short version, *The People's Almanac #2* (Bantam, 1978) by David Wallechinsky and Irving Wallace.

The song "Hell and Texas" is from RCA Victor's album "How the West Was Won" (Radio Corporation of America, 1960).

There seem to be few good books on the Mexican War. Try *The History of American Wars*, op. cit. in Chapters 5 and 6; *The Nation Comes of Age: A People's History of the Ante-Bellum Years*, Vol. 4 (McGraw-Hill, 1981) by Paige Smith; and *The Year of Decision: 1846* (Little, Brown, 1943) by Bernard De Voto.

Perhaps the best way to study the Mexican War is through biographies such as *Grant: A Biography* (Norton, 1981) by William S. McFeely; *Captain Sam Grant* (Little, Brown, 1950); and *Old Rough and Ready* (Vanguard, 1946) by Silas Bent McKinley and Silas Bent. If you can wade through it, you might get a few insights into the war from *Polk: The Diary of a President* (Longman's, Green, 1952) edited by Allan Nevins.

CHAPTER 10

Frontier Living, op. cit. in Chapters 6 and 8, is a marvelous source for anything about the early western frontier. *The Plains Across* (University of Illinois Press, 1979) by John D. Unruh, Jr. is a revisionist history of the emigrant passage, although dry. In *Men to Match My Mountains* (Doubleday, 1952), Irving Stone brings the novelist's touch to the story of the gold rush, Oregon, and the Mormons.

For the gold rush alone, *Gold Dust* (Knopf, 1981) by Donald Dale Jackson is a fine book. *Here They Dug the Gold* (A.L. Burt, 1931) is very old, but still entertaining, as are all of Willison's books.

Any church or mission of the Church of Jesus Christ of Latter-Day Saints will be happy to give you a copy of the booklet I used in part, *Joseph Smith Tells His Own Story*— and as much other material as you want.

CHAPTER 11

No one should ever have trouble finding lots of books on the Civil War, but for interesting and unusual information, I suggest you look up *Our Incredible Civil War* (Holt, Rinehart and Winston, 1961) by Burke Davis, and *The Civil War: An Unvarnished*

Account of the Late But Still Lively Hostilities (Dial Press, 1953) by James Street. Your efforts will be well rewarded.

For the daily toil and tribulation of the private soldier, find *Hardtack and Coffee: The Unwritten Story of Army Life*, told from the Union point of view by John D. Billings, and *Detailed Minutiae of Soldier Life in the Army of Northern Virginia*, written from the Confederate viewpoint by Carlton McCarthy. Both authors were participants in the conflict and both of their books have been published in *Soldier Life in the Union and Confederate Armies*, edited by Philip Van Doren Stern and published by Bonanza Books, 1961, and Fawcett's Premier Civil War classics, 1961. *Grant: A Biography, op. cit.* in Chapter 9, is worth looking into.

The song "How Do You Like The Army" is from the album "Songs of Billy Yank and Johnny Reb" (Radio Corporation of America, 1961) by Jimmy Driftwood.

CHAPTER 12

Handy books on this period are *Centennial: American Life in 1876* (Chilton Book Co., 1969) by William Peirce Randel, and *The Confident Years* (1969) by the editors of *American Heritage*.

For the impeachment of Andrew Johnson, see *The Trial of Andrew Johnson* (Thomas Nelson, 1977) by Noel B. Gerson, and the chapter on Edmund G. Ross in John F. Kennedy's *Profiles in Courage* (Harper and Brothers, 1956).

The disputed election of 1876 is covered especially well in Randel's *Centennial*, but also helpful is the junior book *The Hayes-Tilden Election of 1876* (Franklin Watts, 1972) by Harold Cecil Vaughan.

See *Centennial* for the Grant scandals, plus *Grant: A Biography, op. cit.* in Chapter 9.

The classic study of the moguls is Matthew Josephson's *The Robber Barons* (Harcourt, Brace and World, 1962), but more readable is Stewart H. Holbrook's *The Age of the Moguls* (Doubleday, 1953). Some information of interest may be found in *The Big Change* (Harper and Row, 1952) by Frederick Lewis Allen, and *John D.: Founding Father of the Rockefellers* (Harper and Row, 1980) by David Freeman Hawke.

CHAPTER 13

For the West in general, some useful books are *The Great American West* (Bonanza Books, 1959) by James D. Horan; *The Gunfighters* (Time-Life Books, 1974) by Paul Trachtman; and *The Townsmen* (Time-Life Books, 1957) by Keith Wheeler. (There are other books in Time-Life's western series.) Exploding some of the cowboy myths is *Cowboy Culture* (Knopf, 1981) by David Dary.

For Indians and Indian fighters, *Bury My Heart at Wounded Knee* (Holt, Rinehart and Winston, 1970), the best-seller by Dee Brown; *Sitting Bull* (Putnam's, 1973) by Alexander B. Adams; and *The American Heritage Book of Indians, op. cit.* in Chapter l. *War Cries on Horseback* (Doubleday, 1970) by Stephen Longstreet is a general summary of the Indian wars and contains some interesting sidelights I have not seen elsewhere, but the book is poorly written and even more poorly organized.

You can find an account of the Custer massacre in all the books in the above paragraph and in *The Battle of the Little Bighorn* (Lippincott, 1966) by Mari Sandoz, and *The Story of the Little Big Horn* (Bonanza Books, 1926) by Colonel W.A. Graham. (You can, apparently, spell the name of the river however you choose, as one word or two.) Most accounts of the battle are confusing; you might do better to look into *Custer and the Little Big Horn: A Psychobiographical Inquiry* (Wayne State University Press, 1981) by Dr. Charles K. Hofling.

You can also peruse some books from the horses' mouths: *My Life on the Plains* (new edition by the University of Oklahoma Press, 1962) by the general himself, and *Boots and Saddles* (new edition by Cornerhouse Publishers, 1969) by Elizabeth Custer, the general's devoted wife. Needless to say, it is likely you will find some bias in these two.

CHAPTER 14

William Peirce Randel's *Centennial, op. cit.* in Chapter 12, is good for the period. *A Streak of Luck* (Seaview Books, 1979) by Robert Conot is an excellent book on Edison. The Bell Telephone Company has a good booklet, *Alexander Graham Bell: Inventor of the Telephone.* They will give you all the copies you want.

For cars in general, I used two old books, *Our Times* Vol. 1 (Scribners, 1920) by Mark Sullivan, and *Not So Long Ago* (Random House, 1949) by Lloyd Morris. You can find information in these books that isn't in others; both are full of good verse.

For Henry Ford in particular, I used *Henry's Wonderful Model T* (Bonanza Books, 1954) by Floyd Clymer, and *Ford: The Times, The Man, The Company* (Scribners, 1954) by Allan Nevins. *Not So Long Ago* is also useful.

An excellent book on the coming of the air age is Arch Whitehouse's *The Early Birds* (Doubleday, 1965). *Kill Devil Hill: Discovering the Secret of the Wright Brothers* (Houghton Mifflin, 1979) by Harry Combs is too technical in spots, but is still a good book. For the Wrights, I also used Orville's article "How I Learned To Fly" that originally appeared in the September 1914 issue of *Boy's Life* and was reprinted in October 1953.

CHAPTER 15

Edmund Morris's *The Rise of Theodore Roosevelt* (Coward, McCann and Geoghegan, 1979), winner of both the National Book Award and the Pulitzer Prize for biography in

1980, is an engrossing study of T.R.'s early life and career up to the time of McKinley's assassination.

For the Spanish-American War there are two aging classics, *The Splendid Little War* (Little, Brown, 1958) by Frank Freidel, and the serio-comic version by Walter Millis, *The Martial Spirit* (Houghton Mifflin, 1931). A more recent work, and a good one, is *Roosevelt's Rough Riders* (Doubleday, 1971) by Virgil Carrington Jones.

For an inside view of the war from the common soldier's angle, see *The Little War of Private Post* (Little, Brown, 1960) by Charles Johnson Post.

The material on William Randolph Hearst's role in starting the war came from *Citizen Hearst* (Scribners, 1961) by W.A. Swanberg. The Dewey material is from *Our Times* Vol. I, *op. cit.* in Chapter 12.

The quotes on America from Spanish newspapers came from *Who Rush to Glory: The Cowboy Volunteers of 1898* (Caxton Printers, Caldwell, Idaho, 1958) by Clifford P. Westermeier. The book is dull otherwise.

A good book on the period from 1900 to World War I is Walter Lord's *The Good Years* (Harper and Row, 1960; Bantam paperback, 1962).

CHAPTER 16

For a secondary-school teacher's purposes, the best book on World War I that I know of—by far the best—is *Hurrah for Peace! Hurrah for War!* (Knopf, 1971; New American Library paperback, 1978) by Steven Jantzen. It is chock full of good stuff.

For a quick—and very readable—review of the war, the best book is James L. Stokesbury's *A Short History of World War I* (William Morrow, 1981).

John Toland's *No Man's Land* (Doubleday, 1980) is useful mostly for the political aspects of the war. I don't recommend it for junior high teachers and doubt it would be of much use to senior high teachers except in upper-level classes.

Other books include *Mr. Wilson's War* (Doubleday, 1962) by John Dos Passos; *Over Here* (Scribners, 1933), which is Vol. V of Mark Sullivan's *Our Times*; and *Over There* (Bramhill House, 1964) by Frank Freidel.

General Douglas MacArthur's autobiography, *Reminiscences* (McGraw-Hill, 1964; Crest paperback, 1965) has a short section on World War I, as does William Manchester's biography of the general, *American Caesar* (Little, Brown, 1978).

For the air war, you can check with two authorities: General William "Billy" Mitchell's *Memoirs of World War I* (Random House, 1928, 1956, 1960), and *Fighting the Flying Circus* (Doubleday, 1919 and 1965) and *Rickenbacker* (Prentice-Hall, 1967) both by Edward V. Rickenbacker.

You may also profit from reading a couple of junior books on the air fighting: *Flying Aces of World War I* (Scholastic Book Services paperback, 1965) by Gene Gurney, and *They Flew to Glory: The Story of the Lafayette Flying Corps* (Lothrop, Lee and Shepard, 1965) by Robert Sidney Bowen.

Two good books of fiction are Dos Passos's *Three Soldiers* and the latter-day classic by Erich Maria Remarque, *All Quiet on the Western Front.*

CHAPTER 17

I had three main sources for this chapter: *Ardent Spirits: the Rise and Fall of Prohibition* (Putnam's, 1973) by John Kohler; *Only Yesterday* (Harper's, 1931) by Frederick Lewis Allen; and *The Aspirin Age: 1919–1941* (Simon and Schuster, 1949) by Isabel Leighton. *Only Yesterday*, an old standard, is a wonderful social history of the '20s. *The Aspirin Age* is good for Izzy and Moe, Harding and Coolidge, the Ku Klux Klan, Sacco and Vanzetti, and Lindbergh.

Other useful books are *The Ohio Gang: The World of Warren G. Harding* (Evans Publishing Co., 1981) by Charles L. Mee, Jr.; Mark Sullivan's *Our Times* Vol. VI (Scribners, 1935); and *The Time Between the Wars* (Doubleday, 1966) by Jonathan Daniels.

The End of the Roaring Twenties: Prohibition and Repeal (Julian Messner, 1969) by Bill Severn is useful, as are Time-Life's *Time Capsule* books on each year of the decade.

CHAPTER 18

The best general book on the Depression that I know of is *A Nation in Torment* (Coward, McCann and Geoghegan, 1970) by Robb Ellis. It is a big book and rather dreary reading in places, but interspersed throughout are wonderful anecdotes.

The first hundred pages or so of William Manchester's narrative history of America from 1932 to 1972, *The Glory and the Dream* (Little, Brown, 1973), are also good. And, of course there is Studs Terkel's best-seller, *Hard Times: An Oral History of the Great Depression* (Random House's Pantheon Books, 1970).

Other good books are *The Invisible Scar* (David McKay, 1966) by Caroline Bird; Frederick Lewis Allen's sequel to *Only Yesterday, Since Yesterday* (Harper and Brothers, 1939); and the junior book, *The Hungry Years* (Chilton Book Co., 1967) by Adrian A. Paradis.

You might find some use for James D. Horan's picture book, *The Desperate Years* (Bonanza Books, 1962), and there are also the *Time Capsules* for the 1930s.

Dust Bowl: The Southern Plains in the 1930s (Oxford University Press, 1979) by David Worster is short and a bit scholarly, but helpful. Also useful is *The Day the*

Bubble Burst: A Social History of the Wall Street Crash of 1929 (Doubleday, 1979) by Gordon Thomas and Max Morgan-Witts.

For more—lots more—on Franklin Roosevelt's critics see *All But the People: Franklin Roosevelt and His Critics, 1931–1939* (Macmillan, 1960) by George Wolfskill and John A. Hudson.

CHAPTER 19

There are, of course, thousands of books on World War II. For a simple recounting of events, there is no better book than *A Short History of World War II* (William Morrow, 1980) by James L. Stokesbury.

For Hitler and the Nazis, I like best a marvelous little book by an authority in the field: *Hitler and Nazism* (Franklin Watts, 1961; paperback by Bantam, 1967) by Louis L. Snyder. It is supposed to be a junior book, but I have not found the story told better anywhere, and certainly not as interestingly.

For a more exhaustive study of *Der Fuehrer*, see John Toland's *Adolf Hitler* (Doubleday, 1967, two volumes).

Louis Snyder's *The War: A Concise History, 1939–1945* (Julian Messner, 1970) is excellent on the fighting. John Toland's *The Rising Sun* (Random House, 1970) won the Pulitzer Prize for its retelling of the Pacific War from the Japanese point of view. There is also good information in William Manchester's *American Caesar, op. cit.* in Chapter 16, and his *The Glory and the Dream, op. cit.* in Chapter 18.

The best sources I have found for the home front are *The Home Front, USA: World War II* (Time-Life Books, 1978) by Roland H. Bailey, and *Days of Sadness, Years of Triumph: The American People, 1939–1945* (Coward, McCann and Geoghegan, 1970) by Geoffrey Perrett.

CHAPTER 20

The principal references for this chapter were *My Soul Is Rested: Movement Days in the Deep South Remembered* (G.P. Putnam's Sons, 1977; Bantam paperback, 1978) by Howell Raines, and *Fire in the Streets: America in the 1960s* (Simon and Schuster, 1979) by Milton Viorst. *My Soul Is Rested*, the best book on the Black Revolution I have come across, is in the oral interview format.

Other books are *The Long Shadow of Little Rock* (David McKay, 1962) by Daisey Bates; *Freedom Summer* (Viking, 1965) by Sally Belfrage; *Watts: The Aftermath* (Grove Press, 1969) by Paul Bullock; *Burn, Baby, Burn!* (Dutton, 1966) by Jerry Cohen and William S. Murphy; *The Negro in American History* (Encyclopaedia Britannica, 1969, 1972) general editor, Mortimer J. Adler; *Robert Kennedy and His Times* (Houghton Mifflin,

1978, two vols.) by Arthur M. Schlesinger, Jr.; *Wallace* (World Pub. Co., 1968) by Marshall Frady; and *The Glory and the Dream, op. cit.* in Chapters 18 and 19.

CHAPTER 21

Good books on the Korean War are in short supply. The ones I used are *The Glory and the Dream, op. cit.* in Chapters 18 and 19; *The Truman Presidency: The History of a Triumphant Succession* (Macmillan, 1966) by Cabell Phillips; *Plain Speaking: An Oral Biography of Harry S Truman* (Berkley Medallion Books, 1974) by Merle Miller; MacArthur's *Reminiscences, op. cit.* in Chapters 16; *American Caesar, op. cit.* in Chapters 16 and 19; and *Time Capsules* for 1950–1953.

A brand-new and excellent book on Korea is Joseph C. Goulden's *Korea: The Untold Story of the War* (Quadrangle/New York Times Books, 1982).

CHAPTER 22

President Kennedy: Profile of Power (Simon & Schuster, 1993) by Robert Reeves is a fine book on JFK's career and reveals hitherto unknown facts on his health; books on his assassination include *Rush to Judgment* (Thunder's Mouth, 1966), the first book to question the official version of the assassination; *The JFK Assassination: The Facts and the Theories* (Signet Books, 1992) by Carl Oglesby offers an outline of the matter; and *Case Closed* (Random House, 1993) by Gerald L. Posner concludes that there was no assassination plot.

Material for other assassinations came from *The People's Almanac #1* (Doubleday, 1975) by David Wallechinsky and Irving Wallace, pp. 597–608.

CHAPTER 23

Two good books on the Vietnam War came out in 1981, both of them in the oral history format. They are *Nam* (Morrow) by Mark Baker, and the best-seller *Everything We Had* (Random House) by Al Santoli. Another good book, by young war correspondent Michael Herr, has won several awards: *Dispatches* (Knopf, 1968, 1969, 1970, 1977; Avon paperback, 1978). *G.I. Diary* (Harper and Row, 1968) by David Parks is brief but the young author has something to say about the role of blacks in the war.

Other books I found useful are *Fire in the Lake* (Little, Brown, 1972), a political study of the war by Frances Fitzgerald; *Chance and Circumstance* (Knopf, 1978), a study of protest and draft evasion by Lawrence M. Baskir and William A. Strauss; and *The Best and the Brightest* (Random House, 1969, 1971, 1972) by David Halberstam, which covers the war and many other aspects of the Kennedy and Johnson administrations with considerable insight.

James Michener's *Kent State: What Happened and Why* (Random House, 1971) provides insight into the entire problem of dissent.

Later books are *Vietnam at War: The History* (Oxford University Press, 1988) by Philip B. Davidson; *Bloods: An Oral History of the Vietnam War by Black Veterans* (Random House, 1984) by Wallace Terry; and especially *Vietnam: A History* (Viking, 1991) by Stanley Karnow.

CHAPTER 24

Most of this chapter came from *For All Mankind* (Atlantic Monthly Press, 1988) by Harry Hurt III, with some help from *The People's Almanac #1* (Doubleday, 1975) by David Wallechinsky and Irving Wallace, pp. 510–512.

CHAPTER 25

For a straight rundown on Watergate from start to finish, I recommend *Watergate: America in Crisis* (Thomas Y. Crowell, 1975) by Jules Archer.

To find out how two investigative reporters for the *Washington Post* started it all, read *All the President's Men* (Simon and Schuster, 1974; Warner Books paperback, 1975) by Carl Bernstein and Bob Woodward.

Another useful book is Theodore H. White's *Breach of Faith: The Fall of Richard Nixon* (Atheneum, 1975).

Then there are the many books by the participants themselves: John Dean, *Blind Ambition* (Simon and Schuster, 1976); Jeb Stuart Magruder, *An American Life* (Atheneum, 1974); G. Gordon Liddy, *Will* (St. Martin's, 1980); H. R. Haldeman, *The Ends of Power* (Quadrangle/ New York Times Books, 1978); John J. Sirica, *To Set the Record Straight* (Norton, 1979); Leon Jaworski, *The Right and the Power: The Prosecution of Watergate* (Reader's Digest Press, 1976); and Samuel Dash, *Chief Counsel: Inside the Ervin Committee—The Untold Story of Watergate* (Random House, 1976).

Other books you might want to look into are *The Time of Illusion* (Knopf, 1976) by Jonathan Schell; *Richard Nixon: The Shaping of His Character* (Norton, 1981) by Fawn N. Brodie; *Perfectly Clear: Nixon from Whittier to Watergate* (Quadrangle/New York Times Books, 1973) by Frank Mankiewicz, who was George McGovern's campaign manager, and who lists among his honors a high position on the White House enemies list; and *The Palace Guard* (Harper and Row, 1974), the inside story of the men around Nixon by television correspondent Dan Rather with Gary Paul Gates.

Index